THE LAW OF KARMA

The Law of Karma

A Philosophical Study

by

Bruce R. Reichenbach

UNIVERSITY OF HAWAII PRESS
HONOLULU

Published in the United States by
University of Hawaii Press
2840 Kolowalu Street
Honolulu, Hawaii 96822

Published in Great Britain by
MACMILLAN ACADEMIC AND PROFESSIONAL LTD
Houndmills, Basingstoke, Hampshire RG21 2XS
and London

Printed in Great Britain

Library of Congress Cataloging-in-Publication Data
Reichenbach, Bruce R.
The law of karma: a philosophical study / by Bruce R. Reichenbach.
p. cm.
Includes bibliographical references and index.
ISBN 0-8248-1352-9
1. Karma. 2. Philosophy, Indic. I. Title.
BL2015.K3R45 1991
291.2'2—dc20 90-41032
CIP

for Rachel, bringer of joys

May the wind blow you joy,
may the sun shine down joy on you,
may your days pass with joy,
may the night be a gift of joyful peace!
May the dawn bring you joy at its coming!

(Atharva Veda *VII, 69)*

Contents

Preface

There are a number of ways to mine the rich concept of the law of karma. Though each way has its special resources and unique methods for treating the material, it is also true that each supplements the other. In the past decade, two approaches have been pursued effectively. The historical approach, with its reliance on carefully exegeting primary source materials, is exemplified in Wendy D. O'Flaherty's excellent *Karma and Rebirth in Classical Indian Traditions* and Ronald Neufeldt's *Karma and Rebirth: Post Classical Developments*, as well as in Kewal Anand's *Indian Philosophy: The Concept of Karma*. The anthropological approach, with its descriptions of karma-associated practices and believer reports, is well represented by Charles Keyes's and E.V. Daniel's *Karma—An Anthropological Inquiry*.

But there is a third approach which, though employed to a limited extent in various journal articles, has not been fully pursued. This approach treats the law of karma as a philosophical thesis important both in its own right and as a unifying concept within certain religious-philosophical systems. The concept is central to those systems because of both its explanatory power and its connection to other significant concepts and critical issues—to causation, freedom, fatalism, the existence and role of God, the problem of pleasure and suffering, the nature of the human person, justice, the moral law, rebirth, liberation, and immortality, to name only a few. The burden of this perspective is to discern what has been and is being said about the law of karma, interpret what is or might be meant by what is said, reconstruct how the various pieces of the philosophical puzzle might be fitted together, analytically explore its ramifications for conceptually associated theses, and evaluate the inner logic of the concept. Though this approach builds on the historical texts and anthropological data, it is not meant primarily to provide a historical treatment or anthropological guide to how different individuals or traditions have viewed the law of karma or to the various subtle differences between them. Rather, in generalizing, it takes the concept in broader strokes and ultimately inquires about its meaning, truth, and consistency.

This, which might be termed the philosophical approach, is the one we will employ. In effect, what follows represents an extended essay on the law of karma. Since it is an attempt to understand the law of karma as a philosophical idea, I have not restricted my discussion to the classical documents of Hinduism, Buddhism and Jainism, but have included expressions of it by persons living and writing in the twentieth century. This, I think, is fair, considering that the concept is not a hardened fossil but a living thesis.

There will be disagreement as to whether certain contemporaries correctly ascertain or understand the meaning of the tradition, whether they are consistent with the tradition, or to what extent they can be legitimate spokespersons for the tradition. There will also be disagreement about what the traditions teach, for often the primary sources are far from uniform or, in their aphoristic garb, clear. I intend to be fair to the disagreements, noting where relevant what they are and seeking to incorporate their various insights into the resolution of the difficulties encountered, while at the same time recognizing that treatment of all the permutations would destroy the unity and flow of the book.

Since the book is a philosophical analysis of an idea, readers looking for a historical treatise detailing how the concept is used in particular primary source literature will be better served elsewhere. Neither is this an empirical study directed to ascertain how ordinary practitioners of the various religious faiths interpret the law of karma. It is those who are intrigued with what the concept means and whether it is true, who are interested in what possible ramifications it might have, and who have some concern for evaluating its overall consistency with other, presupposed metaphysical doctrines—in short, those interested in the philosophical issues raised by the concept—who will profit most from the discussion.

This means that our approach has certain limitations which might occasion objection. For one thing, sometimes the questions we raise will not be questions raised within the traditions themselves, or perhaps they will be queries thought not meaningful from certain perspectives (that is, given certain metaphysical presuppositions), or they might be raised in a way different from the ways in which the traditions might pose them. However, I believe that the questions raised below are legitimate when treating the law of karma as a philosophical thesis and deserve careful and considered response.

For another, there will be some objection to the generalized nature of the law of karma as treated here. That is, some might object to treating the law of karma as a single doctrine or concept, since it is expressed with some differences in the different traditions. Yet not only is generalization the very bread and butter of philosophy, but there is enough uniformity in the different presentations of the concept to permit accurate and fruitful generalization. We shall try to note the differences, particularly insofar as they affect the interpretation of the law of karma. But in any treatment of a philosophical or religious theme, there must be some whittling away of the rough edges to obtain a manageable piece which can be analysed and compared with other concepts. In doing so, some might say that this is not exactly what he, she, or someone in the classical tradition (for example, the Upaniṣads, the Buddha, or Patañjali) exactly meant by the doctrine. Perhaps so, but then it is incumbent upon them to give a clear statement of what they or others do mean and how it differs from our treatment. If this book stimulates such a discussion, if it forces people to be clearer as to how particular views of the law of karma differ from each other, all the better.

With a concern for the general reader, I have attempted to keep technical terminology and use of Sanskrit and Pali terms to a minimum. The terms employed will soon become familiar to those who do not already know them. I have italicized Sanskrit terms, since this seems to comport best with contemporary usage.

I wish to thank Augsburg College for providing me both a Faculty Development Grant for the summer of 1983 and a sabbatical for 1984–85, and the Institute for Advanced Christian Study for a major grant in 1984 to work on the manuscript. Without this generosity and released time, the project could never have been undertaken. Thanks are also due to my wife Sharon for her long hours in reading and judging the manuscript for consistency, clarity of style, and comprehensibility. Her numerous criticisms and suggestions have made it more readable and intelligible.

Finally, I want to express my appreciation to the editors of the following publications for permission to reprint articles of mine which they published. Part of Chapter 3 appeared in article form in *Phiiosophy East and West* 38 (Oct. 1988). A slightly shortened version of Chapter 6 was published by *Philosophy East and West* 39 (Apr. 1989). Chapter 8 is reprinted from my contribution to *Death and Immortality in the Religions of the World*, edited by Paul and Linda Badham (Paragon House, 1987).

1

Introduction

Is there a key concept in Hindu, Buddhist and Jaina thought such that the study of it provides ready entrance to their other doctrines? If there is such a key, it is the doctrine of the law of karma. Simply formulated, it states that all actions have consequences which will affect the doer of the action at some future time.

So stated, it might seem that the law of karma is nothing other than the law of universal causation, which affirms that every produce pleasure and pain which either (1) lies outside the individual person, in the environment, or (2) extends through and is effect of a set of causal conditions.

Clearly the two laws are related, though the precise nature of their relation is frequently left unclarified. The law of karma is variously described by different authors as identical with, parallel to, or an application of the law of universal causation.

The relationship is not strict identity. For one thing, the law of karma is not concerned with consequences in general, but with consequences which recoil upon the *doer* of the action, both in the current and in subsequent lives. Secondly, the consequences envisioned by the law of karma encompass more (as well as less) than the observed natural or physical results which follow upon the performance of an action. They especially concern its effects on the dispositions, character, passions and desires of the agent, or the creation of invisible qualities of merit and demerit which adhere to the agent. As such, the proponent of the doctrine will be as much, if not more, concerned with the invisible as with the visible effects of a human action. Thirdly, the law of karma is usually held to apply specifically to the moral sphere. Since the central causal feature of the law of karma is moral, it is not concerned with the *general* relation between actions and their consequences, but rather with the moral quality of the actions and their consequences, such as pain or pleasure and good or bad experiences for the doer of the act.

At the same time, the law of karma applies to more than moral causation. This, as we shall see in Chapter 8, is particularly true in Buddhism, where it is appealed to in order to explain the unity and continuity of the individual. In this context the causal dimension has explanatory power, though it remains the case that insofar as the metaphysical serves moral or salvific purposes, the moral retains ultimate significance. Since the causal element is so central to karmic accounts, the two laws are more than merely parallel.

Consequently, the law of karma is a special application of the law of universal causation, an application which uses the metaphysics of causation both to explain a moral phenomenon and to vindicate the moral order by applying universal justice to human moral actions.

This vindication accords with the fact that the law of karma presupposes an objective ethic. It affirms that intentions and actions can be objectively determined to be right and wrong, so that the proper or just consequences can result or be apportioned. In metaphorical terms, we reap in accord with what we sow.[1] Further, right actions have one kind of effect and wrong another. Since right actions result in good consequences and wrong in bad, the sum total of the good and bad we experience in all our lives must accord with the sum total of our merit and demerit. Finally (generally speaking), we receive the results of our own actions and not another's; the sins of the father are not visited on the children.[2]

In sum, we might say that the law of karma describes or governs (depending on how one views the epistemological status of the law) how certain qualities of consequences, affecting the agent, arise from moral actions and how and to what degree they affect the agent in the current and subsequent lives. The qualities of the consequences are moral-resultant qualities, such as possessed merit and demerit, created dispositions or tendencies to desire, and character, as well as the pleasure and pain they eventually produce.

As one can readily glean from this brief description, the thesis that the law of karma provides an interesting and helpful means of entering the heart of Hindu, Buddhist and Jaina thought holds promise. The law of karma is a *metaphysical* doctrine concerning the nature of reality. Since the law of karma is causal, it provides a way of penetrating Indian philosophical views of causation, and causation (especially in Buddhism[3]) is central to their respective systems. Since it describes (in part) or determines the *modus operandi* of human reincarnations, it opens up discussion of the nature of the human person. And as it relates to human liberation, it leads us to consider the relation between the phenomenal and the noumenal. Secondly, maintaining that right and wrong actions can be objectively determined, that such actions have actual, unseen (moral) effects, and that the universal law of justice must be upheld, introduces the consideration of *ethics*. Consequently an exploration of the doctrine should enable us to ascertain something about the respective ethical views of the systems which advocate the law of karma, and specifically something about their views of justice. We also want to understand how we can come to know the doctrine and what its status is as an item of human knowledge. Thus it provides a convenient entry into concerns about the nature of *human knowledge*—its modes, forms, and limitations. Finally, the doctrine of the law of karma is intrinsically connected to their respective views of the human predicament and *salvation*. Indeed, we cannot understand what salvation is and how it can be attained in the various traditions without at the same time exploring the meaning and significance of the law of karma. In short, because the doctrine of the law of karma stands as a central teaching in the various Hindu, Jaina and Buddhist philosophical-religious systems, consideration of it provides a key to understanding their philosophical and religious beliefs.

Thus, in many ways discussion of the law of karma nicely introduces Hindu, Jaina and Buddhist thought. However, to provide such an introduction by reploughing the furrows of the classical systems and the Sanskrit and Pali texts is not my primary intent. Rather, my purpose is broader, to reflect on the law of karma and its associated doctrines as an interesting and important philosophical thesis, to understand how it functions and is connected with other themes, and to reflect critically on its meaning and truth. It is to look at the logic of the concept.

METHOD

How do I intend to approach the law of karma? What will my method be? My contention is that, even though advanced as a moral doctrine, the law of karma has distinctive metaphysical presuppositions and ontological commitments. I intend to explore not only the moral structures of the law, but the ontology which lies behind it as well. That is, I intend to treat it as a metaphysical and not merely a moral doctrine. My concern will be to analyze the meaning of the doctrine and inquire into its truth in terms of its internal logical consistency, its consistency with associated and presupposed doctrines, and its empirical adequacy.

It might be suggested that our project is fatally flawed even before it gets under way. First, we propose to speak about a law which is held to govern the workings of individual human experience. But (it is often suggested in Indian philosophy) the phenomenal world is suspect. The phenomenal world is not real but rather mere appearance or the product of ignorance. Reality is noumenal, transcendent to individual experience. Thus to devote a book to the doctrine of karma would seem to do little more than compound the ignorance and exacerbate the bondage which is due to our preoccupation with the phenomenal.

My response to this is to suggest that even if there are these two levels, this does not relieve us of concern for either level. The philosopher of the transcendent might do well to bring us to a realisation of the character of ultimate reality, of the abiding Being which is beyond all being, of the Self which is true self. Of this I shall have little to say. On the other hand, since most of us function in the phenomenal world, and since the law of karma has been suggested as a hypothesis to help us understand and explain that human experience, it is necessary that we as phenomenally existent philosophers discourse from that level about that level. We need to ask what hypotheses are used to explain our phenomenal experience, how they purportedly aid in our understanding, what these doctrines mean, and whether they are coherent and can be supported or justified. We might grant that from the transcendent level this is a phenomenal discussion about that which might, in the last analysis, be due to ignorance and illusion. Yet from the phenomenal, the discourse is real and important. Reality, in this sense, is contextual. Thus, from the context of human experience we shall attempt to analyse doctrines which are put forth as explanations of that experience.

Secondly, it might be queried whether the analytic method is a proper attitude to take toward the law of karma. As a fundamental postulate should it not be accepted without having to inquire *how* it operates? To analyse the meaning, nature, and operations of the law of karma is to engage in metaphysics, which for many Buddhist adherents of the doctrine is not only unnecessary but fatally misleading. The person wounded with an arrow does not wait to have it extracted until he finds out the name of the person who shot him, whether he was tall or short or of medium height, what the colour of his skin was, or where he lived. What he wants is to have the arrow extracted. Similarly, discussion of metaphysical dogma does not profit; what is important is explaining the origin, cessation and means to the cessation of misery.[4] The point of the doctrine of karma is to further spiritual liberation from the cycle of rebirths and from desire and craving for existence. Since metaphysical analysis does not lead to the extinction of craving, our work is not spiritually helpful.

Again we might grant that this philosophical treatise might not be directly spiritually uplifting or instrumental in the personal liberation from cravings and desires. On the other hand, it must be admitted that the law of karma, in spite of all the good intentions regarding its spiritual and practical benefit, is precisely what it is, a metaphysical doctrine. Furthermore, it is a metaphysical doctrine of significant import and centrality, both in openly metaphysically and openly non-metaphysically inclined religious systems. It is repeatedly appealed to in order to explain certain aspects of human experience, including personal fortune and misfortune and pain and pleasure. But in this explanatory role it functions not only morally and religiously—as well it might within religious systems—but also metaphysically. It is alleged to account adequately for certain dimensions of human experience. Thus it is open to the analysis of its meaning and truth from a metaphysical standpoint. Religions, by claiming to be concerned with moral and spiritual liberation, cannot escape scrutiny of their dogmas. Of course, our scrutiny will not directly affect whether those dogmas are believed and influential in the practice of the believer. However, the question of their meaning and truth is of substantial significance, particularly if, as is claimed, ignorance lies at the root of our misery. In this sense any attempt to arrive at the truth advances the cause of human liberation.

Of course, the approach I am taking would not necessarily be the approach taken by many Hindu or Buddhist thinkers, though I do not think it is entirely antithetical. There is in non-Western thought, as in Western, a diversity of approaches and methods. That is, I am not purporting to claim that the way I deal with the law of karma or the questions I raise would be their way or their questions. Generally speaking, the law of karma has not been approached in this manner; otherwise there would be no need to write this book. Nonetheless, the approach taken is legitimate and the questions raised need to be asked.

PROGRAM OF THE BOOK

In the remainder of the book I want to take a closer look at specific issues which the doctrine of karma raises. The book is divided into two parts. The first three chapters are largely expository. They attempt to delineate a general concept of the law of karma, note its metaphysical presuppositions, and say something about its epistemological status. The second part, Chapters 4–11, is largely analytical and interpretative. We will explore criticisms of the concept, its consistency with associated concepts, its ability to explain certain phenomena such as pleasure and pain, and how certain subsidiary interpretations can be understood and defended.

In Chapter 2 I will briefly note the debate over the origin of the doctrine, and then spell out some of the metaphysical doctrines presupposed by the law of karma. These presuppositions include beliefs about the relations holding between actions and their consequences, the ontology of moral effects, the nature of the human person, and the possibility of life after death.

In Chapter 3 I will take up the question of the relation of the law of karma to the law of causation and then turn to the question of the epistemological status of the law of karma. As I have already noted, there are some substantial differences between the law of causation and the law of karma. Accordingly, a careful analysis of the relation between these two laws is required, not only to determine to what extent the law of karma is a specific application of the causal law (that is, to determine its proper relationship), but also to ascertain its proper epistemological and metaphysical status.

In Chapter 4 I will turn to the question whether the doctrine of karma is essentially fatalistic. The law of karma has a long history of association with fatalism, especially in popular thought. Yet philosophers have consistently denied that it entails fatalism. To support their claim they have appealed to the fact of human freedom. We will see that human freedom is understood differently in the various systems, and will analyse how the law of karma comports with determinist, libertarian and compatibilist views of human freedom.

The doctrine of karma was introduced to provide a resolution of the problem of the unequal and apparently random distribution of human pain and pleasure, fortune and misfortune. In this it constitutes an explanation of evil. In Chapter 5 we will begin our consideration of the adequacy of the law of karma to explain the human predicament. Western philosophers and theologians have sometimes invoked the law of karma to provide a theodicy for evil. We will raise questions about this easy transfer between traditions by focusing on how the problem of evil to be resolved in karmic systems differs from the problem as found in Western philosophical theology, and on how the concept of God functions in Indian systems.

Evaluation of the adequacy of the law of karma to explain evil involves questions concerning how karmic consequences arise. This will occupy our attention in Chapter 6. Karma is administered generally in the reincarnate stage; how then can the action of the cause be preserved in exact, proportionate amounts for this indefinite time span? Though this is reasonable when the cause and effect are proximate, this becomes problematic when the time between cause and effect is greatly disparate. If the issue merely concerned the impact of karmic actions upon human dispositions, this would not seem so problematic, for as with the seed, the dispositional effects might lie dormant within the human person for a period of time. But since the effects are cosmic as well as dispositional, such that the cosmic brings about experiences or states of affairs which affect individuals, the explanation of dormant effects is not fully adequate. In the light of this difficulty, some Indian philosophers have suggested that there is a God who administers karmic justice. But does the appeal to God as a karmic administrator provide an adequate explanation for evil and good?

In Chapters 7 and 8 we will take up the question of the nature of the self which the law of karma presupposes. In the former chapter we will explore the Hindu view of the self as a persistent, immaterial consciousness or substance. We will raise questions about what evidence there is for the existence of such a self, and what arguments are given to support the thesis that the self is an immaterial being rather than the psychophysical body of human experience.

In Chapter 8 we will take up the question of the nature of the self as found in Buddhism. For Buddhists there is no persistent self (*ātman*). Thus any continuity, as a basis for the continuance of karmic effects, must be accounted for by the transference of influence of some sort between sets of aggregates (*skandhas*). But is this Buddhist view of the human person adequate *vis-à-vis* their advocacy of the moral accountability of the person and the karmic doctrine? Where continuity replaces identity, where each existent bequeaths its dispositions or tendencies to the next existent but where nothing is carried over, are there grounds for a view of karma where the effects of actions recoil on the actor? We will explore the role karma plays in the explanation of the unity and continuity of the aggregates (*skandhas*) which are, for convenience, designated as the self, and see what implications this has for their view of rebirth.

In Chapter 9 we will turn our attention to matters of ethics. The law of karma presupposes that there is universal justice, that right deeds will be rewarded with pleasure and wrong deeds with pain. What reason is there for thinking that there is such a thing as universal or cosmic justice? One answer is that unless we believe that right will be rewarded and evil punished, there is no reason to do the right. But this reduces moral concerns to concerns for advantage and bases morality on self-interest. This concern for self-interest also comes out in the contention that there is little motive for performing meritorious deeds on behalf of others apart from the motive of selfishness—my own liberation. But is this focus on self-interest consistent with the other claims associated with the law of karma, especially the concern for acting without passions and desire for the fruits of the action?

This leads to the suggestion that the law of karma works juridically rather than morally, that is, it forces us to see ourselves as agents of karmic law rather than as genuinely altruistic agents of the other's good. This can also be seen in that, since the consequences of our actions affect us in subsequent lives and since in those lives we have no recollection of our previous lives and their constituent actions, there can be, in the present life, no repentance for past deeds, no feeling of moral accountability for the deeds which occasioned the present circumstances, and no reformation with respect to those acts. Thus, the doctrine of karma cannot affect our present moral attitude toward the past beyond a general regret that whatever we did landed us in our present predicament. In Chapter 10 we shall see how this contrasts sharply with the theses that the law of karma is primarily a moral doctrine and that it provides a formidable redoubt for defenders of an objective ethic.

Finally, what is the relation of the law of karma to human liberation? There appears to be a tension between the karmic and the nirvanic spheres, especially with respect to ethical considerations. Thus an exploration of the relation between the karmic and nirvanic is required. Further, since karma is the force that drives the continuing cycle of rebirths, liberation is held to occur only when accumulated karma is exhausted. This means that the goal of the person seeking salvation is to acquire an empty or zero pool of karma. But is not the aim of seeking a zero karmic pool rather than acquiring merit contrary to an adequate ethic? And how do we know when we have attained the status of a zero karmic pool? In Chapter 11 we will respond to these questions and consider the general relation of the law of karma to human liberation and *Nirvāṇa*. In the Epilogue we will ask what can be learned from the law of karma and provide some overall perspective on both the value of and the problems facing the law of karma.

This study should allow us to gain a better perspective on both the law of karma and its philosophical adequacy. It should lead to greater understanding, better interpretation and clearer critical evaluation of the meaning and truth of the law. If we are successful, some progress will have been made in understanding and evaluating a central facet of Indian thought.

2

Metaphysical Presuppositions of the Law of Karma

To achieve understanding of a concept, it is often helpful to discern something of its origin. However, considerations of origins can be misleading, for concepts change both in content and function. Hence, to avoid any taint of the genetic fallacy, origins must be considered for the insights they can render, not for any evaluative conclusions which can be drawn from them. On the other hand, it is not merely helpful but necessary to ascertain the concept's metaphysical presuppositions. In this chapter we shall begin with a short discussion of the possible origins of the doctrine of the law of karma and then consider some of its presuppositions.

ORIGINS OF THE DOCTRINE

The origins of the doctrine of the law of karma lie shrouded in Indian history. It was unknown to the writers of the Vedas and only a veiled hint is found in the *Brāhmaṇas*. The *Śatapatha Brāhmaṇa* refers to a series of deaths which the person undergoes, thus implying transmigration, but this brief allusion is not strong enough to support any thesis that the doctrine of karma had any currency during this period.[1] However, there is enough evidence to assert that the people of this period had confidence that their ritual actions had consequences which were sufficient to affect their life after death.[2] Specifically, rites were performed to prevent the ancestors from leaving some sort of heaven and thus suffering repeated deaths.[3]

In lieu of any forthright mention of the doctrine of karma in the pre-Upaniṣadic literature, some Indologists have sought its source in other Vedic concepts. Sarvepalli Radhakrishnan traces it to the concept of an Eternal Law or *Ṛta*.[4] *Ṛta* is the order manifested in nature (for example, in the movements of the heavenly bodies and the agricultural cycles), in patterns of human conduct, and in sacrificial acts. The gods were charged with guarding and maintaining this sacred order, which in turn, as the moral order, provides for humans and gods alike the standard of right conduct. Though this quasi-ethical notion degenerated gradually to mean simply the correct, ordered performance of the sacrificial ritual, this supplied the foundation for the later development of the law of karma, which presupposes an underlying cosmic and moral order.

A.B. Keith, on the other hand, discerns its ancestry in the sacrificial notion of *Iṣṭāpūrta*. *Iṣṭi* refers to the sacrifice offered to the gods, while *pūrta* refers to the gifts given to the priests. *Iṣṭāpūrta* or the merit resulting from these sacrificial acts, though not be be conceived in any ethical sense, was held to precede individuals to the world beyond death and there to prepare for them a blissful state.[5] The focus of the concept of consequential merit gradually shifted from some heavenly realm to an intermediate state of heavens and hells where the person suffered or was rewarded until the merit or demerit was exhausted and reincarnation occurred, and finally to the reincarnated state itself.[6]

Some have seen the connection between merit transfer and rebirth mediated through the *śrāddha* or post-cremation rite performed by the son at the death of his father. First, the rite involved a transfer of merit through food. This transfer was necessary to assure that the deceased would get another body. Secondly, there are interesting parallels between the ten-day ritual of *śrāddha* and the ten days of offering following the birth of a child. 'In each case, following the day of birth/death there are ten days of offerings of rice, sesame, etc., ten being a homology to the human gestation period of ten (lunar) months. It may well be the case, then, that the completion of the temporary body on the tenth day [of the *śrāddha* ritual] is an intentional *re*birth expression.'[7] Thirdly, the *piṇḍa* offering used during the *śrāddha* ceremony has symbolic connections with pregnancy. This ball of cooked rice mixed with other ingredients was to be eaten by the sacrificer's wife if she wanted to have a son.[8]

It is in the Upaniṣads that the doctrine of karma first appears in clearly recognizable form, though presented as an esoteric teaching. But to what extent it was an accepted doctrine remains problematic.[9] Some hold that the doctrine's appearance in the older Upaniṣads indicates the age of the doctrine and infer from this that during this time it began to be propagated to the masses.[10] Others suggest that the Upaniṣads add little to the sketchy accounts of life after death found in the *Brāhmaṇas*[11]

It has also been suggested that the doctrine of karma is not of Āryan derivation at all, but rather was incorporated from the religion of the indigenous people. That it is not Dravidian in origin has been argued on the ground that the Tamils, the descendants of the Dravidians, incorporated the theory of reincarnation at a late date (fifth century AD), under the influence of Buddhism and Jainism.[12] Further, its possible connection with the *śrāddha* rite and *piṇḍa* offering possibly has geographical and historical implications. 'The rice imagery raises several possible historical questions. . . The prevalence of the rice imagery seems to exclude the Indus Valley as a source of the karma theory, for this was a wheat-growing civilization. Rice was developed on the other side of the Gangetic plain, among tribal peoples dwelling on the borderlands of South and Southeast Asia— tribes among whom an aboriginal idea of merit for the dead also occurs.'[13] This suggests tribal origins for the doctrine. On the other hand, others see the karmic doctrine as a later development brought about by the transformation of tribal beliefs. Gananath Obeyesekere agrees that the concept of rebirth was part of the religion of the tribes in the Gangetic region. However, their concept of rebirth lacked what he calls 'ethicization'. That is, the tribes believed that rebirth transferred individuals to some other world, where they stayed until they were reborn. But where they went after death was not determined by their moral acts; neither was it a place of reward or punishment. Ethicization—the imposition of religious assessment of moral action—was accomplished either by the activity of a highly specialized priesthood (as in Hinduism), by the development of ethical asceticism, or by Indian religious philosophers to meet their special proselytization needs. And it was ethicization that led to the transformation of a tribal, non-ethical rebirth eschatology into the karma eschatology.[14]

Whether the doctrine was of Āryan import or borrowed in whole or in part from the indigenous people, and if of Āryan origin and development whether it was developed by the Kṣatriyan or by the Brahmin caste,[15] are matters for the historian of Indian philosophy and not germane to our analytic consideration of the doctrine. Suffice it to say that by the time of the flowering of the heterodox systems, the doctrine was fully developed and widely accepted in both Indian thought and Indian culture.

Whatever the specific origins of the doctrine, it is clear that the original concept of karma as action was later applied specifically to the moral sphere of human action and conjoined with the doctrines of transmigration and reincarnation of the soul. From the very character of the law, we might speculate that the reason for its development had to do with a very pressing problem. The problem which confronted the Indian was how rationally to account for the diversity of circumstances and situations into which sentient creatures were born, or for the natural events experienced during one's lifetime which affected one person propitiously and another adversely. There appeared to be no obvious, prima-facie connection between the good fortune of one individual and his personal worth, or between the ill fortune of another and his worth. Accordingly, it was postulated that there is a law which governs the kind of birth, qualities of character and temperament, and subsequent circumstances that a person experiences. Thus, it was in the context of attempting to resolve a problem which was both theoretical and existential that the doctrine of karma had its inception. And indeed, beyond all else, it is its alleged explanatory power in this regard which has gained for it adherents through the centuries.

METAPHYSICAL PRESUPPOSITIONS

The law of karma comes embedded in a body of philosophical and religious doctrines. Five should be noted.

1. All actions for which we can be held morally accountable and which are done out of desire for their fruits have consequences.

Though one can find statements to the effect that all actions for which humans can be held morally accountable have consequences,[16] in fact the formulation of the law of karma is much more subtle. It is actions which are performed with an interest in achieving some result or which arise from desire and passion which bring about karmic effects. Actions which are performed in a disinterested way, which stem from no desire for the fruits of the action or which are offered to *Īśvara*, have no karmic effects (though they may have effects *per se*).

This description of the scope of the law of karma is reflected in the teaching of the *Bhagavad-Gítā*, according to which actions are to be done in such a way that the doer manifests no concern for the personal result or outcome of the action.[17] Only if an individual performs his duty in a non-attached or disinterested fashion can he cultivate the requisite attitude of desirelessness and equanimity. Such actions do not result in any karmic effects, either in this life or the next.[18]

A similar view regarding actions not performed out of desire is present in Buddhism. 'When a man's deeds, O priests, are performed without covetousness [hatred, infatuation], arise without covetousness [hatred, infatuation], are occasioned without covetousness [hatred, infatuation], originate without covetousness [hatred, infatuation], then, inasmuch as covetousness [hatred, infatuation] is gone, those deeds are abandoned, uprooted, pulled out of the ground like a palmyra-tree, and become non-existent and not liable to spring up again in the future.'[19]

Jainism reiterates the theme. Karmic matter is attracted to the soul either because of its vibrations (*yoga*) or its passions. The vibrations come from the activity of the soul, which is caused by its passions. When the passions are stilled, the person can still be active. This means that karmic matter can still be attracted to the soul. However, the karma attracted by passionless actions is non-affecting karma; the bondage thereby created lasts only an instant.

According to the law of karma, then, whether or not our actions have consequences of a karmic sort is not simply a product of the action itself but also of the attitude from which we do the act. If we have certain passions or desires for the object or the fruit of the action, the action has karmic consequences; failure to have desires for the fruits obstructs the formation of karmic consequences. This means that the law of karma differs from the causal account of human action, according to which an action has consequences simply because some action has been performed, irrespective of the particular attitude of the doer. This is not surprising, considering the fact that the law of karma is rooted in ethical considerations, whereas causal relations obtain irrespective of ethical considerations. In ethics, our intentions and desires matter in determining not only our responsibility for, but the very character and ultimate moral evaluation of, the action. The first is generally non-controversial. Where the outcome was unintended, the moral responsibility for it is lessened, though of course the causal responsibility remains.[20] The second, however, is disputed, in particular by those arguing from a strict consequentialist ethical position. Their contention is that incorporating evaluation of intentions into the evaluation of the act confuses matters of a person's virtue with objective moral evaluations of actions *per se*. Actions are to be separated from the agent for purposes of determining their rightness. As we shall see, the doctrine of karma is not committed to such a narrowing of the evaluative perspective. In figuring the moral qualities or virtues of the agent into the evaluation of the entire act-sequence it rejects this strict dichotomy between person and act.

> 2. Moral actions, as actions, have consequences according to the character of the actions performed: right actions have good consequences, wrong actions bad consequences.

Though this formulation seems to suggest a distinctly teleological ethic, this is not the case. That actions have corresponding consequences does not entail that the moral character of the actions is determined by those consequences. Rather, the reverse is true: the consequences are determined by the moral character of the actions performed.

Statement 2 again raises the question of the relation of the law of karma to the law of causation. Since according to the law of karma right actions bring forth good fruit or effects while wrong actions produce bad fruit, there is a kind of moral uniformity in the cosmic order. The very same valuational quality of the action is produced in the effect. Whether this is also characteristic of the causal relation depends upon whether the cause can produce a novel effect. This, in part, depends upon whether the effect is already contained within and emerges from the cause or whether the cause can bring about a quality which it does not contain. This was a hotly debated issue in Indian philosophy.[21]

In any case, this feature of the law of karma accounts for the fact that it is seen to encompass the law of retribution. The retributive theory of punishment holds that justice requires that the guilty should suffer for their evil actions. Whereas in Western penal theory the connection between the evil deed and the punishment is made by the conscious intervention of an agent of punishment, according to the law of karma this requirement of justice is borne out naturally in the course of events.[22] Since the law of karma is inviolable, it is inevitable that individual human persons will suffer for the evil performed, and in suffering, the persons will be punished. On the positive side, persons will be rewarded for the good they have done. The reward will be a natural outworking of their actions; right actions produce good fruit in the future. Thus, the doctrines of retributive punishment and reward are supported by the contention of the karmic law that the moral quality of the act is passed on in such a way as to affect the doer of the action at a subsequent time.

The law of karma should be distinguished from the view which holds that people receive compensation for the bad experienced in this life. According to such a view, not all of our pain and suffering is deserved. Consequently, we will receive good experiences in future existences to compensate for it.[23] This is held to be concordant with the principle of universal justice presupposed by the law of karma.

This view, however, does not comport well with the law of karma, which is essentially a causal-type law, for compensation of this sort (good for evil) requires that the effect be different from the cause in terms of its quality. If the cause be painful, unpleasant, debilitating or harmful, the effect must be pleasant and propitious. But then the natural causal relation which is held to obtain between cause and effect disappears, for if this be combined with a retributive/reward theory, effects of either homogeneous or heterogeneous quality can follow actions—homogeneous if considered retributive or rewarding, heterogeneous if considered compensatory. But this ambiguity of the consequential properties destroys the natural implementation accorded to the law of karma, for there is now no regularity of result, that is, no ordered, qualitative sequencing from cause to effect. Both qualitatively like and unlike consequences can follow an action, and one would be hard pressed to discern anything from the action itself which would determine which kind of consequential property would predominate. Only in a theistic system, where God compensates the individual for wrongs unjustly suffered, would the compensation of good for evil experienced be considered feasible.

Further, compensatory good karma for evil experienced is incompatible with the basic intent of the law of karma. According to the law of karma, our present circumstances are the *result* of past actions. However, if compensation in the future is stressed, it follows that the circumstances in which we currently find ourselves might not be the result of past deeds; otherwise compensation would not be required. That is, our present experience, situation or status might really not be merited. But this introduces the very thing that the law of karma was supposed to eliminate, namely, the role of chance in our life. If our present state is not merited, it is the result of chance. This surely violates both the purpose of the karmic system and its fundamental presupposition of cosmic, causal, moral order. In short, compensation considered in terms of making up for unmerited deficiencies experienced now is incompatible with the law of karma which holds that our present circumstances are a result of our past deeds. Only if compensation is seen in terms of reward for good actions or punishment for evil actions is it consistent with the law of karma interpreted non-theistically.

> 3. Some consequences are manifested immediately or in this life, some in the next life, and some remotely.

That is, while the agent will experience some of the consequences in this life, many of the consequences are such that they will affect the agent sometime in his future lives.[24]

This thesis again suggests comparison of the law of karma with the law of causation. The law of causation applies to two events or things that are temporally conjoined. But the law of karma states that some effects are manifested at some time in the distant future, either in the next life or in more temporally remote lives. Thus the immediacy of the temporal relation found in the causal law is absent in the law of karma. The obvious solution to this is to postulate intermediate bearers of the karmic element from the original act to ultimate consequences. The nature of these and the problems which arise will be discussed in chapters 3 and 6.

4. The effects of karmic actions can be accumulated.

Various ways of classifying karma are suggested by the philosophical systems, the Jainas showing the greatest propensity for making distinctions. They have different names for karma, depending upon the effect which the karmic action produces. There are four kinds of karma which act to keep the self in bondage (called obscuring-karma). These are the karma which produces false views or delusion (*mohanīya*), karma which clouds our knowledge (*jñānāvaraṉīya*), karma which clouds perception or intuition (*darśanāvaraṇiya*), and karma which restricts the quality of energy and restricts its enjoyment of wealth and power (*antarāya*). There is also the karma which does not obscure any inherent soul qualities, but rather is responsible for the mechanism of rebirth and re-embodiment (non-obscuring karma). *Nāma-karma* determines ninety-eight different aspects of the future body, including its type (whether human, insect, or animal), sex and colour; *gotra-karma* determines the environment into which one is born, including the family, race, and caste; *vedanīya-karma* produces 'either pleasant or unpleasant feelings in response to the environment, hence the level of happiness or unhappiness which characterizes an individual'; *āyuh-karma*, which is generally acquired in the last third of our life, determines the length of the next life, measured by the number of breaths we will take.[25]

Another classification is given in terms of the moral quality of the karmic action, whether good or bad. Black karma is karma created by evil persons doing evil acts. White karma is karma achieved through penance, study, and meditation by persons who have purified themselves. Generally it is held that this karma can only occur in the form of mental states, since all external actions cause some harm to other living beings. Black and white karma are created by acts which produce both good and bad effects. Even good acts, though beneficial generally, usually bring about pain and suffering, perhaps even death, to other living creatures. An example is given of accidentally killing ants while pounding rice. Finally, there is neither-white-nor-black karma. This is the karma of those who have renounced everything. They are completely above black karma; white and black karma cannot occur because in their asceticism they no longer use external means to achieve anything; white karma does not accrue because they renounce all the fruit of their actions (for example, by offering it to *Īśvara*).[26] In effect, producing neither-black-nor-white karma is equivalent to producing no karma at all.[27]

A third classification refers to the temporal status of the karmic effects *vis-à-vis* our present existence. *Prārabdha* karma is karma which has matured and whose fruits we are currently experiencing. This karma is inescapable; it is like the 'wheel of a potter which has been already turned; [it] comes to a stop only when the momentum imparted to it becomes exhausted'.[28] *Sañcita* karma is karma which has accrued in the past and is ready to mature. This karma can be averted; if it is good karma, bad karma will help nullify it, and vice versa if it is bad karma. Finally, *āgami* or *sañcīyamāna* karma is karma which we are laying up in our present existence. The actions performed now determine the contents of this karma. The importance of this last category is that it leaves open the possibility that we can affect at least some of the karma that we have built up but have not yet experienced. The significance of this will become clear when we raise the common charge of fatalism against the law of karma in chapter 4.

This brief account of the kinds of karma not only shows the human ability to classify, but also reveals something about the nature of karma, namely, that karma-producing actions often are considered jointly and not individually in bringing about subsequent events.[29] More specifically, karmic consequences are often understood in terms of the *saṃskāras* created in the doer of the action. *Saṃskāras* are the invisible, stored tendencies and dispositions in the agent to repeat the kind of action which was done, whether good or bad, at some subsequent, appropriate time.[30] For example, an action performed out of greed creates or enhances a greedy disposition. The karmic consequences accumulate in the sense that the tendencies get stronger and bear fruit. An individual's karmic residues, on this account, appear as a pool of dispositions which has been filled by prior actions of the individual. That pool is composed of specific tendencies: tendencies to be greedy, generous, cruel, loving, jealous, forgiving, forgetful, lustful, and so on. This pool continues to be affected by the ongoing free actions of the individual. A person may add to this pool by performing actions, either right or wrong, consonant with the primary character of the pool. The pool may also be drained by actualizing the karmic residues already in it. Or by performing actions to counteract the karmic residues already in the pool a person may dilute the pool, wrong actions diluting the good pool, right the bad.[31] On this view individual actions are not preserved. What they do is contribute in their own way to this pool of tendencies or dispositions found within the individual human person. Accordingly, the events which we experience have no unique connection with any particular, prior action, but rather with the pool as a whole. Thus we know that we cannot experience any pain or pleasure greater than allowed by the pool, though we could experience less at any given time. We also know that to be liberated, all good or bad karma must be exhausted; the amount in the pool must be zero, the point where there is no more karma to be worked off.

Now this notion, which seems most consistent with attempts to spell out the working of the law of karma, differs substantially from many descriptions of the law's implementation. Accounts purporting to explain particular cases of good or bad experiences often appeal to specific, prior instances. For example, in the Buddha's account of Moggallāna's death both his death and its specific mode (being slain by highwaymen) are explained by the story of how, goaded by the wife forced on him by his parents, he imitated the sound of highwaymen and slew his blind parents in order to achieve domestic tranquillity.[32] A similar story is told to King Pasenadi the Kosalan to answer his query why a particular householder, who was treasurer in Sāvatthi, lived a life of abject poverty despite being tremendously wealthy, and died leaving no son. The reason given is that because he rued giving alms to the monks rather than to his servants and murdered his brother's son for the inheritance, he was averse to sumptuous food, clothing, and living, died childless in seven successive existences, and suffered excruciating tortures in hell for thousands of years.[33] There are also detailed lists of connections between specific acts and particular types of reincarnated existences.[34] For example, for stealing grain a person will be reincarnated as a rat, for stealing linen as a frog, and for eating forbidden food as a worm.

What these accounts suggest is that there is a correlation between the quality of previous acts (good or bad) and the types of resulting experiences (pleasurable or painful), the quantity of evil done and the amount of pain and pleasure experienced, and (at times) the kind of karmic action done (for example, murder, theft, beatings, and so on) or the way it was done (as with

Moggallāna imitating the highwaymen) and the kind of experiences one has as a result.

A possible solution to this apparent discrepancy is that, though karma generally must be viewed as a pool from which we draw, yet there are some acts which are so powerful in creating karmic residues that their effects can be specially traced back to the original act. For example, the karmic residues created maintain a kind of separate existence, to become causally effective at some later date, or again, the effects are imprinted into the dispositional character of the individual in such a way and to such a degree that at some future date they mature in a manner which can be explained only by the karmic residues of this particular act. This might be the case, for example, in those instances where our final thoughts are held to be determinative of our future existence,[35] or where the action we did was so distinctive that it remains emblazoned on our subconscious in such a way that even in later lives it can be recalled. However the two differing accounts are reconciled, any explanation of how the law of karma operates must explain both the general and the specific accounts of the connection between the karmic act and the effects experienced in later lives.

Though appeal to a cumulative pool of dispositional tendencies provides an account of how our previous acts affect our current behaviour, it would appear that a dispositional theory by itself is unable to account for all the evil (pain, suffering, dysfunction) which we encounter. It would account for the moral evils (evils for which the individual can be held morally accountable) that we do to one another and to ourselves. In this regard it explains why we (mis)treat others or our environment as we do and so bring pleasure or pain upon ourselves. But it cannot account for the evils which are done to us which have nothing to do with our dispositions. Consider the following case. Suppose my house burns to the ground in a raging forest fire ignited by lightning. Since this is a bad experience for me, the karmic theorist would appeal to my previous karmic acts and/or the pool created by them to explain why it burned. But in this case, what causally links my previous actions and the karmic pool they created with the lightning and the forest fire? In what way did the previous act and/or pool function as the or a cause of the fire itself? What is there in the pool which made me suffer the burning of my house rather than another calamity? What caused the fire, not only to strike me, but to do so with the particular intensity it did? The causal link with the previous act and/or pool of karma we have accumulated does not seem to be in the realm of the *saṃskāras*, for it has nothing to do with my behaviour. It would seem odd indeed to say that I have a disposition to have my house burned down by forest fires.

To resolve this, some, such as the Vaiśeṣikas, have appealed to an invisible moral force or potency (*adṛṣṭa*), which bears the merit and demerit of the karmic act. This moral force or quality attaches to, and can be accumulated and stored as a quality of, the self or *ātman*. Since the self is omnipresent, it is capable through its qualities of having effects in the physical universe outside of the particular body with which it is associated. In particular, the *adṛṣṭa* either can function as a particular causal condition for any event, or can represent a higher level of causality which ultimately allows or counteracts other causal conditions.[36] In our example, *adṛṣṭa* would be causally efficacious in creating the forest fire which burned our house or at least letting it burn down our particular house (for example, by removing obstructions to the fire burning in our direction). But in what way does *adṛṣṭa* causally condition any given event in the universe? This is particularly troublesome since *adṛṣṭa* is invisible and hence not subject to empirical verification. And is the concept of an omnipresent self unobjectionable? We shall take up these issues in chapters 6 and 7 respectively.

5. Human persons are reborn into this world.

The doctrine of karma took root historically alongside the doctrines of transmigration, reincarnation and rebirth, and it is not difficult to see why. Unless the very same person experiences a sequential series of lives, of which birth and death of the body are mere features of experience, the justice element is compromised, for justice requires that it be the *same* person who is either rewarded or punished for the past deeds he has done. Thus the law of karma presupposes that the human person is capable of undergoing a series of transmigrations or rebirths. It also seems to imply certain things about the nature of the person who is to be reborn, in particular, that this person is a substantial self with certain (to be further specified) continuous features.

These features must account both for personal identity over time and for continuity of dispositions. We shall examine this thesis more closely in chapters 7 and 8 when we examine the doctrines of *ātman* (self) and *anātman* (no self) insofar as they relate to the law of karma.

CONCLUSION

Our sketch of some of the presuppositions of the law of karma substantiates our claim that the law of karma is a metaphysical doctrine. It has brought to the fore metaphysical problems and issues with which we must deal if we are to agree to the doctrine. These issues include the nature of causation which the law of karma presupposes, the manner in which the law is implemented, the nature of the human person who is reborn, and how merit and demerit become connected with our good and bad experiences. Before we undertake the investigation of these and other issues, however, something must be said about the relation of the law of karma to the law of causation (for the law of causation has been a constant companion in our discussion) and the epistemic status of the law of karma. To this we turn in the next chapter.

3

The Laws of Karma and Causation

In the previous chapters we raised questions concerning the relation of the law of karma to the law of universal causation. In this chapter it will be our intent first to clarify the relation between these two laws. Then we will inquire concerning the epistemological status of the law of karma. Is the law of karma a convenient fiction which, though it enables the believer to resolve certain philosophical and practical problems, is not descriptive of empirical states of affairs? Or is it an empirical generalization from certain experiences known by a person whose self-advancement makes possible extraordinary perceptual states? Or is it to be considered a necessary, presuppositional postulate with empirical content? The answer to this question should help us to understand better how the law of karma is to function in discussions which invoke it and provide direction for the remainder of our study.

THE RELATION OF THE LAW OF KARMA TO THE LAW OF UNIVERSAL CAUSATION

In Chapter 1 we argued that the law of karma is a causal law. Actions performed with certain attitudes cause karmic effects. For example, particular actions produce in us particular karmic residues which affect our behaviour later in this and subsequent lives. However, we have also noted that the law of karma is not strictly identical with the law of universal causation. The reasons for this claim should be apparent from our above discussion. First, whereas the causal law is concerned with producing results regardless of whom they affect, the law of karma is concerned with the effects of the action insofar as they ultimately impinge upon the doer of the action. Second, whereas according to the law of universal causation the production of effects does not depend on the intentions of the agent (except as they are causally related to actions) but on his action, the karmic relation depends upon both. As we have seen, it is held that actions which are not performed out of desire for their fruits have no karmic consequences, even though they have causal consequences. Third, according to the law of karma like causes produce like effects. Right actions produce good consequences, wrong actions bad consequences. However, it is not obvious that like producing like is a characteristic of all causation. Fourth, whereas the causal law holds irrespective of moral judgements, the causal feature which is central to the law of karma is a moral one. That is, it is not concerned with the general relation between actions and their consequences, but with a specific aspect of certain actions, namely, the moral aspect and its consequences for human happiness and unhappiness. Fifth, the law of causation applies to two events or things that are temporally conjoined, whereas the law of karma states that the effects are manifested at some time in the distant future, either in the next life or in more temporally remote lives. Thus the immediacy of the temporal relation found in the causal law is absent in the law of karma.

In short, there is good reason to think that, though the law of karma is a causal law, it is not identical with the law of universal causation. But if we conclude that the law of karma is an application of the law of universal causation to moral causation, how can we account for the differences between them? Is any kind of reconciliation possible?

One possibility is to make a distinction between two kinds of effects, which we might term *phalas* and *saṃskāras*. Phalas include all the immediate effects, visible and invisible, which actions produce or bring about. They are often referred to as the results or fruits of an action. *Saṃskāras* are the invisible dispositions or tendencies to act, think, experience, or interpret experiences in ways which are conducive to one's happiness or unhappiness, produced in the agent as a result of the action.[1] They constitute, in effect, special modifications of the agent.

Using this distinction, one can argue that the laws are consistent. The law of universal causation speaks to the production of *phalas:* every act produces *phalas* (results) in the world. The law of karma, however, speaks to the production of *saṃskāras*: every karmic act produces *saṃskāras* in the agent. The two laws are related in that the law of karma is the application of the law of universal causation, which deals in general with the relation between the act and its effects, to a specific aspect of certain kinds of actions. It concerns the disposition- or *saṃskāras*-producing aspect of disposition-producing actions. The law of karma, then, is the more limited law.

This distinction between *phalas* and *saṃskāras* holds promise for resolving the differences between the laws noted above. First, it accounts for the specificity, found in the law of karma, of who is affected by the results. Since the law of karma focuses on the formation of *saṃskāras*, its concern is with the *agent's saṃskāras* and not another's.

Secondly, it accounts for the fact that in karmic causation the arising of the effect depends on the intention of the agent, for the formation of the disposition follows properly on the original intention. All actions have *phalas*, but only actions produced from desire recoil on the doer of the action. Only when action is performed out of some desire to realize a worldly end is the corresponding disposition or tendency to repeat the same kind of action in future lives produced. This seems reasonable, for dispositions are formed consistent with the attitude in which the original act was performed. Actions performed out of greed tend to produce a greedy disposition; but an action performed out of no desire for personal gain but to please others or for the good of the work would tend to produce a disposition of wanting to please others or to work skilfully. And it might be reasonable to hold that actions produced from complete equanimity produce no dispositions at all.

Thirdly, it accounts for the fact that, in karmic causation, like produces like, for actions of one sort, for example, done spitefully, will produce like dispositions, for example, to act spitefully. This, in turn, accounts for the fourth difference, that is, for the relevance of the moral feature in karmic causation. Intentions are particularly important for determining the moral quality, if not of the action, at least of the agent who performed the action. A person who performs an action which results in bringing about good but which was done to bring harm is immoral because he engaged in it for that reason. In karmic actions, since the resulting disposition correlates in kind with the intentions which the agent had in performing the action, the moral quality (in the form of a potency) is passed on and preserved. Acts performed with right intentions lead to dispositions to perform like acts; acts performed with the wrong intent produce corresponding dispositions.

Finally, this distinction also solves the problem of immediate versus delayed results. All effects, including *saṃskāras*, are immediately produced. But though produced immediately, *saṃskāras* (as tendencies or potencies) are not actualized until some future time when the proper actualizing conditions are present. This interpretation is confirmed by frequent references likening karmic fruits to seeds which, though produced at a particular time, lie dormant until the appropriate conditions for germination occur.

CAN WE RESTRICT KARMA TO *SAṂSKĀRAS*?

Unhappily though, promising as it is, this resolution is not without difficulties.

1. First, if only *saṃskāras* have relevance, what is important in karmic considerations is what forms dispositions. Future dispositions or tendencies arise not from the results of the act, but from the dispositions or intentions out of which we acted. If so, what matter are the attitudes, desires, passions, dispositions, and general character with which we perform the action and not the actions *per se* and their general results. That is, the karma produced by an action is determined largely by the intentions, dispositions, desires, character and moral virtue of the agent.

This emphasis on formative dispositions, desires, and intentions seems to accord well with the Buddhist emphasis on will or intentional impulse (*cetanā*). In early Buddhism, *kamma* is virtually defined as *cetanā*: 'I say, monks, that *cetanā* is *kamma*; having intended, one does a deed by body, word, or thought'.[2] Actions performed without intention produce no karma, whereas intention alone is capable of producing it. That is, intention is not only a necessary condition for considering an act to be moral or immoral, it is sometimes held to be sufficient.[3]

However, such an emphasis on originating dispositions and intentions as determinative of moral quality implies that it matters little *what* we do. Consequently, with respect to our accumulation of karma it would mean we could do the most despicable acts, so long as our attitude and dispositions were correct. Even though consequences might be partially determinative of the morality of an act, they can be irrelevant or minimally relevant to karmic considerations. This begins to drive a wedge between the law of karma and the moral law governing actions it is sworn to uphold.

Further, it is inconsistent with the fourfold classification of karma in terms of consequences, noted in chapter 2, found in both Hinduism and Buddhism. For example, acts which have good intentions but which also have bad consequences, intentional or unintentional, are classified not as white karma (which would be the case if only the intention mattered) but as black and white karma.

We cannot so easily separate intentions from action. In Buddhism, for example, though some, such as Vasubandhu, make *cetanā* a mental act and distinguish it from the physical and vocal acts which follow from it, others interpret *cetanā* more broadly to include both the intention and the resultant actions. 'Mental acts are pure intentional impulse, while acts of body and voice are intentional impulses which put the body and voice in motion, not simply the actions ensuant upon such impluses.'[4] The vocal or physical act is, as it were, the thought or intention incarnate. Buddhism refuses to make the clear-cut distinction between mental act and bodily and vocal acts found in Western action theory. Thus even where intention is determinative, the intrinsic connection between intention and act, where act is intention made manifest, makes it impossible that a good intention is knowingly and willingly followed by an evil act.[5]

Put more broadly in a different framework, though it is true that right intentions are necessary for building character, they are not sufficient. Frequent reference is made to a stage of the path to liberation where the person has the right knowledge and intention, but lacks sufficient spiritual strength to carry out the intention. If the intention is not implemented sufficiently, this will affect the intentions of the agent, for he will begin to question whether he should bother to form the intention since he regularly fails to act on it. Persistent right intentions without implementation lead to regression; it is not a stage at which one can remain. It is like the traditional making of New Year's resolutions. After a while, if there is no serious attempt to keep the resolutions, the making of the resolutions is either foregone, or it becomes a ritualistic game with no moral significance for the maker. Rather, it is the brunt of a bad joke.

2. A second objection to the restriction of karmic efficacy to *saṃskāras* is that this denial of karmic efficacy to *phalas* in general

separates two things which are functionally inseparable in the doctrine of karma, namely the visible or physical and the invisible and moral. It is precisely the strength of the doctrine of karma that it links the pain and pleasure that we experience with cosmic or environmental conditions, and these conditions in turn with the moral quality of actions performed. But this distinction between *phalas* and *saṃskāras* severs that connection. *Phalas* now seem to function in their own sphere, immediate, short-lived, affecting the agent as one among others and other things, whereas *saṃskāras*, which are the proper concern of the law of karma, are the seeds sown to bear fruit in future experiences. But our human predicament is not merely the product of our dispositions and tendencies; it is also the product of our environment.

It might be argued in response that pain and pleasure are not objective but subjective. We experience pain and pleasure because that is the way in which we interpret our experiences, and this interpretative perspective arises from our dispositions, which are caused by our karma. Accordingly, if we can control the way we view our experiences, we can control and eventually eliminate pain and pleasure from our existence. In effect, then, *phalas* in themselves are irrelevant to our future, karmically caused experiences. What really matters is internal to us, that is, the dispositions and tendencies we create within ourselves which affect our interpretation and understanding of our experiences.

This view is consistent with the Buddhist emphasis upon adopting the proper inner attitude and spirit and with certain important Buddhist teachings,[6] including the doctrine of Dependent Origination. According to this, we have contact with the environment, and this causes us to crave or desire things, which in turn causes grasping or clinging to things, which finally brings rebirth, misery, and sorrow. If we can eliminate the cravings, we can eliminate both the search for satisfaction and the frustrations of dissatisfaction, and this in turn will mean the elimination of pain and misery. And cravings are eliminated through terminating the *saṃskāras*—the drives, impulses, and dispositions karmically produced in us, and this through overcoming ignorance about our true nature and condition and following the Eightfold Path. Note that in all this, the primary source of pain and pleasure is not objective or external (though of course the external or environmental is a condition or occasion for it), but subjective or internal. That is, pain and pleasure are created by us as we react to our circumstances. We are disposed to interpret our experiences in this way. Thus, by controlling our reactions and the desires from which they stem, we can control our responses of pain and pleasure and ultimately eliminate both. This goal is achieved in adopting the attitude of equanimity toward all events.

Yoga might also be interpreted as offering, at least in part, a subjective view of pleasure and pain, though in a different vein. Yoga too has a cycle or 'six-spoked wheel' driven by ignorance. From virtue and vice come pleasure and pain; from these come respectively the *saṃskāras* of attachment and aversion. From these *saṃskāras* come effort, and from effort action by mind, body and speech. This action favours or injures others, creating virtue and vice, and the cycle begins anew.[7] Here the experiences of pleasure and pain are causes of the dispositions, and not their results. Hence pleasure and pain are not attitudes but experiences which result from our actions. Exactly how pain and pleasure arise from virtue and vice is unclear, though what is clear is the presupposition that virtue is rewarded with pleasure and vice with pain.[8]

Where then is the subjective flavour? It arises in the discussion, not concerning the causes of pleasure and pain, but concerning how to eliminate them. In the Yoga account the *saṃskāras*, along with the other named afflictions (ignorance in taking the non-eternal, impure, painful, and non-self to be eternal, pure, pleasurable, and the self; egoism; and love of life) are responsible for our accumulation of merit and demerit (called the vehicle of actions). This accumulation determines our subsequent birth(s), the length of our lives, and our experiences of pleasure and pain. Insofar as ignorance is the breeding-ground or field for the afflictions, and these bear fruit in pain and pleasure, the latter can be ended through proper 'cultivation' of that field. That is, pleasure and pain can be eliminated by the separation of the knower from that which is knowable, the cognizer or self from the field of its experience, and this can be done by meditation.[9] Pain and pleasure, then, are subjective, not in the sense that they are attitudes which we adopt, but in that they can be eliminated though gaining control over the mind (detachment, becoming one-pointed) and restraining and ultimately ceasing its modifications.

That karma works only subjectively is an important possibility, for it means that our painful and pleasant experiences are our own responsibility. Pain and pleasure, though in one sense resulting from our experiences, are in another and most real sense created by us out of our dispositions and tendencies both to have desires and to view the world in this way. Our environment provides only a setting, a backdrop against which we react. Thus there is both individual responsibility for interpreting the world in a certain way and the promise of being able to alter that interpretation through removing those dispositions through the removal of ignorance and desire, or by separating the self from the world entirely.

However, even supposing that pain and pleasure are subjective, it is difficult to isolate pain and pleasure from the environmental instruments which occasion them. Indeed, it is generally held that karma affects these as well. Length of life, health and sickness, handsomeness or beauty and ugliness, social position, wealth and poverty, the kind of body and intellectual ability acquired at birth, fortune and misfortune, all are believed to be caused by karma.[10] As we noted in chapter 2, in Jainism in addition to the subjectively-operative obscuring karma, there is the objectively-operative non-obscuring karma which is responsible for the mechanisms and objective features of rebirth. Even in the *Yoga-Sūtra* the karmic residues (vehicle of action) ripen into a determination of our quantity of existence.[11]

There are, in effect, two stories, the subjective and the objective. According to the first, karma works through us, creating dispositions and tendencies, merit and demerit, which in turn affect our desires, passions, and perspective on the world. So seen, karma disposes us to interpret our experiences and to act in ways which bring us pain and pleasure. Here the appeal to *saṃskāras* (or something similar) provides a reasonable basis for constructing a naturalistic account of the causal operations of karma. According to the second, our karmic acts affect the instruments of our experiences, from our own bodies to the world around us. They help determine, among other things, the kinds of bodies with which we are reborn, our social status, and how other persons and things in the environment act on us. These instruments mediate properly determined karma to us, so that one can say that we deserve what happens to us. Here the saṃskāric account by itself is inadequate. Since both accounts are part of the tradition, an explanation of how karma affects objective as well as subjective conditions is necessary.

In chapter 6 we shall look at the attempt to re-establish the linkage between the environment and the dispositional. What is suggested is that karma is propagated through the dispositions until such time as it bears fruit when the person with a given set of dispositions creates (in part) his environment. Our environmental conditions are a product, in part, of our current actions and dispositions. This environment will in turn affect us, both in forming the context for our karma-producing actions and in being the instrument for the appropriate recompense for our past deeds. The adequacy, then, of this reconciliation of the two laws by the distinction between *phalas* and *saṃskāras* rests on the adequacy of the account which brings the dispositional and the environmental-physical back together.

3. Finally, the restriction of karmic concerns to *saṃskāras* proves unsatisfactory in cases where the action bears fruit in ways which have no obvious connection with the action, or where the happiness or unhappiness experienced and its causes have nothing to do with dispositions or tendencies. Let us consider two cases to illustrate these.

Suppose we contract malaria. As an unpleasant experience, this must be the just recompense for some previous misdeed(s). On the account of the law of karma just given, our contracting malaria might be explained in terms of some *saṃskāra*, for example, our susceptibility to the disease. This susceptibility, resulting from some action(s) done in this or previous lives, has remained dormant until we encountered malaria-carrying mosquitoes in our environment. There is a continuous causal chain from our action(s) to our disease; they are connected causally by the susceptibility which resides in us. But what is the causal connection between the original act(s) and our susceptibility to *malaria*? What is there about what we have done which brings about this susceptibility rather than another? And what is there causally to justify the thesis that this susceptibility rather than another is morally justified in terms of the demerit accruing to our action(s)? The causal connection between the original action(s) and the susceptibility which arises is unaccounted for.

Consider a second case, mentioned in chapter 2. My house burns to the ground in a raging forest fire ignited by lightning. Since this is a bad experience, the karmic theorist would appeal to some of my previous action(s) to explain why it burned. But in this case, what causally links my previous actions(s) and the burning of my house? That is, why did the house burn rather than another calamity strike, and what caused the fire to burn my house (and not another's) or to destroy it rather than fill it with smoke? How am I a cause of the fire and/or of its burning my house? Since the lightning, forest fire, and house burning have nothing to do with my dispositions, the causal link here is not in the realm of the *saṃskāras* but the *phalas*, visible or invisible. One possible response to both cases is to expand the concept of *saṃskāra* to include special modifications of the agent other than simply dispositions and tendencies. As we shall see in chapter 6, there are various interpretations as to how karmic residues are stored in the agent. This includes, in addition to dispositions and tendencies, the storing of special, invisible moral potencies or forces (*adṛṣṭa*) or the accumulation of invisible karmic matter which our passions and actions attract to us and which forms a 'subtle body' that accompanies the soul. Using this broadened notion of special modifications to the agent, one could argue that the contracting of malaria or the burning of the house was caused by the special moral quality which existed in us.

Yet the problems remain. Why do our action(s) occasion malaria or the burning of our house rather than another calamity? Further, how does this moral or physical quality connect with establishing this as the appropriate and just recompense? That is, what is the connection between a so-called moral quality and the justness of an event which it causes? In ordinary causation, the mere fact that the cause has a property does not entail that the effect will possess it as well. For example, that the hammer is made of grey, hardened metal tells us nothing about the colour or composition of the things it affects. And finally, what is the *causal* connection between these special modifications and the environment which caused the fire? Here we return again to the issue raised above, for it is not obvious how, for example, *moral* qualities existing in the agent can cause forest fires or houses to burn or remove impediments to such.

We conclude, then, that *phalas* in general *are* relevant to rebirth. If so, then karmic consideration must be paid to the general consequences of the act as well as to the specific, saṃskāric consequences which are produced in the agent.

PROBLEMS WITH EXTENDING KARMA TO *PHALAS*

The contention that *phalas* in general are relevant to rebirth is also not without difficulty. For one thing, since according to the law of universal causation all acts have *phalas* or consequences, the very actions performed in order to live will have results. Will another rebirth be necessary to fulfill the consequences of these acts? If so, the question arises whether escape from *saṃsāra*, even for those well on their way to enlightenment or *Nirvāṇa*, is possible.

One possible solution is simply to deny the universality of the law of causation. That is, if one affirms that some acts have no effects or *phalas*, the acts of the saint about to be liberated could be of this sort and thus create no karma. However, many advocates of the law of karma wish to maintain the law of universal causation, especially since a denial of this law could in turn be used against the universality of the law of karma.

A different resolution is suggested by the Jainas. They argue that the perfect state is realized in the cessation of all activity, when no more karma is accumulated. And we cease activity when we liberate the soul from the passions which delude it and obscure and distort its capacities. The passionless saint on the verge of emancipation still acts, but these acts create only momentary karma, which is quickly and immediately exhausted. The final acts, if not much of the life, of such a person would be of minimal moment, producing as little as possible of what can be immediately used up. Indeed, he would be largely engaged in meditation. As the one about to be liberated gradually approaches inactivity, he uses up the remaining karma, as passionless creates no new significant karma, and in his acts produces results with only momentary karma, until finally activity itself ceases.[12]

One can find a similar view in Yoga. The *yogin* in his final stage, who has rooted out the afflictions, renounced all actions, and whose present life will be his last, performs no actions which depend upon external means. By meditation alone he destroys the last vestiges of karma while accumulating no new karma, since the fruits of his mental actions are offered to *Īśvara*.[13]

A third reply would be that the final rebirth would be one where the individual suffers—and thus completes the karmic debt—but where the individual does not act—and thus fails to accrue further karmic debt. Since it is impossible for an individual to live as a person and not act, the final reincarnation would be in a lower form of life which would suffer the final karmic debt. As a lower form of life it would not accumulate further debt, since only conscious actions or actions for which the individual can be held morally accountable create karma. The story of the Emperor Aśoka, who was incarnated briefly as a maggot before being transformed into a deity, illustrates the point, though it hardly makes it more believable. This response suggests, however, that reincarnation in lower forms of life may play a more significant role in karmic systems than generally allowed.

There is, however, a more serious problem with this view. How do the karmic aspects of the general effects impinge on the agent? In particular how are the appropriate and just deserts meted out through insentient nature? We will suggest in chapter 6 that some kind of conscious agent seems necessary to administer the unconscious law of karma, that is, both to be aware of these *phalas* and to apportion out their effects.

In sum, it seems reasonable to contend that the law of karma is a special application of the law of universal causation. In particular, it refers to some special modification of the agent which includes, among other things, dispositions and tendencies which have an important connection with moral actions. But what remains to be explained is the relation between these special modifications and the environmental effects which cause in us good or bad experiences. We shall take up this central issue in chapter 6.

KARMA AND HEREDITY

Discussion of the causal law and the production of *saṃskāras* in future existents raises an interesting question: what is the relation of the law of karma to contemporary theories of heredity?

That there are differences in explanation is obvious. For one thing, according to genetic theory, inherited characteristics are derived from beings who are causally related to, though ontologically distinct from, the one affected. But the law of karma deals not with two separate individuals but with one: the doer of the action and the person who is consequently disposed to act in certain ways are the same person. The doer exists in one life;

the disposed exists both in that life and in subsequent lives.

For another, geneticists contend that much of who we are, both actual and potential, is a product of the genetic code which we have inherited from our parents. Our genes, to a great extent, determine our size, colour of eyes, hair and skin, physical shape, development of our sense organs, mental capacity, susceptibility or immunity to certain diseases, tendencies to certain emotional states, personality traits, and much more. According to the law of karma, however, the psychophysical traits of the newborn are the product of the person who is to be reborn. That is, though the parents might function in some intermediary role, yet what traits are transmitted are the effect of the child's previous moral actions and accumulated karma.[14]

How is genetic theory to be reconciled with the view that it is our karmic residues which determine these very features? To resolve the difficulty, could we understand our *saṃskāras* or tendencies in terms of the genetic heritage deposited in us? It seems not, for such a move to reduce the *saṃskāras* to the genetic would call into question the law of karma. Its purpose is to explain the evils that we suffer. But if our body, circumstances or our birth, dispositional traits, and psychophysical characteristics are due to our parents, then the explanation of why we are afflicted with a certain body or an inherited disease apparently has nothing to do with karma, or at least our karma. Of course, it might have to do with the karma of our parents, which then devolves upon us. But this alters the usual view that our experiences are individually merited, for now my experiences have nothing to do with my previous actions, but with those of my parents. This not only entails a sweeping revision of the law of karma, but also introduces the view that the transmission of karmic residues from one person to another is consistent with justice, a position which is generally denied, especially when it involves the transfer of negative attributes.[15]

Another possible response is that the reincarnated self, which takes up its existence in the conceptus, works (in either a conscious or more likely an unconscious, causal way) with this genetic material to create a psychophysical organism consistent with previous karmic acts or the pool of karma. That is, though one might suggest that the parents through the transmission of certain genes caused the child to have certain characteristics, this is not the complete story, for the very determination of these traits—especially as they affect the pleasure and pain or good and bad fortune experienced by the child—is the result of the child's own previous wilful acts. The question then becomes how the wilful actions of the child and the karmic residues (or the karma formed in the pool) can affect the transmitted genetic material to bring about the appropriate effects. Somehow the genes must work with the elements which transmigrate to produce their result. If, as Advaita Vedānta and Sāṅkhya hold, that which transmigrates does so via the semen and includes the physical in subtle form, this would provide for some kind of causal connection between the transmigrating self and the genetic heritage from the parents. The final product—the new person—is consequently a result of the combined action of the father through the genetic contribution found in the sperm, the mother through the genetic contribution contained in the ovum, and the transmigrating self with its subtle body. Obviously, then, though heredity will affect certain of the person's traits, how it works depends on the qualities of the transmigrating self, and these qualities have been determined by previous karmic actions.

Whether this answer is viable depends, for one thing, on the reasonableness of the contention that there is a transmigrating self with a subtle body, a matter we will take up in chapter 7. It also must explain why there is so much genetic regularity between parents and offspring, something which one would not expect if the transmigrating self plays such a central role in determining which genetic features will be transmitted and in what ways they will be effectual. For example, this view of the transmigrating self co-operating with and acting on genetic materials seems incompatible with the certainty with which we can breed animals (and perhaps humans) to have certain characteristics. Finally, it must explain why we can cure genetic diseases or prevent susceptibility merely by altering the transmitted genetic material. If the law of karma determines these qualities of every rebirth, it would seem that we should not be able to tamper with that feature by merely altering the genes. Or if the transmigrating self helped create or determine the character of the genetic material in the first place, it should be able to react in ways which would counter the genetic manipulation and preserve intact the karmic consequences and dispositions, despite the efforts of others to alter it. This would also appear to be an unacceptable tampering with the law of karma, for in altering persons before they have acted, we have tampered with their karmic dispositions or character, or at the very least the vehicle with which they approach the environment (that is, what they are susceptible to which is designed to bring appropriately proportioned pain or pleasure in this life.[16]

STATUS OF THE LAW OF KARMA

It is time to turn to our second major question, namely, what is the epistemological status of the law of karma?

1. Eliot Deutsch has argued that the law of karma is a convenient fiction. This, he says, means that the law of karma is indemonstrable and hence cannot be shown to be either true or false.[17] If this is all he means by the term 'fiction', it would be clearer to say simply that the law of karma is indemonstrable, a thesis which is not in dispute. However, at one point he states that to assert the doctrine 'as a literal truth [describing relations between lives] would involve an unjustified extrapolation from a limited phenomenal fact'. The law, then, as a fiction does not describe the empirical course of events, but is a 'rational concept or idea' which, in a Kantian sense, is useful in helping us 'interpret human experience'.[18] In short, as a fiction the law speaks to the way in which we understand and interpret our experience; it is not meant actually to describe the way the world operates.[19]

For Deutsch, the law of karma serves several functions. First, it can be used to instil in us the awareness that actions performed out of desire continue our bondage, and that only as we become aware of this and seek to reduce and ultimately eliminate our desires can we make progress toward liberation. It thus becomes a conceptual tool to help us understand both bondage and liberation. Secondly, it aids in persuading persons to 'live a moral life. . . If men feel that a tremendous importance is attached to every moral act and decision, that whatever they do will yield results that have an influence on the entire nature of their being, now and in the future, they will think twice about leading anything other than a moral life'.[20] Thirdly, the doctrine of karma resolves the difficulty of keeping the seeker after liberation diligent at his task by claiming that no effort toward controlling one's desires is ever lost. 'What one cannot attain in this life, one will attain, or be better prepared to attain, in another life.'[21] Finally, it provides a solution to the problem of evil, of pain, suffering and misfortune.

The reason he concludes that the doctrine is a fiction is that it fails to satisfy any of the six *pramāṇas* or modes of valid knowledge and consequently stands undemonstrated and undemonstrable. It cannot be known by perception because the law of karma is not an object, quality or relation which can be made apparent to the senses. Perception cannot 'yield knowledge of law-like relations between objects in Nature'.[22] Likewise it cannot be known by comparison and non-cognition (which also rely upon perceptual experience) because it is not the subject of a judgement of similarity or of non-existence at a particular time and place. In sum, it cannot be asserted as a literal truth about our experience because it cannot be empirically validated. It cannot be known by inference 'for the simple reason that the nature of inferential reasoning in Indian philosophy precludes the possibility of a universal proposition or law being the conclusion of an inference. It might be the result of induction but not of deduction'.[23] It is not a postulation (in the sense that one postulates 'one fact in order to make another fact intelligible') because as a relative truth about the phenomena it is not deducible from the fundamental metaphysical principles, for example, that *Ātman* is *Brahman*, and its denial does not entail a contradiction. And finally, it is not the subject of testimony because accepting testimony involves accepting scriptural authority, and 'scriptural authority is accepted only for those truths which transcend reason and the senses and are derived from spiritual experience. . . In terms of spiritual experience an idea may be considered demonstrated or validated for the Advaita only if, phenomenologically, it describes a "content" of that experience'.[24] But in spiritual experience the phenomenal disappears from consciousness and hence there can be no spiritual experience of one's empirical existence. Since the empirical is the realm where the law of karma operates, the law of karma cannot be a subject of spiritual experience.

Deutsch's argument, however, encounters difficulties at several points. First, he equivocates on the term 'spiritual experience'. On the one hand, it refers to the knowledge that a person obtains regarding that which is unknowable through perception or the use of reason, for example, the nature of reality (the absolute unity of all being), that the phenomenal world is *māyā* (illusion), and that our bondage is only a matter of our ignorance of reality. On this view of spiritual experience, the enlightened can know that the phenomenal world operates according to the law of karma and that this law only applies to the phenomenal and not to the noumenal. This is the teaching of the scriptures and can be known from them. On the other hand, he uses 'spiritual experience' in the sense of knowledge (not personal) in which all that is phenomenal disappears from consciousness and one is no longer aware of any distinctness or differentiation. In this sense one would not know the law of karma or anything about the phenomenal; from the absolute standpoint all *pramāṇas* lose their relative validity.[25] But it is unlikely that this is the sense in which the *pramāṇa* of testimony is to be understood, for the very *pramāṇas* themselves, as ways in which the individual, phenomenal person comes to knowledge, are matters of the phenomenal and not the noumenal. Further, knowledge received through testimony, though it is new and extra-empirical in the sense that it cannot be ascertained by empirical experience, is not unrelated to human experience. 'When we take the condition of novelty along with this fact that the terms in which transcendental truth is communicated must necessarily be known to us, we see that what is revealed, so far at least as philosophic truth is concerned, cannot be altogether new, but can only be a new *way* of construing our experience.'[26] Thus the mere fact that knowledge of the doctrine of karma comes from testimony does not entail that it must be treated as a fiction, as not literally true about our experience. In fact, to the contrary, if it fails to connect with the empirical and experiential, it cannot be a genuine item of knowledge by testimony.

Secondly, Deutsch rejects the thesis that the law of karma can be a matter of knowledge by postulation on the grounds that other hypotheses might be suggested to account for the data. He assumes that that which is postulated to make another fact intelligible must be unique, the only supposition possible. But for any given set of facts which are to be explained or made intelligible another hypothesis might be suggested which would likewise account for the data. This *pramāṇa* does not depend upon there being no other possible hypothesis; rather, it depends upon the suggested hypothesis being the best hypothesis, that is, the one which makes the evidence or data to be explained (generally two truths which appear mutually incompatible) the most intelligible. For example, the hypothesis that Devadatta must be elsewhere since he is alive and we do not find him in his house is not the only hypothesis which makes intelligible his absence. One might also hypothesize that he was hiding in his house and we failed to observe him. That the law of karma makes intelligible the apparent contradiction found in the human experience of good persons suffering misfortune or evil persons experiencing good fortune is precisely what advocates of the doctrine of karma maintain. Thus the degree to which the doctrine can function as a postulate depends upon the degree to which it adequately explains or makes intelligible the data, which is precisely the point of the present study. But merely to suggest that there are other hypotheses possible does not mean that it cannot be an item of knowledge in the manner of a postulate.

Finally, supposing that the law of karma failed to meet all of these *pramāṇas*, would that in itself entail that it was not literally true and hence a fiction? I think not. All that would follow would be that the law of karma is as yet undemonstrated, not that it is not a literal truth about our experience. Indeed, Deutsch admits that the law of karma is at least partially demonstrable in this life in that 'one can, in principle, see if one's conduct determines one's being in one's "present life"; one can see whether one's actions do reverberate back into one's nature and condition one's personality'.[27] But this, at least, makes possible a partial verification of the law of karma, which means that the law has empirical content and is more than merely an interpretative concept. Deutsch, of course, might reply that there is partial verification, but that what is thereby preserved as empirically true is not in doubt nor powerfully explanatory. Neither the interesting part of the law having to do with relations between lives nor the universality of the law has been validated. But granted Deutsch's reply, the fact that there is possible a verification of the law of karma in one restricted sphere does establish its character as a law which is meant to be true about our experience and not merely an interpretative concept.

2. On the other hand, the law of karma is not an empirical generalization, for we lack sufficient experiences of instantiations of the law of karma to be able to construct such a generalization. Even granted certain cases of rebirth as being known by parapsychology or by yogic experience, these cases are by no means sufficient to enable us to construct any kind of empirical

generalization, either about rebirth or the law of karma.

3. Our emphasis on the empiricality of the law of karma, while denying that it is an empirical generalization, suggests that the law must be treated as both empirical (in that it is an informative hypothesis which explains human experience) and necessary. This means that we must take exception to Karl Potter's contention that the law of karma is not a descriptive law about human experience. According to him, descriptive laws are the result of a sequence of events that have been observed to occur with unvarying uniformity under the same conditions. A descriptive law 'is arrived at when a hypothesis is constantly confirmed and never falsified'. But the law of karma, like the law of causation, is not of this sort, for 'just as the causal principle. . . exhorts us to keep on seeking explanations for physical occurrences, so the karmic principle exhorts us to keep on seeking explanations for what [might be called] "moral" occurrences'.[28] That is, nothing in experience is taken to falsify the law of karma. Should we discover cases where the pain and pleasure experienced did not result from past actions, the defender of the law of karma would not sacrifice the law, but rather would assert that the causes of the phenomena in question have not been adequately ferreted out.[29]

But is it a necessary feature of a descriptive law that it be arrived at by consistent verification? If it is, Potter is correct: the law of karma, like the causal law, is not a law but a principle encouraging us to seek explanations of a certain sort. But not all descriptive laws need meet this condition; laws can be necessary and yet be descriptive. Such laws are necessary *de re*.[30] That is, they are necessary truths which possess empirical content.

The causal law, for example, can be held to be a universal and necessary truth which explains certain features of reality. It does more than encourage us to look for causes when we have an effect without an apparent cause. It has empirical import in that it describes an aspect of the world: every event or contingent being has a cause. And we look for the cause because we believe that in the world necessarily all events have a cause.

Similarly with the law of karma. On the one hand, it is used to explain human experience. It is true that in its most interesting aspects it is non-verifiable by ordinary human experience. Though it is purportedly experienced by those with extra-sensory perception (*rāja-yogis*), their experience generally is not used to verify the hypothesis. Yet it is not merely an encouragement to cause-searching of a certain sort; it is meant to explain the empirical workings of moral causation. On the other hand, it is taken to be both universal and necessary; all karmic acts necessarily have appropriate consequences.

If it is a necessarily true, non-verifiable law about the relation between certain facts, can one then evaluate it? The answer, I think, is yes. Any evaluation must be carried out in terms of its ability to provide an explanation which both is internally consistent (logically coherent) and makes intelligible certain aspects of human phenomenal experience (is empirically adequate).[31]

It is to the claim that the law of karma is internally consistent and makes intelligible certain aspects of human experience that the remainder of this book is addressed. We shall examine various aspects of the law, to see how and how well they function in the context suggested for them.

4

Karma and Fatalism

A common criticism of the doctrine of karma is that it entails fatalism. Sarvepalli Radhakrishnan writes, 'Unfortunately, the theory of Karma became confused with fatality in India when man himself grew feeble and was disinclined to do his best'.[1] Another philosopher writes, 'If we are justified in our acceptance of the causal dogma, there does not seem to be any legitimate way to avoid fatalism. If the present is determined by the past, so as to admit of an accurate prediction of the past (the failure of accuracy being due solely to our ignorance of the data), how can we avoid the conclusion that the future is similarly determined by the past and the present?'[2] And A.B. Keith echoes the same theme:

> The conception of *Karman* serves indeed in an excellent way to defend and protect the established order of things, but it is essentially fatalistic; and fatalism is not for a normal mind a good incentive to moral progress. If, on the one hand, the doing of an evil deed is restrained by the thought that it will be punished in another life, it is equally true that reflection shows that the actor has really no option in his act and is an absolutely predetermined person, whose former acts produce his present motive and reasonings without the possibility of intervention of any kind on his part.[3]

In what follows I want to explore whether the charge against the law of karma, that it is necessarily fatalistic, can be sustained.[4] If the law does entail fatalism, the philosophical consequences for the objectivist ethic which it is held to support are substantial, for any moral injunctions which would follow from such an ethic would have no import. If we are fated to act as we do, we cannot change our behaviour, but must resign ourselves to our fate.

DEFINITIONS

To begin, some preliminary distinctions are in order. First, we must distinguish three points of view relating freedom and causation: the libertarian or indeterminist, determinist, and compatibilist. According to the libertarian view, persons are free when the causal conditions are not sufficient to cause, determine or coerce them to choose or act in a certain fashion. Where causal conditions are sufficient to determine the outcome, we lack the ability to evaluate the influences conditioning us and to select between alternative courses of action. And without the ability to make meaningful choices, we are not free. If we are free, then given the same (non-subsequent) conditions, we could have chosen or done otherwise than we did. Of course, this should not be taken to mean that freedom is the absence of influences, either external or internal. For someone to act, certain causal conditions are necessary. Rather, it means that these do not determine our choices or actions.

On the other hand, the determinist maintains that for everything that happens, there are necessary and sufficient conditions or causes such that, given them, only this effect could happen and nothing else. For something different to happen, a different set of causal conditions must be present. Since freedom is the absence of sufficient causal conditions, freedom is only apparent, not real.

From this it is clear that the libertarian and determinist views are incompatible. Both maintain that if our choice or action follows necessarily from external or internal determinants, it is not free. The difference between them is that, while the determinist maintains that all events have sufficient causal conditions which determine them and freedom is merely apparent, the libertarian holds that some do not have sufficient causal conditions which determine them so that in these cases we are truly free.

This last formulation of the libertarian position is subject to a number of different interpretations and possibly is misleading. Libertarians adopt several different perspectives regarding the role of causal conditions. Some deny that all events have sufficient causes. Among these events is choosing. This sort of libertarian feels comfortable appealing to confirming evidence from quantum physics. If there is causal indeterminacy on the sub-atomic level, they argue, indeterminacy can also occur above that level, that is, on the level of human choice. Others (with the determinist) maintain that all events have causes, but hold either that choosing is not an event and hence escape causal determinism, or else that not all events have *events* as their sufficient cause. In the latter case, choosing is an event whose cause is not another event, but an agent. This latter view is termed agent causation. In agent causation, contrary to determinism, the choice does not follow necessarily from the existence and state of the agent, along with the external causal conditions. Neither are agents caused to act as they do, though of course they might have good reason to act so. Given the same non-subsequent causal conditions, agents, if free, could have done other than they did. Whatever the particulars of the libertarian view, whereas the determinist holds that all human actions have necessary and sufficient causal conditions (such that given those conditions the event cannot but occur), the libertarian holds that some human actions are chosen or performed without there being sufficient causal conditions either *simpliciter* or other than the agent (such that given the conditions present, the agent could have chosen other than he did).

The third position is compatibilism. Compatibilists, like determinists, hold that all events follow necessarily from their respective causal conditions. However, like libertarians, they contend that individuals can be free. We are free when we are not coerced (by external forces) to choose or act contrary to the way we want to act. If we are free, in a given instance we could have done otherwise than we did. But compatibilists understand 'could have done otherwise' in a hypothetical sense. By 'could have done otherwise' they mean such things as 'if we had wanted to' or 'if we had tried'. By using the hypothetical sense of 'could have done otherwise' freedom is viewed as compatible with determinism. For the compatibilist, whether we act freely stands independent of the presence or absence of non-subsequent causal conditions, for 'being able to do otherwise if. . . ' in no way precludes that our action is the necessary result of non-subsequent causal conditions. Rather, whether we act freely depends upon whether we are able to act as we want. When we are prevented by external coercion from acting as we want, we cannot act differently and hence are not free.

The compatibilist is particularly concerned with moral contexts and the ascription of moral responsibility. We are morally responsible when we could have done something other than we did had we wanted to or tried. For example, we ascribe responsibility in those cases where the individual can be brought to do things differently, for example by instituting rewards or punishments. Where the person does the same thing no matter what conditions are altered—for example, no matter what threats of punishment are brought to bear or rewards offered—the person is not morally responsible, for he could not (presumably) have done anything else even if he tried. What matters with respect to ascribing moral responsibility is not whether the decision made or action taken is causally determined, but whether it accords with what the person wanted.

We have, then, three positions. Indeterminism holds that we are free when human decision-making lies outside the deterministic causal chain; if a person is free, given the same causal conditions, he could have done otherwise than he did. Determinism likewise holds that we are free when human decision-making lies outside the deterministic causal chain. But freedom is merely an appearance; phenomenally we are free, but in fact our decision-making is determined by non-subsequent causal conditions. Given the same causal conditions, we could not have done otherwise than we did. Compatibilism holds both that we are causally determined in that all our decision-making and acts have their place within the chain of deterministic causal conditions, and that we are free when we are not coerced by anything external to us, that is, when we can do what we want.

The other distinction is between determinism and fatalism. As we have seen, determinists claim that every event is determined by sufficient causal conditions, such that given these conditions, a certain effect, and only that effect, must occur. Fatalists also hold that the future is determined and that humans are not free to affect the future as they wish, and in this they wage common cause with determinists. However, the grounds of their battle differ. Whereas determinists deny human freedom on the basis of their claim regarding the sufficiency of causes, fatalists argue that since it is now true that some event will occur, that event must occur. And if it must occur, there is nothing anyone, including ourselves, can do to prevent it. The future is already determined or established and we cannot change or prevent it. We are not free; whatever we will do we must do.

The fatalist argument leads to a state of mind which accepts everything that happens as being determined by forces outside our control and hence bound to happen. The sequence of events is determined beforehand or from all eternity by the gods,[5] time, karma, or a significant prior event, and individuals are powerless to alter or change that sequence. They merely must accept the course of events as it occurs, as a leaf would fall into the stream and float, having no power to influence whether it will be stranded on a rock or washed up on shore by the current. The attitude determinists take, on the other hand, is open. They might adopt a fatalist position. But they also might believe that what they do here and now has a causal impact on the future; a person's actions and behaviour are causes which condition subsequent events. Thus one's participation in the causal sequence is not superfluous, even though it is caused by other non-subsequent conditions.

Our first task must be to decide whether advocates of the law of karma promote or deny human freedom. If they maintain humans are free, there is no need to pursue the question whether or not they are fatalists. If they deny that humans are free and hold that the future is determined, then the question of fatalism must be raised, for it must be ascertained on what grounds human freedom is denied.

DETERMINISM AND THE LAW OF KARMA

There is ample evidence that the law of karma is associated with a deterministic view of the world. This is hinted at in the *Bṛhad-āraṇyaka Upaniṣad*: 'What they said was karma and what they praised was karma. Truly one becomes good by good action, bad by bad action'.[6] It comes out more clearly in the *Bhagavad-Gītā*, where Krishna declares, 'If, in your vanity, you say: "I will not fight," your resolve is in vain. Your own nature will drive you to the act. For you yourself have created the karma that binds you. You are helpless in its power. And you will do that very thing which your ignorance seeks to avoid'.[7]

The same theme is echoed in contemporary authors. Radhakrishnan writes, 'Every act is the inevitable outcome of the preceding conditions'.[8] And Abhedananda:

> The character of an individual is again subject to the law of *Karma* because it is the aggregate of a large number of minute activities of the mind-substance to which we give different

> names such as desires, tendencies, thoughts, ideas and impressions every one of which is governed by the law of action and reaction. Each character or personality is the grand total result of previous mental actions, and is also the cause of future changes in the character. . . It is our own *Karma* that produces its results in the form of joy or sorrow, pleasure or pain, happiness or unhappiness. . . Every thing that we possess in this life, is the effect of our previous *Karma* or action, both mental and physical. Our present character is the resultant of our past and our future will be determined by our present acts. . . We cannot arrest our external work so long as there is mental activity. We are impelled to some kind of exertion by our own inner nature. . . Unable, therefore, to resist this inner force, we are bound to do that which we are doing.[9]

Note that we are not simply bound to do, but we are bound to do a particular thing.

In Buddhism, karma causes dispositions, and according to the doctrine of Dependent Origination, dispositions in turn condition sense contact, desire or craving, clinging to the objects of enjoyment, rebirth and misery. But these events do not occur in a haphazard fashion. Rather, they proceed in an orderly causal chain. 'When this is present, that comes to be; from the arising of this, that arises. When this is absent, that does not come to be; on the cessation of this, that ceases.'[10] There is, then, a causal determinism. The effect can be altered or avoided, but only by the removal of one of the causal conditions.

Further, we argued in chapter 3 that the law of karma is the application of the causal law to the moral sphere. Now if the law of causation is a universal law governing all events, then since the law of causation is deterministic in character, it would follow that the law of karma is likewise. In short, the very placing of the law of karma within the larger metaphysic of universal causation argues for a deterministic perspective.

But the story is not this simple. In almost the same breath that it is suggested that the law of karma is determinstic, it is argued that there is human freedom and moral accountability for the acts committed. We are individually (or, for some persons, corporately) responsible for what we do, and this responsibility carries over into subsequent lives where we receive compensation—good or evil—for the actions we performed in previous lives. For example, the *Bṛhad-āraṇyaka Upaniṣad* continues shortly after the above-quoted passage: 'According as one acts, according as one behaves, so does he become. The doer of good becomes good, the doer of evil becomes evil. One becomes virtuous by virtuous action, bad by bad action. Others, however, say that a person consists of desires. As is his desire so is his will; as is his will, so is the deed he does, whatever deed he does, that he attains'.[11] Krishna in the *Bhagavad-Gītā* instructs Arjuna to ponder all this but then act, not only according to his duty but also in devotion to Krishna.[12] Radhakrishnan continues in the passage quoted above.

> If the spirit, which is on a higher plane than nature, does not assert its freedom, past conduct and present environment will account completely for the actions of man. Man is not a mere product of nature. He is mightier than his karma. If the law is all, then there is no real freedom possible. Man's life is not the working of merely mechanical relations. There are different levels—the mechanical, the vital, the sentient, the intellectual and the spiritual—these currents cross and recross and interpenetrate each other. The law of karma, which rules the lower nature of man, has nothing to do with the spiritual in him. . . The essence of spirit is freedom. By its exercise man can check and control his natural impulses.[13]

Similarly Abhedananda, immediately after affirming that 'each character or personality is the grand total result of previous mental actions', that 'every thing we possess in this life, is the effect of our previous *Karma*', goes on to assert that 'a believer in the law of Karma is a free agent and is responsible for all the good and bad results of his own actions that attend to his life'.[14] Thus what started out looking like a clear-cut case of determinism is less so upon further study. And further study is precisely what is necessary to untangle the claims made on behalf of the law of karma. In particular, we must look at three things: what is affected by karmic actions, to what degree are these affected, and what remains outside karmic influence.

WHAT IS AFFECTED BY KARMA?

Descriptions of the effects of karma-producing actions suggest that everything in human experience can be affected by them. Karma certainly affects our innate tendencies and dispositions, desires, and passions. The actions we performed in previous lives create in us the disposition to desire similar things or to continue to perform similar acts: good acts if the original acts are good, actions stemming from desire if the original acts so stemmed.

As we argued in chapter 3, however, the effects of karma are not merely subjective. Our pleasure and pain are mediated through our physical environment as well as through our dispositions and/or *adṛṣṭa*. Hence anything which produces pain or pleasure, good or bad, is affected.[15] Since nature is such a source, the affected would include such things as earthquakes, floods, fires, pestilences, rain, sunshine and the fertility of our fields. Likewise we are affected by the things we create, like the functioning of our automobiles, appliances, machines and computers. The kinds, amount and quality of our property or material possessions likewise are results of the actions done in our previous lives.[16] Karma also affects our personal physical existence.[17] The size, shape, weight, colour and appearance of our body, the number and functioning quality of its appendages and organs, and our length and quality of life are conditioned by our karma. Karma also determines our social position, including the class or caste into which we are born.[18] It even affects whether we are reborn as human or as some lower or higher form of life.[19]

In short, it is maintained that every aspect of our existence is conditioned by the karma we have built up by past actions. Nothing that we are or experience which relates to our pleasure or pain escapes the pervasive causal power of karma. Our environment, body, intellectual faculties and abilities, dispositions, passions, desires and character, all stand under the universal sway of the law of karma.

TO WHAT DEGREE?

Secondly, to what degree is all this affected? With respect to the world around us, the law of universal causation is invoked: all events or things are causally conditioned. However, the prior actions of any given individual constitute only one of the causal conditions which might (if relevant) be given for any event. For example, the earthquake which destroys a particular person's house at a particular time and place has among its causal conditions both the karmic influence of that person as well as that of others so affected. But its causes also include the normal physical conditions of plate-sliding, fault-tension, and the like. That is, while every action produces environmental effects, these effects are not completely conditioned by that action; other causal conditions are necessary for their production.

Now these environmental conditions in turn affect our present existence; they provide the context for both our existence and our current moral actions. Our body and mind, the social class into which we are born, our good and bad fortune to date, the property we already possess, what we have encountered in our environment, all are the given product of certain prior causes, and cannot now be affected.

Yet however much our past and present environment is now determined and unavoidable, our future environment is still malleable. Our present actions are counter-acting or reinforcing past karma and are building up our future karma. Consequently the results of our present actions will have a direct bearing on our future environment, embodiment and character, both in the current and in subsequent lives. This is not to deny, of course, that these features have other causal conditions; it is rather to affirm that one of their causal conditions is our own action. Consequently, what is critical to answer our query about degree is to focus on the attitude taken toward the agency of the human person.

This brings us to the self and its dispositions and tendencies. Are we determined in our character, desires, dispositions and choices by the choices made in previous lives? The response generally is in the negative. The psychological or internal effects of past acts are at most tendencies or dispositions to act. They help mould our desires and influence our conduct, and as powerful forces move us in their direction. But we can control these tendencies and dispositions. They are ours either to follow or to alter by attaining self-knowledge, self-discipline, and self-control.

In short, the doctrine of karma is almost always found in philosophical circles in the company of an affirmation of human free agency. And free agency is understood in the sense that the dispositional tendencies inherited from past karmic actions are not deterministic. What we are disposed to do, whether good or bad, can be resisted; our future even now remains in our own hands. Thus the individual is capable of responding to the situation in which he finds himself and by his response can affect future situations. For example, by good acts he can relieve previously accumulated negative karma. Accordingly, since the human person is free, both strict determinism and fatalism are excluded. But how are we to understand the metaphysical position which underlies this freedom? Is it a case of indeterminism or of compatibilism?

THE SELF AND LIBERTARIANISM

Before we proceed to answer this question, it is necessary to pause for a moment to note that the question which we are posing is not posed in this way by the classical Indian writers. When they consider freedom, they are not interested primarily in the freedom which is necessary for ascribing moral accountability, that is, with free agency. Rather, their overriding interests concern what might be termed spiritual freedom, that is, freedom or liberation from that which binds us to the cycle of rebirths and human misery. Spiritual freedom will inevitably take us beyond the laws of karma and ethics which govern *saṃsāra*. Thus, the answer to our question will not be found by discovering their explicit response to the problem posed, but must be inferred from the views of the self invoked by advocates of the law of karma.

The answer to our question depends—not unexpectedly—on the metaphysical system which underlies the affirmation of human freedom. According to Hinduism there is a self (*ātman*) which functions in several capacities. In its pure or noumenal form, as sentience or substance, it transcends the sphere of karma and moral determination. This state must be possible, it is argued, else liberation from the saṃsāric cycle is impossible.

However, when the self is linked in some way or other (depending on the system described) with the physical, it as the empirical self (*jīva*), associated now with various material psychophysical organs, can decide, choose, act and create its own future. True, it is faced with a given environment and situation. It finds itself associated in a particular manner with a particular body (or bodies, if one also considers the subtle body), and it must deal with certain strong dispositions and tendencies to repeat the deeds done in previous lives. Yet none of this is fully determining. The created *saṃskāras* only dispose the empirical self to act in certain ways.

But what is this self which remains free? In Advaita Vedānta it is important to distinguish two senses of the self and two senses of freedom. The noumenal self (*Ātman*) cannot act, for in realizing its essential identity with *Brahman* it has transcended all sense of agency. The Absolute Self is absolutely free: free from all ignorance, change, willing, activity, and anything that would limit it. However, since the highest Self is not an agent, this sense of freedom (what we termed above spiritual freedom) is not relevant to the doctrine of karma (except as a goal), morals, and to our problem of human agency. Karma and ethics are, from the noumenal perspective, unreal; their laws apply strictly to the phenomenal realm.

The self with which we are concerned is the *phenomenal* self. This self is not real but 'fictitiously hypostatized by the *buddhi*'.[20] This self is grounded in ignorance and, particularly related to our issue, in the error of *adhyāsa*—imposing on oneself agency. That is, the phenomenal or empirical self sees itself as an agent.[21] But its agency is not founded on its real nature. Else there could be no liberation. Its agency, then, is due to attributing adjuncts to the self.

However, from the phenomenal perspective, the self is an agent. Otherwise, the commands (for instance, the Vedic command to sacrifice) and moral obligations would have no import. As such, it is an agent which is free to choose between options. It is not absolutely free, for it acts in conjunction with other causal conditions. Śaṅkara gives the example of the cook who also requires fuel and water. But the agent, in cooking, is free to cook what he wants, or even not to cook, within those limiting conditions.[22]

It would seem that it is the indeterminist view of freedom which underlies this claim. The individual self is the highest Self: 'That thou art'. As such, it participates in or reflects the latter's immateriality or spirituality. This character of the self becomes particularly evident in the last two of the four states of consciousness, that of deep sleep (where the self is a witness to the ignorance which is the cause of all distinctions) and transcendental consciousness (viewed from the perspective of the *jīva* as a determinate spiritual experience).[23] Consequently, insofar as the phenomenal self is the noumenal self (as limited by the physical adjuncts or reflected in them), there is a dimension to it which stands outside the deterministic causal chain. True, as linked with the psychophysical or internal organ, it is disposed to act in certain ways and is not completely free. Yet as immaterial or spirit it is sufficiently free to be able to choose meaningfully between options and correspondingly be held morally accountable for its acts, for it is this empirical self which is subject to *saṃsāra* because of its karmic acts.

As with Advaita Vedānta, so with Nyāya-Vaiśeṣika it is important to distinguish two senses of freedom, as well as what are regarded here as two states of the self. When it has attained freedom or liberation from the cycle of rebirths, the self (*ātman*) realizes its true nature. In this state it is pure substance, devoid of consciousness and affective states (desire or aversion), undergoing no experiences, activity or change, and possessing no properties. Again, since the *ātman* in the liberated state is neither an agent nor has any moral responsibility, this is not the sense of freedom with which we are concerned in this chapter, though of course it is a primary concern of the Naiyāyikas and Vaiśeṣikas.[24]

Our concern, then, is with the unliberated or empirical self and the freedom it has which makes it possible to ascribe intentional action and karmic accountability to it. This self, which in contrast to Advaita Vedānta we might call the *related* self since no noumenal/phenomenal distinction is invoked here, is associated with the body through its instrument, the mind or internal organ (*manas*). The mind, which is a material, atomic substance, is its constant companion through transmigration. The mind is passive and, as physical, cannot be the ground or subject of consciousness. Supplying this is the role of the *ātman*.

The *ātman*, when conjoined with the mind, functions as the conscious experiencer of the world and the intelligent, guiding agent of the body. As agent, it is responsible for our cognitive, volitional and affective activities. In the latter case, because of its desires it seeks to experience the pleasant and avoid the painful, and this leads to continued activity, which brings the accumulation of merit and demerit, which in turn results in rebirth and sorrow. In the state of bondage, then, the self is both the agent of action and the recipient of the fruit of action. But the *ātman* is not to be identified with the body, for it is the 'I' for which the body is an object. Nor is it physical, for consciousness cannot be a property of material bodies.[25] It is rather the immaterial substance which is the subject of all experiences, volitions and affective states.

Human intentional action, then, is understood in terms of an immaterial agent which is responsible for cognition, volition and desiring. Though it uses the physical as its instrument and is influenced by physical causes and dispositions, yet as an immaterial substance it stands outside the physical chain of causation. It is reasonable to conclude, then, that human action is here explicated in terms of agent causation. This means that for Nyāya-Vaiśeṣika the self as agent is free in an indeterminist sense.

Similar themes come through Sāṅkhya-Yoga, though perhaps less clearly. The self (*puruṣa*) is not a substance, as in Nyāya-Vaiśesika, but pure sentience. It is the sentience which is required by every non-sentient thing to experience it. Yet by itself it has no cognitive states, for these require association with the *buddhi* (intellect). It is eternal, omnipresent, changeless, external to everything else. And it is passive, the sentient experiencer or witness without being a doer or agent.[26] Again, then, the transcendent self (*puruṣa*) is not our concern here, for as inactive it is not truly an agent and thus not related to karmic or moral concerns. Karma only affects primal nature (*prakṛti*), not the *puruṣa*. Morality and the law of karma have significance only on the empirical plane. Indeed, no *puruṣa* is ever bound, transmigrates, or is liberated; to think that it is, is the product of ignorance.[27]

The empirical self is the *reflected* self. Human persons, as part of evolving *prakṛti*, are physical beings. But since the physical cannot be conscious but can only appear to be so, the conscious dimension must be supplied by something outside the physical, namely, the *puruṣa*. On the other hand, since the *puruṣa* is inactive, the activity associated with agency must be supplied by the physical, in this case, the *buddhi* or intellect. However, the *puruṣa* cannot come in contact with the physical; between the physical (*prakṛti*) and sentience (*puruṣa*) a great gulf is fixed. Thus, individual conscious experience and agency arise only when the *puruṣa* is reflected in the *buddhi*.[28]

What then of the freedom involved in moral concerns? Again, the empirical self, though in part characterized by the physical and hence formed in part by the causal chain, is not fully encompassed by the physical, for it contains the reflection of the *puruṣa* which is external to everything, which in itself is experient but unaffected by all changes and alterations. The empirical self, then, though affected by causal conditions, is not completely determined by such. It is not that there is an immaterial agent, but rather that the self, through the reflection of the *puruṣa*, can act freely. Again, the libertarian perspective is in view.

In short, in stark contrast to the alleged fatalism believed necessarily to infect the doctrine of karma, the very opposite proves to be true. Rather than leading to a fatalistic view of human existence, Hinduism affirms that human persons in their empirical existence are free to act within certain limiting conditions. Humans are not completely free, of course, for among other things there is our accumulated (*sañicita*) karma to be faced. Merit and demerit (*dharma* and *adharma*) adhere to the self or are modes of the intellect which are mistakenly believed to belong to the *puruṣa* (in Sāṅkhya-Yoga). But in the phenomenal world, in the face of the given environment and tendencies resulting from past actions, we can choose between various courses of actions. We are disposed but not caused to act in any particular way. We can, for example, either follow our dispositions to perform acts similar to those which endowed us with our dispositions, or we can choose to act in a contrary fashion. That is, given the same set of causal conditions, we can choose various courses of action which will condition our future state. And this is the heart of the libertarian thesis.

The ontological basis for this is that persons are free because the empirical self is not wholly physical, but is in some respect (either in substance, as identical with the noumenal self, or as a reflection of the pure, unmoved self) an immaterial existent which is not determined by the causal conditions which govern that which it experiences or upon which it acts. At the same time, this immaterial self, as sentience or the ground of sentience, limited by, in conjunction with or through its reflection in the material organs of mind or intellect, can experience the world and act as an agent in it.[29] It grounds and is the subject of cognitions, volitions and desires, which in turn make intentional action possible. Because of this, it makes sense to claim that Hinduism understands the freedom of human agency in a libertarian or indeterminist sense.

NO-SELF AND COMPATIBILISM

Not all advocates of the doctrine of karma are sanguine concerning this indeterminism. Above we noted that there are two different positions which maintain that we are genuinely free: the libertarian and the compatibilist. The view which we have just developed and which is generally characteristic of Hindu philosophy is the indeterminist viewpoint, which, as we have seen, is incompatible with complete determinism. But compatibilism is more consistent with other views of the human person, particularly those found in Buddhism.

For Buddhists there is no spiritual *ātman* which stands outside the chain of causes and is the possessor of the tendencies. There is no persistent self or soul which decides which reasons are to be accepted and which rejected. The self is a fiction. What we call the individual person is merely a transitory or impermanent aggregate or bundle of the five *skandhas* (body, perceptions and volitions, feelings, dispositions and consciousness).[30] The *skandhas* follow one another, not in the sense that some thing undergoes change, but in that one attribute state is followed by another attribute state.

This succession proceeds according to the causal principle. Each state is causally conditioned by the previous state, such that it would neither exist nor be what it is apart from these conditions. Indeed, it is the causation of karma which is held to account for the continuity which obtains between the discrete, dependent (in later Buddhism, momentary) existences.[31] Yet the Buddha held that the individual can direct his will and action so as to free himself from the causal chain of Dependent Origination. In particular, right purpose and right effort are part of the eightfold path which leads to the destruction of selfish craving and brings liberation.

Thus Buddhists search for a middle ground.[32] This middle ground lies between a causal determinism which denies real human freedom and moral responsibility on the one hand, and a libertarianism which, on the other, denies that all events follow necessarily from sufficient causal conditions. If to exist is to be caused and to cause, the causal principle must be affirmed.[33] And if religious life and extinction of misery is to be possible, there must be human freedom.[34] Accordingly, the middle ground or Middle Doctrine must assert both freedom and causal determinism, which is compatibilism.

Since there is no persistent self or *ātman*, there is no agent that can exist outside the causal chain. All that exists are events, which are causally conditioned by prior events. Consequently, as proponents of the doctrine of no-self who advocate freedom, Buddhism requires a compatibilist view of freedom.

The compatibilist theme sounds forth clearly in the Mahāyāna thought of D. T. Suzuki. The law of karma is 'irrefragable'. 'If we could record all our previous karma from time immemorial and all its consequences both on ourselves and on those who come in contact with us, there would be no difficulty in determining our future life with utmost certainty. . . [F]rom the divine point of view, determinism seems to be perfectly justified. . . ' Yet there is room for freedom. 'Insofar as we confine ourselves to a general superficial view of the theory of karma, it leads to a form of determinism, but in our practical life which is a product of extremely complicated factors, the doctrine of karma allows in us all kinds of possibilities and all chances of development. We thus escape the mechanical conception of life.'[35] What Suzuki seems to be suggesting is that whereas on the ontological or psychophysical level we are determined in that all events are conditioned causally by prior events, practically (in the moral sphere) we are free to decide how we are to act. That is, determinism in the psychophysical sphere is compatible with freedom in the sphere of human moral action. And this is precisely the position of the compatibilist.

Is compatibilism, however, a viable alternative? The compatibilist makes two claims: first, that all events have sufficient causal conditions, and secondly, that an act is free if it is not performed under external duress or compulsion. According to the first claim, not only are the prevailing external conditions causally determined, but so are our internal states. This means that there is a non-subsequent set of conditions individually necessary and jointly sufficient to cause or determine the choices made. For Buddhists, these prior causal conditions include (but are not restricted to) the acts performed in this and prior lives by the individual.[36]

With respect to the second claim, it is true that not being performed under external compulsion is a necessary condition for an action to be free; the question is whether it is a sufficient condition. The compatibilist argues that not only are internal states present when we make choices, but they are the immediate cause of our decisions. We choose as we do because we are disposed to choose that way or because we have certain beliefs, desires, feelings, intentions, or wants. Our decision is not uncaused, else it would not occur, for all existence is causally conditioned. Now these internal states have non-subsequent conditions which cause them, and these are themselves the result of non-subsequent conditions, and so on. How, then, are we to reconcile the causal determinacy of our internal states with our alleged freedom? If we are free, we are able to act otherwise than we did. But under this account it would seem that there is no sense in which we could have done otherwise than we did. Our actions are causally conditioned by prior actions, and these by still prior actions, and so on. But if we cannot have done otherwise than we did, we are not free and hence are not morally responsible for our actions.

Compatibilists respond that though our decisions are conditioned by non-subsequent events, we could have chosen otherwise than we did in those cases where we are free. By 'could have chosen otherwise' they mean 'could have chosen otherwise if we had wanted'. That is, we are free when we can do what we want.

But given the causal determinism sketched above, how could we want to act differently from the way in which we do? For us to have *wanted* to do otherwise, different causal conditions would have had to be present. That is, something would have had to be different from what it was. Thus, 'could have chosen otherwise' means 'could have chosen otherwise if there had been different conditions'. But since everything is the result of non-subsequent causal conditions, nothing could have been different from what it was. Thus, our being able to act or want to act otherwise than we did is not in our power to bring about, but is the result of non-subsequent causal conditions. And as such, we could not have wanted to act other than we wanted nor acted other than we did at the time, and though at the time we were not caused to act by immediately present external forces, considered more ultimately our act was the product of conditions other than those immediately attributable to ourselves. Our karma and other causes which conditioned our choices and actions were the result of prior karma and causal conditions, and these the result of still prior karma and causal conditions. In short, we could not have wanted to act other than we did want, and as such we are not free. That is, mere absence of immediate, external determining causes is not sufficient to account for human freedom. Ultimately the compatibilist's determinism means that there is no genuine human freedom.

To put the argument another way, if every event and thing is caused, then my very choices, beliefs and desires are caused. But if my choosing and desiring are caused, I cannot will, choose, or desire other than I am caused to do. But then the freedom asserted by compatibilists is an illusion, for there is no sense to their analysis of freedom given in terms of what I would have done or chosen to do if I had wanted, for my very wanting is the product of causal conditions.

Thus Buddhism is faced with a dilemma: either it affirms its determinism and gives up real human freedom, moral accountability, the religious life and the intentional actions which bring about the elimination of misery, or else it affirms genuine freedom and sacrifices its causal determinism. Neither, of course, is acceptable to Buddhism. The first would destroy its moral and religious system, which is predicated on moral accountability and eliminating misery and ills. The second, as we shall see in chapter 8, would jeopardize its view of the human person and reality, for all existence is analyzed in terms of causation. Thus, though with its compatibilism Buddhism escapes fatalism, the complications prove as bad as the disease.

CONCLUSION

The results of our analysis show that any charge which necessarily links the law of karma with fatalism fails to understand the law of karma. This is not to say that there is not a streak of fatalism in Hindu thought.[37] Indeed, fatalism seems to play a substantial role in the thought of the commoner.[38] But be this as it may, philosophically the law of karma, instead of necessarily entailing fatalism, affirms the freedom of the human person to determine his or her future destiny. The acts a person performs here and now determine that person's environmental context and future dispositions and tendencies. This freedom may be couched in either an indeterminist or compatibilist framework. But whichever be the case, human freedom is presupposed and fatalism denied.

5

Karma and the Problem of Evil

The doctrine of karma continues to be significant because it provides an explanation for both pain, suffering and misfortune on the one hand, and pleasure, happiness and good fortune on the other. Consequently, an assessment of the success of the doctrine in resolving the problem of good and evil will go a long way in enabling us to evaluate the doctrine itself, for should it fail to resolve satisfactorily the problem which it is intended to meet, since as we have seen the law is an explanatory hypothesis proposed to resolve a problem and not empirically verifiable, there would seem to be little reason to advocate the doctrine.

THE PROBLEM OF EVIL

What is the problem that the law of karma was introduced to meet? Though we have no historical records on the matter, it seems to have been introduced to explain why it is that we experience happiness and unhappiness, pleasure and pain, good and bad. These experiences come to us apparently randomly; there is no obvious logic to them or equality in their distribution. Two people are walking down the road in a thunderstorm; one gets struck and killed by lightning, the other escapes unhurt. Two children contract influenza; one dies while the other survives. Two daughters of the same parents have different dispositions, the one obedient and helpful, the other obstinate and selfish. One thing that is obvious is that one's experiences often seem to have no necessary connection with one's present moral qualities or character. Good people sometimes experience good—birth into advantageous settings, healthy bodies, devoted spouses, wealth and prestige—but at other times bad. On the other hand bad people sometimes have bad experiences, but often have good. This suggests that the world is governed by moral chance.

But a world governed by moral chance is unacceptable. For one thing, it violates cosmic or universal justice, according to which each person should have an equal opportunity to achieve happiness and ultimately liberation. There is a reason behind the events which happen to us, a reason which is intrinsically joined to fairness and equality. For another, it eliminates a proffered primary sanction for keeping the moral law, for unless there is a necessary connection between the moral quality of the actions performed and pain and pleasure experienced by the doer of those acts, there is no reason for doing right and avoiding the wrong. Why should we do the right if it fails to bring us happiness or at least avoid pain, suffering and misery?

To avoid this some explanatory hypothesis has to be suggested, a hypothesis which is consistent with universal justice and the moral law. According to this hypothesis, universal justice is preserved by virtue of the fact that the good and bad that we experience are not the result of chance, nor of the acts of others, but of actions we performed at some time in our past. We have brought on our own misery or happiness. Though often there is no immediate or obvious empirical connection between our moral actions and our happiness and unhappiness or good and bad circumstances, the connection is there. Chance is excluded; cosmic justice upheld. Right actions and happiness, wrong actions and misery, are linked.

Likewise, this hypothesis preserves one suggested sanction for keeping the moral law. If we do right, we will be rewarded with pleasure or happiness sometime in the future, though not necessarily in this life; and if we do wrong, we will be punished. If we wish to escape punishment and experience pleasure, we have no choice but to opt for doing the right thing.

Those familiar with the so-called problem of evil as discussed in Western philosophy will immediately notice an obvious difference of focus. In Western thought, the problem of evil usually is formulated in terms of the questioned ability of the theist to justify the actions, character or very existence of God in light of the evil present in the world. Simply put, if God is omnipotent, omniscient and wholly good, why is there evil in the world? The argument from evil has two forms. In its deductive form, the argument asserts that the existence of evil *per se* is inconsistent with a God who is good, omnipotent and omniscient. Persons are considered good when they eliminate evil as far as they can without losing a greater good or producing a greater evil. Since God is omnipotent—the argument goes—one would expect God to eliminate all evil from the world.[1] Since there is evil, God either does not exist or does not possess the properties ascribed to him, namely, omnipotence, omniscience or goodness. In its inductive form, it is not the mere existence of evil that matters, but rather the variety, degree and profusion of evil which make it improbable or unlikely that God exists. The likelihood of there being this much evil in the world given what we know about the world and that God exists is less than the likelihood of there being this much evil and God not existing. That is, if God existed, we should expect there to be much less evil than there currently is. Since there is so much evil and since it is so bad, it is unlikely that God exists or has certain ascribed properties.[2]

It should be readily apparent that both kinds of arguments in Western philosophical theology have to do with the existence and character of God rather than with the question of moral chance. True, there is an attempt to provide an explanation for the evil that afflicts human persons. Yet what is of primary concern is the existence and nature of the deity. Given the presence of evil, does God exist? Is he good? Is he omnipotent? For this reason Western treatments of the problem attempt to construct either a defence of God's existence or possession of certain properties such as goodness, or a theodicy which justifies the ways or actions of God *vis-à-vis* the world and the evil found in it in terms of some morally sufficient reason for evil.[3] Indeed, the very word 'theodicy' (from the Greek for 'God' and 'justice'), which means vindicating the justice of God, indicates this.

But the problem of evil as generally found in Indian philosophical traditions rests not on the question of the existence and nature of God, but rather on the question whether there is universal justice. Evidence for this thesis can be found in the fact that the problem of evil in a theological guise (that is, with reference to God) is rarely treated directly in classical or medieval Indian literature.[4] What this means in effect is that the question of the relation of God to pain, suffering and dysfunction is much less significant or even insignificant in Indian karmic systems. And the reason has to do not so much with the law of karma as with their respective views of God.

Paradoxically, evidence for this is found in the fact that the problem of evil is formulated in identical fashion in Indian philosophy, irrespective of whether the context is theistic or not. For example, the description of the problem to be solved by the law of karma in Theravāda Buddhism, which is not theistic, does not differ from that found in theistic Vedānta. Both want to understand why it is that persons experience pain and pleasure, fortune and misfortune in ways that seem unconnected with the moral quality of their present actions, and ultimately, how this cycle of suffering can be escaped. Justification of divine ways and action is rarely undertaken.

GOD AND THE WORLD

To understand this difference between what I will call the theistic and the non-theistic problems of evil, something must be said about the nature of God and the role which God plays in the theistic systems of Indian thought. In the majority of philosophical systems God does not have the nature or role that is assigned to him in Judaic, Christian or Islamic thought. Primarily he is impersonally cosmogenic and cosmic, rather than the personal creator who providentially intervenes in his world to realize good and redeem humankind from evil.

For example, in the pluralistic system of Nyāya-Vaiśeṣika, the world is an effect, and hence there must be some efficient cause of that effect. This cause is God, whose role is a cosmogenic one. It is God who causes the atoms to collide at the beginning of each cycle, thus initiating world evolution. It is God who is the necessary condition for all action and thus sustains world action. And ultimately God destroys the world, only to restart the process. However, God in this causal role acts for no end or purpose; God possesses no personal, telic will. Rather the evolutionary process depends on the karmic potencies of the individual selves (*ātmans*).[5] God is merely a necessary condition for cosmic existence and movement. God's second function, following upon the first, is to implement the law of karma. Since the law of karma is inactive and non-intelligent, there must be some being which is responsible for seeing to it that cosmic justice is done, that the law of karma is implemented. God, unlike the other *ātmans*, is essentially conscious, controls the process of reincarnation according to the law of karma, and thus in its acts stands subject to it. Thirdly, later in the history of the school and influenced by the *Yoga-sūtras*, it is held that knowledge of God helps in human liberation, not directly, but in that by knowing God wrong attitudes, including passion, hate and delusion, are removed.[6] Generally speaking, God is not personal; it has no *dharma* or *adharma* such that we cannot raise questions about its goodness in light of the character of the world which it evolves. Neither is God providential, bringing forth good for its creatures and being responsible for the evil. Rather it is the 'prime mover' and 'cosmic sustainer' of what exists by implementing the law of karma according to accumulated merit and demerit. God serves a cosmic role but does not directly help in our liberation. As such, the question of reconciling God's existence and goodness with the evil in the world does not, indeed cannot, arise for Nyāya-Vaiśeṣika.

In the non-dualistic systems, the picture is more complicated. In the Upaniṣads there is an underlying concern with a monistic and idealistic view which identifies reality with the Absolute, *Brahman*. Though there are many gods, they are cosmic in character (fire, the earth, the air, the sky, the heavenly bodies, thunder, the ten breaths of a person; or that which is transformed into such). Ultimately, all gods are manifestations of the one *Brahman*.[7] God is *Brahman*.[8] However, since the system is monistic, God is not a being distinct from the self to be worshipped.[9] *Ātman* is *Brahman*. What then is God's (as *Brahman*) position or role? Two different perspectives are suggested. On the one hand, *Brahman* is transcendent to everything. It is beyond all predication, that which the mind cannot comprehend,[10] the noumenal reality behind all phenomena. This is referred to as the acosmic view. On the other hand, *Brahman* is all comprehensive in nature. Its role is cosmogenic; it is that which brings the world out of itself (as the Absolute), sustains it in existence through its immanent activities—as the thread of the universe—and then takes it back into itself.[11] Yet it remains unchanged, persisting through its self-evolution. This is the cosmic or panentheistic view. In this perspective God, insofar as it can be considered, does not act providentially, concerned with human good, but functions 'energistically', that is, as a principle of cosmic unfolding.

One exception to this analysis might be found in the *Śvetāśvatara Upaniṣad*, where God seems to be portrayed on a more individualistic basis and can function as an object of knowledge and devotion.[12] Yet even here the role of God is primarily cosmogenic and cosmic. It is that by which the Brahma-wheel (cosmic process) turns. It covers itself with *prakṛti* (nature, the physical universe) as a spider covers itself with a web. Though hidden in all things, it is the inner self of those things.

According to Advaita Vedānta, reality is noumenal while our empirical existence is phenomenal. As such, there is no real relation between God (as *nirguṇa* Brahman) and the empirical or phenomenal world which contains good and bad, pleasure, pain and suffering. Though from the empirical viewpoint pain and suffering, pleasure and happiness are real, from the absolute perspective, which is that of God as *Brahman*, these are appearances which, by illusion and ignorance, we are deluded into thinking are real. Further, God as the noumenal *Brahman* is beyond all predicates and categories. In particular, it transcends any moral categories or distinctions. Consequently, because of the unpredictable character of the Non-dual Absolute and because of the unique non-relation that it has to the phenomenal wherein are pain and suffering, the question of reconciling the existence, power and goodness of God with the existence of pain and suffering does not arise. Indeed, any explanation of pain and suffering, good and bad fortune, operates only on the phenomenal level, and consequently stands in relation to reality as a mere appearance.

One might ask, however, since *Brahman* appears at the phenomenal level as well, how it is possible to reconcile the existence of the phenomenal *Brahman* with human pain, suffering and misfortune? Phenomenal *Brahman* is seen in two different ways.[13] As *saguṇa* Brahman, it is impersonal consciousness, a 'state of being wherein all distinctions between subject and object are harmonized'.[14] Since in this capacity it is not a personal deity with moral attributes but a philosophical 'Absolute which explains the world-system',[15] there is no divine goodness to be brought into question, and no theistic problem of evil can arise. Phenomenal *Brahman* is also called *Īśvara* or Lord. *Īśvara* is a personal deity who caused the world out of himself. He is the efficient, material and sustaining cause of phenomenal existence.[16] At the end of each world-cycle, he destroys the world by taking it back into himself and brings it again into existence out of himself. Cannot we then raise the theological problem of evil at this juncture? Cannot we wonder how a perfect, good God, free from all evil,[17] can be the cause of a world which contains inequality and suffering? Śaṅkara raises this question and responds by arguing that creation is the 'expansion of *Īśvara*'. 'The activity of the Lord . . . may be supposed to be mere sport, proceeding from his own nature, without reference to any purpose.'[18] Since it is done for no purpose, it is not an intentional action and *Īśvara* bears no moral responsibility for the self-evolution. And without moral responsibility there is no theistic problem of evil.

Śaṅkara does raise the question of God's perfection, but in the context of the question whether *Īśvara* can be the efficient and material cause of the world. The objection is that 'The Lord cannot be the cause of the world, because . . . the reproach of inequality of dispensation and cruelty would attach to him. Some beings . . . he renders eminently happy; others . . . eminently unhappy. Moreover, as the infliction of great pain and the final destruction of all creatures would form part of his dispensation, he would have to be taxed with great cruelty . . .'[19] Śaṅkara raises three problem areas here: the unequal distribution of fortune and misfortune, the fearful miseries we experience, and God's periodic destruction of the world. It is interesting to note that the first of the problems he raises is not the problem of evil (why there is suffering) but the problem of justice (how one can reconcile with justice the apparent unequal distribution of good and bad fortune). This confirms our thesis that the Indian problem of evil differs from the Western in that it is primarily concerned with the universal principle of justice. The third stresses the role of God in the periodic dissolutions of the world. This destruction of the world seems cruel, though it is held by Hindus to be purifying. Again, moral-cosmogenic considerations assume primary importance. In short, he rebuts the charge both that *Īśvara* dispenses goods and evils unequally and is malicious or cruel, not primarily to establish or justify God's goodness *per se*, but in order to show that *Īśvara* is qualified to be the cause of the world.

In the systems which are more theistic, that is to say, more devotion-(*bhakti*-)oriented, the situation is both similar and different. In the *Bhagavad-Gītā* this cosmogenic role is repeated. God is *Brahman*.[20] All things spring from God as their original source, are maintained in their existence, and are eventually dissolved by him. Indeed, his 'body' is the very stuff out of which they evolve and into which they devolve.[21] God is also the energistic or animating principle in everything; it is he that brings all things into existence by his power (*Māyā*).[22]

As both the evolver and evolute of *Brahman*, everything both comes from God and is in God. 'Both whatsoever states are of (the Strand or *guṇa* of) goodness, and those of (the Strands or *guṇas* of) passion and darkness too, know that they are from me alone; but I am not in them; they are in me.'[23] Now the *guṇas* are responsible for the bad as well as the good, that is, for the slothful, evil and resistant as well as for the energetic and passionate, enlightening and good. Elsewhere not only are good things like enlightenment, knowledge, non-delusion and pleasure viewed as coming from God, but so are pain, fear, indifference and ill-repute.[24] As such God is not only the evolver of that which results in evil, these very things are in him. Yet, interestingly enough, none of this seems to bother the author of the *Gītā*. There is little attempt to rescue God's moral character in any way, to disassociate God from these effects, either in terms of the effects themselves or to justify them morally.[25]

It is only when the personal side of God is emphasized that the *Gītā* approaches the Western theodicistic concern. Krishna is the personal manifestation of *Brahman*. In this role he is both the saviour of those who worship him and the corrector of unrighteousness. He is more than merely an object of devotion, knowledge or meditation[26]; he takes an apparent role in controlling moral evil. 'For whenever of the right a languishing appears, a rising up of unright, then I send myself forth. For protection of the good, and for destruction of evil-doers, to make a firm footing for the right, I come into being in age after age.'[27] God in this role comes to save those devoted to him; 'even if a very evil doer reveres me with single devotion, he must be regarded as righteous in spite of all; for he has the right resolution'.[28] God is the God of grace. When God is so described, the theistic problem of evil arises.[29] For if God is omnipotent and the knower of all, why does he not dispense salvific merit more frequently or more effectively?

Finally, in Yoga God's primary function relates to human liberation, though the cosmogenic function comes later. God (*Īśvara*) is a separate, inactive, omniscient self or consciousness (*puruṣa*) who differs from the other *puruṣas* in that he never suffers the afflictions (ignorance, egoism, attachment, aversion and love of life) which affect other *puruṣas*.[30] Thus he never acquires karma nor undergoes *saṃsāra*. *Īśvara's* purposes are three-fold. First, he is that to whom the *yogi* offers the fruits of all his actions, so that his external acts do not result in the accumulation of additional karma to be worked off in this and subsequent lives.[31] In this role, God is simply object, not subject, and consequently *per se* plays at best a tangential or passive role in liberation. According to the second, God is the object of meditation or devotion. By meditating on *Īśvara*, by repeating and understanding the sacred word (*Om*), one obtains self-understanding and the obstacles to attaining true discriminative knowledge—disease, debility, doubt, carelessness, sloth, sensuality, and so on—are overcome.[32] Here the role of God is more ambiguous. He again can be seen as merely a passive object upon whom meditation is appropriate and beneficial. However, later commentators suggest that there is more to it than this, that devotion draws *Īśvara* to the worshipper, and his presence removes the impediments to knowledge. Two qualifications should be added. First, *Īśvara* is not in fact active, since by nature he is inactive. To understand how he removes impediments to knowledge without acting, the analogy of a magnet is used. Secondly, though this is sometimes spoken of as an act of grace on his part, it is grace only in that it speeds up the process. Impediments to knowledge are removed more quickly than would be the case if the devotee had to go through all the meditative stages. But nothing is removed which the devotee does not merit removed in virtue of his karma. Thirdly, God is the teacher of all the ancient teachers in his role as the revealer of the Vedas.[33]

In this schema the problem of reconciling God's existence and 'action' with evil and suffering could only arise with respect to the second function. However, God's grace is dispensed according to merit and not without considerable preparation and meditation on the part of the receiver. Further, though God is conscious and omniscient, as inactive he is incapable of any moral action, either good or bad. Thus, moral predicates cannot be appropriately applied to him. Finally, on the matter of his having a telic will there is substantial ambiguity. He is said to have no desires, yet also said to purpose (and by his presence facilitate) the liberation of all *puruṣas*.[34]

In later Yoga, God again assumes a cosmogenic role in that his presence removes the obstacles in the way of *prakṛti*'s evolution, and consequently provides the stimulus for altering the balance which holds between *prakṛti*'s three constituents (*guṇas*) at the end of an evolutionary cycle. This initiates the evolutionary process. Here again this is not done telically, but under the aegis of the law of karma.

To summarize, first, many Indian systems (Sāṅkhya, Mīmāṃsā, early Vaiśeṣika, Theravāda Buddhism, Jainism[35]) are atheistic. For these systems the theistic problem of evil would never arise. Secondly, when God's existence is envisioned, it's role is primarily cosmic and cosmogenic. In such a capacity it is often held to be impersonal and in essence qualitatively transcendent. Only when a personal, theistic God is envisioned do we begin to find concerns which approach the Western theistic problem of evil. This arises out of two different contexts. On the one hand, we find a concern whether God is qualified in terms of his perfection to be the efficient and material cause of a world which contains inequality of dispensation of good and bad fortune, the miseries of *saṃsāra*, and which he periodically dissolves. Here, though the problem is similar to the Western problem, the primary focus remains cosmogenic. God's perfection is a concern only insofar as it qualifies him to be the cause of the world (though this seems to be a problem for Śaṅkara and Rāmānuja and not for the author of the *Gītā*). However, despite this, the ground is there for raising the theistic problem of evil. It is maintained that God exists; is the efficient and material cause of what exists; is perfect, omniscient and omnipotent; and that pain, suffering and dysfunction abound in the world. Therefore one can ask how God's perfection or other properties can be reconciled with this evil. On the other hand, the theistic problem also arises when God is viewed as a dispenser of grace. Here the theistic problem of evil can be raised by asking why God, who is good and desires the liberation of all, does not dispense more saving grace more effectively. In short, the problem of evil as raised in Indian thought is almost always non-theistic, and where the theistic problem is raised, it is raised as a secondary issue. However, in those theistic systems where God is viewed as personal and as an omnipotent, perfect cause of the world and/or a dispenser of grace, the grounds are present for raising the theistic problem of evil. To put it another way, the theistic problem of evil arises *out of* certain aspects of some Indian philosophies, rather than *in* Indian philosophy.

THE THEISTIC PROBLEM OF EVIL

We have already noted that the law of karma is introduced to resolve the non-theistic problem of evil. Can it also be used to resolve the theistic problem, which attempts to defend or reconcile the existence of a good, omnipotent, omniscient deity with the presence of pain, suffering and misfortune in the world? Since some Western philosophers and theologians think so, it is worth reconstructing what such a solution might look like.

Let us begin with Śaṅkara's brief treatment of the theistic problem.[36] As we noted above, the problem is raised in the context of an objection that God is not qualified to be the cause of the world because good and evil are dispensed unequally, there is great misery in the world, and he periodically destroys the world. Śaṅkara's reply involves an appeal to the law of karma. He contends that all three of these are explained as the recompense of individuals' acts. That is, the evil in the world is due to human merit and demerit accumulated from prior karmic actions.[37] Though God causes what happens (since he is the sole material cause), he has no control over dispensing either fortune or misfortune. He simply acts according to the dictates of the law of karma. The solution to the theistic problem of evil, then, is that God is not morally responsible for the evil in the world because he simply administrates the consequences of our karmic acts. It is the individual agents which are morally accountable. This means, then, that all evil is moral evil, that is, evil for which human agents can be held morally accountable. There is no natural evil *per se*.[38]

Three objections to this can be raised:

1. First, is this subjection of God's acts to the law of karma consistent with his omnipotence? The answer is affirmative, provided one carefully defines omnipotence. If God is omnipotent, then he can do anything which is not or does not entail a contradiction or which he is not excluded from performing.[39] If he is omnipotent but cannot violate the law of karma, there must then be some contradiction in his doing so. There would be a contradiction if the law expresses a necessary truth. That it is treated as doing so we saw in chapter 3. As such, it would be impossible for anything, including God, to break the law. Hence, that God cannot do the impossible does not count against his omnipotence.

2. Second, if all evil ultimately is caused by human persons and if human persons are God's creations, where did the original human desire to do evil come from, and why did God create human persons with the ability to desire and do evil? If the first humans did evil, not because they desired to do so, but accidentally, then they should not be held morally accountable for breaking the moral law and karma should not accumulate. If, on the other hand, they did evil because they were disposed to do evil, then God created them with that disposition and is morally responsible for it. It might be replied that they did evil, not because they were disposed to do so, but of their own free choice. But then why did God create humans with the ability freely to choose and do evil? Some justification of this action of granting persons morally significant choice is required in order to preserve God's goodness and wisdom.

So stated, it appears that the attempt to use a karmic theodicy in the theistic context depends upon a more basic theodicy, such as a free will or soul-building theodicy. That is, some explanation of why God created human persons with the ability to choose and do evil is required, and it is to this issue that non-karmic theodicies are directed.

Śaṅkara and Rāmānuja suggest two answers to the dilemma.

a. First, they maintain that God's causation of the world is not an intentional act. God causes (and in Rāmānuja, sustains and destroys) the world, not purposefully, but out of sport, and thus is not morally accountable for his acts.[40] Generalized to the above problem, this means that the creation of persons with the freedom to make moral decisions was not intended or purposed by God. In fact, God has no intentions or purposes. It is merely the result of his non-intentional or sporting actions. And since he did not intend it, there is no answer to the 'why' question, nor need a moral justification for his actions be sought.

Why do they argue in this fashion? The reason is to avoid a dilemma. On the one hand, if God acts from a purpose or goal, he wants to achieve something. But if he wants to achieve something, he lacks something; he is not self-sufficient, which contradicts his perfection. On the other hand, if he has no purpose, he cannot act except in senseless or spontaneous ways, which contradicts his omniscience.[41] Thus, they want to suggest that there is a class of actions which is neither intentional (in that it has no purpose) nor unintentional (and hence not done senselessly). And this they see manifested in acting out of sport.

But is 'doing something out of sport' equivalent to doing something for no purpose or non-intentionally? To do something out of sport is to do something either for pleasure (for the heck of it) or else to do it for its own sake. But in both cases, a purpose of some sort is involved. To use their example, when nobility engage in sporting activities, they do so for the pleasure they derive from them; from seeing the hounds chase and catch the fox, the falcon swoop down on its prey, or the billiard balls roll into the pocket. That the sport itself has no purpose does not entail that those who engage in it have no purpose in doing so.[42]

What Śaṅkara and Rāmānuja require is an intentional act which is not done for a purpose (and hence out of any lack) and which frees the agent from moral accountability. Interestingly enough, they have such acts at their disposal. As we noted in chapter 2, acts which are performed for their own sake, without any thought of or desire for the results, do not build karma. They are performed not out of desire, necessity or lack, but out of the fullness of being. The acts of God which are other than karma-implementing could be of this non-karma-producing nature. He would be seen as acting simply for the sake of acting, without desires for any end.

This view, of course, has implications for the nature of God. In particular, it removes from God any desires, goals or objectives concerning the world. This, of course, would be consistent with Śaṅkara's and (to a lesser extent) Rāmānuja's view of God.[43] It becomes more problematic, however, for the theist who sees God actively involved in the world. For example, it would not be right to ascribe to him the desire that all persons be liberated. As such, on this account God could not be a God of grace, who intervenes telically on the behalf of those who worship him to relieve them of their suffering and bring liberation.

b. In their next response, they argue that to ask why God created persons as he did is a pseudo-problem because the world is beginningless.[44] All effects are products of causes, which are themselves effects of other causes. Thus there is no question why God brought these particular beings into existence; they have always existed. God simply 'arranges the diversity of the creation in accordance with the different Karman of the individual souls'.[45] God, then, is subject to the law of karma in his dealings with the universe. He is not the teleologically-efficient cause of what exists.

Again, for the theist who sees God involved telically with the creation, this raises the larger question concerning what can be said about God's acts and his relation to the world. Does God do anything but administer the law of karma? If not, and if the law of karma is a necessary truth, then of course the law of karma solves the theistic problem of evil, for all his acts are justified in terms of the karma accumulated by us. But what then happens to the nature of God? He becomes little more than a general cause in the universe. He is, as Śaṅkara notes, a general or 'common' cause, like the god who dispenses rain everywhere regardless of where it is needed. God then creates everything (as a non-teleological material cause) but has no further role to play with the created as individuals.

But this God can hardly be the God of religious worship, the one to whom devotion is paid and requests made. It is not the God who out of love and compassion relieves the suffering of the petitioner or who liberates those who call on him. Indeed, in this view divine grace in any particularized sense is impossible. If the law of karma requires that each person receives his due, and if what is due a person is the result of the actions he has performed, then God can be of little direct aid in removing our acquired karma by divine intervention, mercy and forgiveness. In short, God's role is cosmogenic and administrative and little else.

3. Finally, there is the problem how God as the material cause can avoid sullying his perfection with the evil which evolves. Though the *Bhagavad-Gītā* at times appears nonchalant about the disassociation of God from evolved evil, other personal, theistic systems show more explicit concern. For example, Rāmānuja notes that 'the Supreme *Brahman* is devoid of even the slightest trace of the evil that is found to exist in all the intelligent and non-intelligent things . . . . The Supreme *Brahman* is the opposite of all that is evil and the sole seat of all auspicious qualities. He is entirely distinct from all other things (than Himself)'.[46] The imperfection of the evolved does not affect the perfection of the evolver. However, how his panentheistic deity can remain separate enough from what evolves out of him, which includes evil and imperfection, to be perfect is unclear. *Brahman* and his body (souls and matter) are one, a unity.

It might be thought that the imperfection here is ontological and not moral, and hence not directly germane to the problem of evil.[47] That something is not perfect in its being says nothing about its moral perfection. For example, being crippled and in a wheel chair implies nothing about moral character. But for Rāmānuja, God is the soul or self in each person, just as each is part of his body. But souls or selves perform karmic deeds, both good and bad. As such, it is hard to see how God can escape similar consequences.

In summation, the appeal to the law of karma to resolve the theistic problem of evil has important consequences. First, it either necessitates that the creation of the world and selves is the result of a desireless and purposeless act of God (so that he does not lack self-sufficiency) or that the world and selves are beginningless (so that the evil which we experience is always the result of our prior acts).[48] The former not only leaves many questions unanswerable, including why God made what he did and why he made it as he did, but turns the universe into a grand sporting event. If anything, it trivializes and degrades human existence. The latter is possible, though unlikely, given what we know and can reasonably infer about the history of the universe and life in it. But more importantly it accounts for no other divine acts. Secondly, either all God's acts are governed by the law of karma and hence justified thereby, or else he performs acts which are done to realize no end. Both make it impossible that God is gracious, having pity for miserable mankind and intervening on behalf of those he seeks to save. In effect, if one appeals to the law of karma to explain all evil, then we have a movement towards an impersonal theism, where God's primary roles are non-teleologically cosmogenic and/or administrative. Where we have a personal theism in which God brings selves into being or sustains their existence, or is motivated by a desire to show mercy and intervenes in behalf of their liberation, an appeal to the law of karma must be conjoined with other theodicies (such as the free will or soul-building theodicies) in order to justify either God's creation and sustenance of beings capable of free, moral choice or the degree to which he intervenes. However, this being said, the adequacy of the law of karma within the Hindu/Buddhist context should not be measured on this score, since, as we suggested at the outset, the theistic problem of evil was not the problem it was developed to resolve.

THE NON-THEISTIC PROBLEM OF EVIL

It is time to return to the issue with which we began this chapter. Is the law of karma adequate to solve the non-theistic problem of evil? To evaluate its adequacy, two areas must be addressed. First, some defence of the doctrine of rebirth (in either the Hindu or Buddhist forms) must be made. As we noted in chapter 2, this is a presupposition of the theory. We shall look at this presupposition in detail in chapters 7 and 8. Secondly, the advocate of this explanation of evil must provide an account of the mechanism by which karma is implemented. That is, if the law of karma is to explain all kinds of fortune and misfortune and the evil that we do to one another as well as the evil that results from natural causes, some reasonable description of its workings is requisite. It is to this that we shall turn in the next chapter.

6

Karma, Causation and Divine Intervention

According to the law of karma, our actions have consequences which affect not only our dispositions and tendencies (*saṃskāras*), but also the non-dispositional aspects of our being (for example, our genetic make-up, our physical characteristics, our social status at birth, our length of life) and our environment. The environment is affected in such a way that in some future life it will be instrumental in rewarding or punishing us according to the merit or demerit resulting from our acts. For example, a person might be mauled by a grizzly bear either in retribution for a particular violent act he committed or because of his pool of accumulated karmic residues.

One can understand how desiring to act and then acting in accord with those desires would create dispositions in the person who wills and acts; and where a continuous, substantial self is presupposed, it is reasonable to hold that these dispositions would be preserved and bear fruit in that self at some later time. But that our acts also have cosmic or environmental effects of a specific character in subsequent existences is more problematic. How, it might be wondered, can the acts we performed in some past life affect the present material and physical conditions of our environment or other agents? With the exception of certain theistic systems, about which we shall speak later, karma is held to operate in a naturalistic fashion. That is, prior events effect subsequent events without the intervention of any supernatural agent. But if karma operates naturally, is it reasonable to believe that there is any causal link between the original cause (our doing either one or many acts) and the (pleasurable or painful, advantageous or disadvantageous) effects we experience in a subsequent life? What causal chain can be established between a person's doing good actions in a previous life and the fact that the person has the pleasure of owning a Cadillac, recovered from an attack of influenza, or had a tree blown down by the windstorm miss his house?

The problem is exacerbated by the contention that the law of karma is not empirically verifiable. Yet its constitutive process of cause (one's action) and effect (the pain or pleasure received) cannot be understood in any way other than empirical.

What I intend to explore is the causal relation which is believed to hold between the original action(s) taken by the agent and the effects which impinge on the agent in subsequent lives. To accomplish this, we must begin with an analysis of the nature of the causal relation invoked by karmic accounts.

ACTIONS AND ENVIRONMENTAL CONSEQUENCES

Strange as it may seem, the precise connection between our actions and the events which bring us happiness and unhappiness in subsequent lives is rarely dealt with in the literature of the traditions which invoke the law of karma, Jainism being the exception. What is focused on is the effect (in terms of pain and pleasure) which the original action has on us, not the process. Yet this is not so strange, considering that the primary concern of karmically-oriented philosophies is with how we can bring about our own salvation through renunciation, non-attachment and overcoming ignorance. The literature attends to primary, salvific relationships. Secondary relationships, such as the relation between the original action and the environmental effects, fade into the background, to be focused on only when they illustrate the basic point that our actions will affect us in the future. The 'how' is known perhaps only by *yogis* who have extrasensory intuition and can know the past and future. Yet a description of the way actions cause environmental effects in subsequent lives is necessary if the law of karma is to provide a plausible explanation of our pleasant and painful experiences, that is, if it is to resolve the problem of evil. Indeed, the plausibility of the law of karma itself depends to a great extent upon the plausibility of the accompanying accounts of this causal relation.

Two different directions have been taken to answer the question of how the original act and subsequent environmental effects are related. The commonly held view takes the relation to be natural; less frequent is the appeal to the supernatural. If they are related naturally, then either (1) there is a causal chain (either direct or mediated through a pool of karmic residues) external to the agent from the environmental effects immediately brought about by the original act to the environment which produces his future painful or pleasant experiences, or else (2) the connection is made through the effects made on the agent himself, which in turn produce relevant changes in the environment in subsequent lives. To put it another way, understood naturalistically, there is a causal chain between the karmic acts and the things which produce pleasure and pain which either (1) lies outside the individual person, in the environment, or (2) extends through and is mediated by the person affected. We will first examine the adequacy of these two naturalistic accounts. Should they prove inadequate, we will turn to evaluate the appeal to a supernatural causal connection.

KARMIC RESIDUES IN THE ENVIRONMENT

The first option [(1)] contains two possibilities; let us consider these in turn.

(a) Let us suppose that there exists outside us a chain of causal conditions which directly links the karmic action(s) we performed in one life with the environment we experience painfully or pleasurably in the same or another life. When we perform an action, that action has immediate effects (*phalas*) in the world, and these in turn (along with other conditions) have their subsequent effects, and so on. Eventually, the morally relevant environmental state which affects us as the agent of the original deed is produced. This is not to deny that there are other causal conditions relevant to bringing about the particular situation experienced. It is rather to assert positively that the moral-consequence-bearing aspect could be traced causally to our prior action(s).

This scenario, though logically possible, is implausible. Were the temporal gap between cause and effect restricted to a slice of our present existence, one might reasonably claim that such a connection could be made, though it would become less likely as the time between the original act and the later effect increased. But when the time between the karmic action and the morally relevant consequence is spread over several, if not hundreds of, incarnations, that a direct causal connection could be present in non-conscious, material or physical conditions, and that this causal connection would operate not only on the appropriate moral agent but also to a degree determined by impersonal cosmic justice, is beyond reasonable belief. Yet all three conditions—direct causal relation, action on the agent of the original karmic action(s) and appropriate compensation—are necessary for the implementation of the law of karma. It would appear that a different explanation of the causal relation is necessary for the doctrine of karma to be plausible.

(b) The second possibility under the first option is that the original karmic act contributes to a pool of karmic residues. These residues, which can be accumulated, consist of invisible moral forces, potencies or qualities which exist in things external to us. Things, by virtue of these moral forces, have the ability to cause events in the world.

But this option not only faces the same difficulties which option (a) faced, it encounters the difficulty of explaining how these accumulated forces are created in the first place, in what manner they continue to exist in the universe, and how they affect, in whole or in part, events at some later date. That is, not only is the causal process non-verifiable, but the invisible karmic potencies which are responsible for causing the event (at least in part) are indescribable and non-verifiable.

KARMIC RESIDUES IN THE AGENT

According to the second naturalistic explanation [(2)], karma operates causally through the agent of the original action. The performance of the original action causes effects of a certain kind in the agent, and these effects in turn bring about changes in the agent's environment at an appropriate time. The nature and character of these effects is explained differently within the various traditions. In this and the following section I will piece together in detail how different traditions explain these effects. Following that, I will explore how these effects allegedly condition our environment in karmically relevant ways.

According to the Mīmāṃsākas, a karmic act produces effects in the form of potencies (*apūrva*).[1] Since these potencies are characterized as *dharma* and *adharma* (merit and demerit), the very moral quality of the action is preserved in the form of a potency within the doer of the act. They can be accumulated in units of higher and lower order and exist unseen (*adṛṣṭa*) within the *ātman* until the proper time for fruition, when they causally condition the environment to produce the proper experience for the agent.

A similar view was advocated by the Vaiśeṣkas. According to them, among the effects karmic action creates are special qualities called *adṛṣṭas*. *Adṛṣṭa* refers to invisible qualities of merit and demerit which are capable of producing effects. In the non-moral sphere, *adṛṣṭa* was invoked to account for events which could not be explained by the physical processes already known. For example, it was invoked to explain the ability of magnets to move things, the circulation of sap in trees and plants, the fact that fire rose rather than descended as other things do, and the movement of atoms, including the mind (*manas*).[2] In the moral sphere, it referred to the qualities of merit and demerit which are produced by actions. These special, invisible qualities, which are attached to the self or *ātman*, function as causal conditions, such that like any other causal condition, their presence or absence helps to determine whether an effect will occur or occur in a particular way. Specifically, they condition our desires and aversions, which in turn drive us to further karmic actions.[3]

The Jainas, on the other hand, treat the causal sequence more materialistically. They categorize reality according to two types, *jīva* (spirit or self) and *ajīva* (that which lacks life and consciousness and which can be understood only in contrast with *jīva*). The *jīva* is the self whose essence is knowledge. In the state of perfection, it exists disembodied, free from delusion, loving the truth and knowing everything directly and accurately. However, the present epistemological condition of fragmentary, partial, inaccurate knowledge is due to the impeding activity of karma, which interferes with the *jīva*'s powers of perception and obscures its love for truth. In addition, there are two kinds of karmas. Spiritual karma consists of our passions, privations, and the perversions of our self's capacities. This karma constitutes the bondage of the self. Material karma is a substantive, material force; it is matter in a subtle form which is omnipresent in the world. This is the karma which causes and in turn is caused or attracted by our bondage.

Our actions arise from our passions. These actions and passions, in turn, attract material karma. It is attracted as if magnetically and affixed to the *jīva,* infecting it with liberation-retarding matter. The passions which cause bondage (for example, anger, pride, deceit and greed) are called sticky substances (*kaśāyas*) because they act like glue in making matter-particles stick to the self. According to the varying strengths of the passions, atoms with different units of intensity are attracted.[4] And the stronger the intensity, the greater the bondage and the farther one is from liberation.

The material karma acts directly on and changes the immaterial *jīva,* causing passions and obstructing its knowledge, thus deluding it. These changes are variously described as a coloration (white, black or a mixture of white and black) or an actual weighing down of the *jīva.* However, subtle karmic matter is believed not merely to affect the *jīva,* but to penetrate it, accumulate, and build up a special body called *kārmaṇa-śarīra,* which transmigrates with the self and does not leave it until its final emancipation.[5] The self in bondage, it is held, actually possesses a material form.

There is, then, a cycle: passions attract material karma, which is transformed by the self into a subtle, karmic body, which in turn causes passions, and so on. Eventually karma can overpower and take control of the spiritual self, though the soul never completely loses its knowledge and love for truth. If it did, it would cease to be a self. The cycle is broken and liberation comes, but only when the self regains its purity by eliminating the taint of karma. To do this we must stop the inflow of new karma and destroy the karma which has already accumulated by allowing it to exhaust itself. And this is accomplished by eliminating the passions and activity which attract material karma.

The soul's activities and passions are held to attract karmic matter as a magnet attracts filings or a lamp draws oil into its wick.[6] But what is there about activities and passions which gives them such a power, and what, specifically, is this power? (It should be noted that the power is not merely one of attraction, but of attraction of matter appropriately and justly proportionate to the moral quality of the activity or passion.) Further, how does karmic matter in the subtle body cause the passions and delude the self? Karmic matter, it is said, infects or circumscribes the self; forms a crust on or covers the self; mixes with the self as milk mixes with water or fire with iron; obscures, obstructs and distorts the self's knowledge, intuition, bliss, freedom and energy; pollutes and destroys the purity of the soul.[7] Peering behind the analogies, it is clear that some of the specific activities of karmic matter can be understood causally, for example, how the karmic body might make awakening from sleep difficult, cause pleasant and unpleasant feelings in us, or be a factor in producing our body. But how it deludes knowledge or causes anger, pride, deceit or greed, or 'obstructs the inclination for making gifts and charities,' is more difficult to see. Perhaps one could understand how matter could cause greed, in that when we see the material goods that others have we covet them for ourselves. But this kind of common-sense explanation will not suffice here, for karmic matter is invisible and works more in the sense of an efficient cause. Perhaps the clearest way to understand this is to see the karmic body as limiting the moral energies of the self. Without the unlimited energies it would have in its pure state, the self cannot adequately control its passions and activities. Consequently, it is more easily aroused, enticed and deceived by what it encounters in its environment. It angers more easily, is greedier, displays less concern for the truth, and acts out of pride.

Whatever the true causal account, for our purposes, it is important to note that, for the Jainas, karmic residues are passed on and preserved in the agent as both spiritual and material karma. As spiritual, they are the passions and privations, actual and potential, which exist in the person. Since 'the soul, at any instant of its worldly existence, is the integrated whole of the dispositions, actual and potential',[8] karma is stored in the dispositions to manifest these passions. Even as dispositions they continue to be affected by the material karma which they attract. As material, karmic residues are attracted to and preserved in the person until removed or eliminated. Indeed, they constitute a special, subtle body which accompanies the self and continues to affect it by limiting its moral energy, until its liberation.

KARMA AND CAUSATION IN BUDDHISM

The Buddhist analysis depends upon its own theory of the nature of reality and causation. We will say more about the role of causation in Buddhism in chapter 8; here we will sketch enough to clarify the causal relation between karmic actions, karmic residues and environmental effects.

Reality is analysed, not in terms of static substances, but in terms of events (*dharmas*). Events do not exist without a cause and are in turn, along with other conditions, causes of other events. The effect is conditioned by prior causes in that it would not exist did not these causal conditions exist. That is, events are functionally dependent upon temporally non-subsequent events. 'This being, that occurs' is a recurrent phrase. Second, causation is the relationship which provides the continuity between events. Finally, '[c]ausation is said to have [the characteristics of] objectivity, necessity, invariability and conditionality'.[9] All events, then, are causally conditioned by and causally connected to other events.

How does this apply to the question regarding how karma is passed on? Two of the elements (*skandhas*) which go to make up what is termed the person are dispositions and consciousness (as awareness, acts of the mind, or thoughts). Dispositions are important in explaining an individual's behaviour, particularly because they eventually give rise to desires. And since they condition consciousness, they in part account for a person's psychophysical personality. Our current dispositions and consciousness are caused by prior dispositions and consciousness, and these in turn cause subsequent dispositions and consciousness. Since we act out of our dispositions and consciousness, they become the vehicle through which karma is causally transmitted.

But *how* are karmic residues causally transmitted, particularly if there are no persistent substances, only events? The Buddha asserted that all events are causally conditioned, but at the same time he refused to become embroiled in the metaphysical controversies surrounding contemporary discussions of causation.[10] His was, as David Kalupahana often reminds us, an empirical theory of causation, and the law of karma extends beyond empirical verification. Thus, in effect, how karmic residues in one event affect subsequent events is one of the great mysteries.[11] However, usually the matter is not left here, for simply to describe this fundamental relation as inexplicable raises the question of the intelligibility and sense of the karmic thesis.

The various Buddhist schools developed theories to explain the transmission. Being willing to offer analyses of the process created particular problems for scholastic or Ābhidharma Buddhists, for whom events are momentary and, since production takes time, lack transitive force.[12] The cause and effect are not contemporaneous with each other but are momentary events connected sequentially. Thus how can an event which has ended and disappeared bring about an effect? And how can an event whose only non-arising, decaying or ceasing moment is static have causal efficacy? Further, since nothing exists but momentary or transitory events, there are no permanent, subsistent entities and hence no selves to convey dispositions, consciousness or karmic residues.[13] Yet, they contend that karmic acts and accumulated karma are the causal conditions which in part determine or condition all subsequent human experience. How is this to be explained?

The Vaibhāṣikas, a school of the Sarvāstivādins, attempted to provide an explanation by postulating the existence of an unseen product of a volition (*avijñapti*). Every physical, verbal or mental act must have a result. Often the results are visible, but frequently they are not. This is particularly the case with respect to the production of moral qualities and dispositions in the agent. Hence, they postulated an invisible resultant to explain cases where no result was observed. Some held that this resultant was neither mental nor physical; others held that it was physical when it resulted from physical or verbal acts, and mental when it resulted from mental acts; still others (the Yogācārins) that it was material, dependent on the four fundamental elements (earth, water, fire and air). In any case, it resided in the agent where it functioned as an invisible cause of future events.[14] It was able to cause events at a later time because events are eternal in their ideal being. Both the past and the future exist; only their mode of existence varies. What makes events in the past, present and future differ is not their existence, but their temporal mode. Accordingly, the *avijñapti*, existing through these various modes, can cause effects at times later than its creation. Thus they postulated an existent which, though its mode changes, does not change in substance.

Others, for example the Sautrāntikas, rejected the thesis that all events (past, present and future) exist. Past acts do not exist and cannot directly cause future events. They also rejected the postulation of an unseen entity enduring through various temporal modes. Rather, karmic acts are causally efficacious because they 'perfume' the bundles of *skandhas*, creating in them invisible potencies or traces (*vāsanās*) which later will bear karmic fruit. These potencies exist in and through the five *skandhas*, as seeds waiting to produce their fruit. The seed then is an analogy, a fruitful fiction, to help explain the transmission of karmic residues.

But how is the analogy of the seed to enlighten us as to the nature of the transfer of karma or karmic efficacy? The answer is not always clear. Indeed, it often appears that, as with the concept of *avijñapti*, a kind of substantialist thinking is being used to provide an explanation for that which is allegedly non-substantial, for the seed is at least commonly perceived as a substance, enduring until it ripens. Indeed, the Sautrāntikas approached the substantialist thinking they rejected in others when they introduced a kind of substratum which supported these ongoing potencies.[15] Yet surely the concept of a seed understood as a substance existing over time cannot be used by the non-substantialist Buddhist thinker to explain karmic causation.

The Mahāyāna tradition also appeals to the seed analogy. 'Whatever a man does, the same he in himself will find. The good man, good; and evil he that evil has designed; and so our deeds are all like seeds, and bring forth fruit in kind'.[16] D.T. Suzuki, the twentieth-century popularizer of the Mahāyāna Buddhist tradition, also uses the seed analogy. 'All our mental and spiritual experiences are due to the operation of karma which inherits its efficiency from its previous "seeds of activity" (*karmabīja*), and which has brought the five *skandhas* into the present state of co-ordination. The present karma, while in its force, generates in turn the "seeds of activity" which under favourable conditions grow to maturity again.'[17] He attempts to develop the analogy of the seed non-substantially.

> Another good way of illustrating this doctrine is to follow the growth and perpetuation of the seed. The seed is in fact a concrete expression of karma. When a plant reaches a certain stage of development, it blooms and bears fruit. This fruit contains in it a latent energy which under favourable conditions grows to a mature plant of its own kind . . . . The life of an individual plant cannot be permanent . . . . But this is not the case with the current of an everlasting vitality that has been running in the plant ever since the beginning of the world. This current is not individual in its nature and stands above the vicissitudes which take place in the life of particular plants.

> It may not be manifested in its kinetic form all the time, but potentially it is ever present in the being of the seed. Changes are simply a matter of form, and do not interfere with the current of life in the plant, which is preserved in the universe as the energy of vegetation.[18]

The explanation suggested here is that the *skandhas*, which bundled together are identified as being the individual person, are the field upon which an eternal, karmic force operates. Penetrating the particular, transitory bundles of *skandhas* is a universal force which, by its energy, or better, being energy, brings about or provides the conditions for subsequent 'seeds'. This karmic force, running through the particular, momentary sets of *skandhas*, plays a significant role in the construction or arising of the subsequent *skandhas*.

> There is no irreducible reality in particular existence, so long as they are combinations of several causes and conditions brought together by the principle of karma. Things are here because they are sustained by karma. As soon as its force is exhausted, the conditions that made their existence possible lose efficiency and dissolve, and in their places will follow other conditions and existence.[19]

Suzuki's explanation invokes the concept of a continuing force, energy or vitality which exists in addition to and has duration through a large number of transitory events. This differs from the Theravāda Buddhist denial that causes are forces and that there is something which has duration. Further, when Suzuki refers to this vitality as something which is not individual in nature, he appears to mean that it is a universal, and then goes on to ascribe existence to this universal. Though Suzuki does not directly make the connection, this continuing energy which penetrates everything seems to be identical with or a state of the *Dharmakāya*. *Dharmakāya* is the unconditioned, non-dual, ultimate reality of which everything is a manifestation.[20] What this illustrates, of course, is the Mahāyāna departure from Hīnayāna thought in the formulation and advocacy of an Absolute or Ultimate Principle of the universe.

To return to the question at hand, how does this help us understand how karmic residues are transmitted? Karma is perpetuated through an ongoing vitality which actualizes the seeds. It does this through its own unfolding, for the seeds themselves are stored in that by which they are actualized.[21] The *Ālayavijñāna* is the storehouse of seeds, not as physical objects, but as ideal possibilities. Consistent with Vijñānavāda Buddhism, Suzuki gives the *Ālayavijñāna* a double sense. Vijñānavāda Buddhists interpret reality on the model of the psychological individual. The psychological individual is the microcosm; ultimate reality the macrocosm. The principles, stages and operations of the one are mirrored in the other. This is legitimate for them because ultimately there is no difference between the microcosm and macrocosm, except for the role that ignorance plays in the development of the former out of the latter. To put it another way, the psychological models the other because it is a transformation or projection of it. The psychological states and processes of the individual soul or consciousness parallel those of Absolute Consciousness seen as transforming.

What, then, is this double sense? On the one hand, the *Ālayavijñāna* is not a universal but particular.[22] It is the soul or self as it evolves or transforms from the state of pure consciousness to the state of mental activity. In this stage or state, the dispositions or tendencies are preserved in an ideal or mental form, until they are actualized by the soul in its later stages of development. On the other hand, the *Ālayavijñāna* is more than the particularized self; it is the supra-individual or universal mind or soul which, by illusion or ignorance, is a particularized transformation of the *Dharmakāya* or Absolute.[23] It is a state of Suchness, the non-dual Absolute Mind or Pure Consciousness. Pure Consciousness lacks particularity or differentiation of any kind. It is only when it evolves as the *Ālayavijñāna* that it becomes the repository of seminal ideas and dispositions. The *Ālayavijñāna* contains the seeds of all things as ideal beings. In our ignorance, we take these ideas to be real, as physical objects, and project these seeds into the world to create an objective world. In effect, in this second view, Suzuki is saying that our karma, which is part of this projected world, is stored in this transformation of the Absolute, and since everything evolves from and is a part of it, our karma is preserved in the very evolving universe. In short, our karma, as seeds or potencies, is preserved both in the individual consciousness as ideal potencies and, since our consciousness is an evolute of Absolute Consciousness, in the transformed Consciouness as seminal ideas or potencies.

But if the individual's karma is stored in this modification or evolute of Absolute Consciousness or Mind, how is it implemented in the individual? The answer depends on the relation of the individual to this transformation of the Absolute. On the one hand, Suzuki stresses the point that all is one, that anything other than it is an illusion created by ignorance. Thus, from the perspective of the higher stages of evolution, everything below it is unreal.[24] As such, the objective world does not really exist but is a subjective illusion created by ignorance.[25] In this case, it is difficult to see how individual karma can be stored in or implemented from the *Ālayavijñāna*, since all objective reality from its perspective is illusory. Though we grant that ignorance is a cause, how can ignorance which has the status of an illusion act as a cause on that which from that same perspective is real? On the other hand, though all is one, Suzuki sees the universe as a phenomenal manifestation of the Absolute.[26] The *Dharmakāya* reveals itself in the phenomenal realm by taking various forms. Out of it everything evolves and to it all will return. Here individual karma is a modification or transformation of the universal karma. Again, however, it is difficult to see how karma is preserved and implemented so as to affect the individual proportionately and justly. The reason is because it is difficult to understand the role of the individual in a monistic system, to see how the many can be preserved along with the One without destroying either. If all are modifications of the One, which is undifferentiated, how can the differentiatedness of the many be appropriately determined karmically? Even if we grant the continuing karmic energy, what is there is its undifferentiated wholeness which differentiates it? To reply that it is individual karma begs the very issue.

But beyond all this, the introduction of a repository or storehouse of seeds or dispositions, even if they are ideal, again introduces substance-thinking into Buddhism. The *Ālayavijñāna* is a durational consciousness which, as a seed bed, stores the dispositions until they are projected by ignorance into the objective world. Substance or durational thinking has not been successfully overcome in unpacking the concept of the seed which causes future results.

However, one interesting direction remains. As we noted above, the *Dharmakāya* is not strictly impersonal, but has or is will, intelligence and love. But if our karma is preserved in personal being, we begin to leave the naturalistic explanation of the workings of karma for the theistic, which we shall take up shortly.

To avoid substantialist language and yet retain the significance of the seed analogy is difficult. The seed represents our potencies, dispositions and consciousness which are causally conditioned by previous events. It, as functionally dependent upon and occasioned by prior, skandhic conditions, lies in and works through the complex of *skandhas*, to mature and bear fruit in the proper circumstances.

This, of course, does not explain *how* dispositions and the other *skandhas* are conditioned to exist, for an analysis of causation in terms of functional dependence is circular. Causation is defined as a functional relationship of dependence between events. But what kind of dependence is this? Clearly, it must be a causal one. But then, contrary to what might appear, we have not been provided with any analysis of causation. Rather, causation is a primitive in terms of which other analyses are understood. In effect, according to the Buddhist account, since causation is a primitive or basic relational concept, no further explanation of the causal conditioning of human dispositions and tendencies is possible.

This can be seen in another way. To be real is to be a cause. But when it is noted by the Ābhidharmists that what is real is momentary and consequently inactive (since being momentary it lacks the time necessary to do anything), the response is that its causal activity or efficiency is its very existence. Causation is identical with reality.[27] Causation, then, must be a primitive or basic relational concept, not further analysable into anything more fundamental.

There is, of course, no problem in treating causation as primitive. What creates the difficulty is coupling this causal perspective with a metaphysic which denies the existence of persisting substances. Though Buddhists are clear that karmic residues continue to exist in individuals as dispositions and consciousness, how this can occur given an event metaphysic is left unexplained, except that these are conditioned by prior dispositions and consciousness. The problem is that it is difficult to understand how events (and this is compounded if they are momentary) can condition other events in any way which involves their production.

To summarize the last two sections, we have seen that there is a variety of interpretations concerning the manner in which karmic residues are transmitted from the original act to subsequent experiences of the agent. What all these views have in common is that causation is a feature of (phenomenal) reality, that karmic residues are transmitted through the agent, that the medium of transmission is invisible, and that justice in the form of retribution and reward is preserved in the very passage of karmic residues from the original act to subsequent states of affairs. Where they differ concerns the nature of the karmic quality. For all except Jainism (for whom the moral quality is also embodied in the physical), the causation under consideration is the passing on of a moral, psychic or dispositional quality rather than a physical quality. It is either an invisible moral potency or quality of merit and demerit, a disposition or tendency which either exists in a persistent self or is causally conditioned by prior elements of the person, a subtle material quality, or a combination of these.

THE ENVIRONMENT AND NATURAL GOOD AND EVIL

Were we to understand the workings of karma strictly subjectively, we could stop here. Our acts create dispositions or accumulations of merit and demerit which cause us to act in ways which bring us pleasure and pain, to interpret our experiences in terms of pleasure and pain, or to be vulnerable to certain things in the environment (such as diseases) which affect our body or mind and thus bring pleasure and pain. These accumulations or dispositions affect our experiences and their interpretations until we eliminate them, as the metaphor goes, burning out both the seed (using up the accumulated karma) and its roots (destroying the dispositions and not creating new ones). This is accomplished when we achieve a proper understanding of the self, no longer act out of desire for any fruits, have equanimity toward all events, or cease mental modifications.

That this is a reasonable explanation of karma interpreted subjectively does not however mean that it is without difficulty. The major difficulty is to be found in assuring that the produced dispositions, whether behavioural or bodily, and resultant pain and pleasure, are justly appropriate to the karmic act. We have no scale which correlates the amount of pleasure and pain to be received with the moral quality of the act performed. And even were we provided with one, it would be difficult if not impossible to carry out the relevant calculations. Pleasure and pain are notoriously difficult to quantify accurately.

But as we argued in chapter 3, subjectively transmitted karma, the appeal to dispositions or special moral qualities, is only the first step in explaining how the law of karma operates naturalistically. Karma also affects us as embodied and the environment which mediates or is an instrument of karmic justice. Karmic residues, whether found as unique moral qualities (*adṛṣṭa*), as invisible material bodies (*kārmana-śarīra*), as dispositions (*saṃskāras*), or as karmic seeds (*karmabīja*), condition events in the environment which bring pain and pleasure to the agent. That is, they are in part responsible for certain events occurring as they do or things being as they are. What, then, is the relationship between this moral, material or dispositional quality which exists in the person and the material environment? The response is that this subtle karmic influence, at the appropriate time, disposes us to act or itself acts on the environment to produce the appropriate state which causally contributes to punishing or rewarding us for our prior action(s).

For example, 'The creative power of ethically relevant actions is as axiomatic to the Buddhists, as it is strange to us. The environment in which beings have to live is to a great extent, especially in regard to its pleasantness or unpleasantness, determined by their deeds (karma). The various hells, for instance, are *produced* by the deeds of the creatures who are reborn there. We have waterless deserts in our world because of our small merit. The world of things is really nothing more than a kind of reflex of peoples' deeds.[28]

There is, it is held, a symbiotic relationship between human actions and the environment. And this is to be seen in terms of a causal chain. Our actions produce moral qualities or condition tendencies or dispositions to act. These bear fruit later in actions. These actions, in turn, create or causally condition events in our environment. These events in turn affect us, bringing us pleasure or pain according to our karmic merit or demerit. Thus our good and bad experiences and the ensuing pain and pleasure have been brought upon us by our own deeds.[29]

But how do human actions condition the environment? We noted above that some Buddhists attempted to provide an explanation by postulating the existence of an unseen product of a volition (*avijñapti*) which resided in agents, where it functions as an invisible cause which emanated from persons to affect their environment. But the postulation of this unseen result helps us no better to explain how we can be a causal condition of our environment than the postulation of phlogiston helps us to understand how things burn. Clearly the *avijñapti* is a theoretical construct rather than something for which there is empirical evidence. Indeed, this was precisely the Yogācārins' contention against the Sarvāstivādins; the former held that, due to the non-empirical character, it was only the product of a creative imagination.

Now it is true to say that my actions can affect my environment, and that my environment, in turn, has a bearing on my happiness. For example, in a fit of rage I might destroy a work of art, an act which, when I return to my senses, I greatly regret, or again, by our greedy timbering of the Amazon we are rapidly creating an inhospitable desert. But though we might affirm this connection for some of our experiences, it is difficult to see how our actions can have the cosmic implications necessary to account for all natural evils. How can our *saṃskāras* or *adṛṣṭas* have the causal efficacy to occasion natural evils such as earthquakes, tornadoes, genetic deficiencies and the like?[30]

Vaiśeṣikas attempt to make this claim plausible by suggesting that the self or *ātman* is omnipresent and eternal. As omnipresent, its activity is not restricted by the particular body to which it is connected by the *manas*. It can act on all things. As eternal, its action can cover spans of time and incarnations. Since *adṛṣṭa* is a quality of the self, by means of this quality the self can causally affect all of nature, and thus bring about earthquakes, fires, diseases and the like. 'An illustration of this is given in Uddyotakara's *Nyāyavārttika* [4.1.47]: if somebody waters a tree, the success of his action, that is, the process of fertilization and growth, may be influenced by the karma of the person who at a later time will eat the fruits of the tree; it becomes the function of the tree, directed by the karmic potential of a soul which may or may not be that of the person who watered the tree, to provide an opportunity of retributive experience, of enjoyment.'[31] As such, the dispositions or moral qualities of the person directly affect things in the environment and function as a causal condition of their acting, both in general and on the agent. The gap between self and environment is overcome.

The viability of this solution depends on the adequacy of Vaiśeṣika's description of the self as pure substance, omnipresent and eternal. We shall argue in the next chapter that there are serious difficulties with this view. In particular, if each self is substance only, underlying cognitive qualities but itself possessing no essential psychological or physical qualities, how can there be a plurality of such substances? Are we not reduced to a monism Vaiśeṣika rejects in Advaita Vedānta?

Beyond the particular problems elucidated, the underlying and fundamental question concerns the claim that moral calculations can be preserved naturally. If one appeals to distinctive moral qualities, are there such things in the universe? How do karmic actions create them? And how do they affect the environment so as to produce precisely the appropriate experiences for the agent? If one appeals to dispositions and tendencies, to potencies and seeds, or to subtle material bodies, how are merits and demerits not only preserved in them but transferred to the environment and returned in *appropriate* and *just* proportions of happiness or unhappiness? For example, how can the postulation of the *avijñapti* assure that the external situation it conditions will cause the appropriate and just experience for the agent? That is, the naturalistic explanation of the implementation of precise moral calculations through the intermediating agency of the environment is inadequate.

THEISTIC EXPLANATIONS

Because of the difficulty of accounting for the action of the law of karma naturalistically, some have argued that a god of some sort is a necessary component of any system which advocates the law of karma. There must be a theistic administrator or supervisor for karma. For example, Śaṅkara argues that the original karmic actions themselves cannot bring about the proper results at some future time; neither can supersensuous, non-intelligent qualities like *apūrva* or *adṛṣṭa* by themselves mediate the appropriate, justly deserved pleasure and pain. The fruits, then, must be administered through the action of a conscious agent, namely, God (*Īśvara*).[32] Thinking in a similar vein, Nyāya uses this as one of its arguments for the existence of God.[33] Our karmic acts result in merits and demerits. Since unconscious things generally do not move except when caused by a conscious agent (the axe moves only when swung by an agent), and since the law of karma is an unintelligent and unconscious law, there must be a conscious God who knows the merits and demerits which persons have earned by their actions, and who functions as an instrumental cause in helping individuals reap their appropriate fruits. Though immobile, he affects the person's environment, even to its atoms, and for the reincarnate produces the appropriate rebirth body, all in order that the agent might have the karmically appropriate experiences.[34]

The law of karma thus is a functioning law of God's action in the world. The critical issue now becomes how to characterize this law of karma as applied to God. Is the law merely descriptive of God's activity, portraying how in general God brings about effects, that is, in a rewarding and retributive manner and generally according to a constant regularity? If so, then the law must be understood as merely contingent, one which can be transgressed by God as he wills according to his purpose to liberate us from the rebirth cycle. Or is the law normative and hence necessary, so that God's operations in the world must accord with its dictates? If so, then God cannot alter it by his will or actions, but stands merely as the implementer of an irrefragable law of karma.

A great deal rides on how one characterizes the relation of God to the law of karma. Not only is the character of the law as necessary or contingent at issue, but also the analysis of the way God relates to the world.[35]

THE LAW OF KARMA AND GRACE

This issue can be clarified by asking whether there is room for grace and forgiveness in a theistic system which invokes the law of karma. The answer depends upon how the law of karma is viewed.

On the one hand, if the law of karma is held to be inviolable or necessary, there would be no room for individual acts of divine grace and forgiveness. Each cause would have its appropriate effect; each individual would get the fruits of his actions, according to the principle of just deserts. Grace and forgiveness would be out of place. In fact, the inviolability of the law of karma is often appealed to in order to show the superiority of karmic systems over grace systems, for in a system which allows God to intervene at his own initiative to dispense grace to those whom he would, unfairness and injustice are introduced into the world order. The law of karma, on the other hand, is held to support fairness and justice. 'What sort of a world is to be created? What is to be the destiny of each creature in it? What direction is history to take? These matters are not planned and decided by God in advance . . . . The force of Karma determines the direction of things to come . . . . There is nothing arbitrary about it. God creates a world which will give to every individual what he deserves and give him also scope to escape from the working of the law of Karma, fulfil his destiny and become free . . . . He creates with the help of the law of Karma . . . . If we do not accept the law, the whole responsibility for evil and suffering in the world is God's.'[36]

On the other hand, if forgiveness and grace are possible, then the law of karma is violable or contingent. That is, a person might receive less or more than the strict compensation which he ought to receive for his deeds. This is important, it is argued, for if God cannot intervene in human affairs according to his will and contrary to the rigid dictate of the law of karma, what value is there to religious observances and especially to petitionary prayer?

But then one major reason for the introduction of the law of karma disappears, for the purported strength of the law is that it resolves the problem of human pain and suffering by holding that what we suffer are the just deserts of our former lives. If God can and does intervene graciously at times on our behalf, the connection between our previous acts and our present condition is partially severed, and one now has to ask why God intervenes as he does and why he does not intervene more often to reduce the enormous pain and suffering extant in the world. In short, the problem of producing an adequate account of human suffering and pleasure is reintroduced. Indeed, the problem of evil is now moved to a new level. No longer are we explaining why humans suffer or experience pleasure. We now want to know why *God* brings about or allows our suffering. And since the law of karma depends upon God's will and action, it does not provide an answer to this question.

The point of the dilemma is that if the law of karma is inviolable or necessary, it functions to resolve the problem it was introduced to solve, namely, the problem of evil. But then divinity can play little role in the religious life. If the law of karma is violable or contingent, worship of divinity has its place, but the law of karma no longer solves the problem of evil.

Is there a way out of this dilemma? One possibility involves making a careful distinction in the concept of grace. God's grace must not be understood as affecting the merit or demerit earned *per se*. He neither gives a person less or more than his karma merits, nor does he forgive accumulated karma. Rather, his grace comes through the removal of impediments to attaining proper insight into the nature of oneself and the one-pointed mind necessary to achieve liberation.[37] God facilitates liberation by helping the devotee speed up the karma-eliminating process. But nothing is removed or facilitated which the devotee does not merit. That is why he does not release all persons from *saṃsāra*. The recipient of grace must meet certain conditions to receive God's grace. He must have purified himself from all evil tendencies, impurities and desires, and he must have perfectly surrendered himself to God, and so deserve and be willing to receive grace.

It might be objected that the dilemma has not been escaped, but merely moved to a different level. The question no longer concerns the original accumulation of karma, which both sides grant must be accounted for, but now concerns the additional conditions preparatory for divine intervention. With respect to these conditions, is divine intervention to facilitate the liberative process by removing impediments an act of grace or not? If the devotee worships God, purifies and surrenders himself in the appropriate way, and requests aid, could God refuse? If the devotee merits this intervention, then God cannot refuse and the intervention is not an act of grace. Where the preparatory acts of the person are sufficient for divine intervention, there is no grace. If the devotee does not merit this intervention, that is, if his preparatory acts are necessary but not sufficient, then God's intervention is gracious, but then the question arises as to why God does not intervene for others as well who do not merit it.

The problem of evil re-emerges on another level.

The other possible response to the dilemma is that grace is not specifically directed to one person, but generally distributed. Divine grace is likened to the sun which shines on all equally. Only those who are properly, karmically and spiritually, ready, like the mature plant, can receive and use it.[38] Thus the criticism that God gives it to some and withholds it from others is groundless. Grace is simply there for the meritorious to take; it is another external condition which saints can appropriate to further their own salvation. But this too diminishes the religious significance of God; he retreats into the background as more or less the generic cause of the world, the administrator of karma, and the creator of this external, general condition. In short, the dilemma remains, so that the theistic account of the implementation of karma likewise is fraught with difficulty.

To summarize, we first explored naturalistic accounts of the workings of karma. However, the problems of explaining the causal operation of the law of karma and of accounting for the precise moral calculations it requires have led to the appeal to a theistic administrator. But the theistic view has its own problems, not of causation, but of the status of the law of karma. If the law of karma is inviolable, there seems to be no room for the divine grace and forgiveness essential to a religious system. If there is room for personal grace and forgiveness, the law of karma is not inviolable, but the ability of the law of karma to provide a reasonable and compelling explanation of human pain and pleasure is lost. In short, both naturalistic and supernaturalistic accounts occasion difficulties. In later chapters we shall have occasion to reflect further on this dilemma.

7

Hinduism and the Enduring Self

According to Hinduism and Jainism, we can experience the effects of our karma in subsequent lives because there is a self which survives death and bears its karma into the next life. Throughout our discussion we have referred or alluded to the existence of a persistent self and in chapter 4 we considered it as touching on the question of human free agency. It is now time to focus on this crucial presupposition, to say more about its nature, and ask why anyone should believe that it exists.

However, several programmatic problems confront us at this point. First, there is no such thing as *the* Hindu view of the self. Different traditions and schools put forth differing views; even members of the same school diverge in their analyses. Since our purpose is to analyse why one should believe that a persistent self, which experiences rebirth and can be affected by karmic residues, exists, it will be enough to obtain a general idea of the nature of this self. This will be possible because there is sufficient common ground between the views on the points relevant to our karmic concerns. For ease of handling and clarity, we shall restrict our discussion to Hinduism in general, and, to provide a contrast of views, to the orthodox Hindu schools of Vaiśeṣika-Nyāya and Advaita Vedānta in particular. A survey of all the positions and their permutations is beyond both our scope and our purpose. Those interested in detailed statements of the various classical views should consult the standard texts.

THE SELF

1. What is the fundamental nature of the self? According to Vaiśeṣika-Nyāya, the self (*ātman*) is an imperceptible,[1] immaterial substance which, moved by desire, acts on the physical through the internal organ or mind (*manas*). Each self relates through one

internal organ, which constitutes its instrument of knowing and, as connected to the body, acting in the world. As pure substance, it is in essence devoid of qualities. Thus *via negativa* is the most appropriate mode of its essential predication. However, it does possess contingent qualities, such as separateness, contact, judgement, pleasure and pain, desire and aversion, and merit and demerit.[2]

For Advaita Vedānta, on the other hand, the situation is more complex. It is necessary to distinguish the *ātman* (the non-empirical self) from the *jīva* (the empirical self). The *ātman* is the essential being of the individual, the foundational reality which undergirds the conscious powers of the individual. It is not the object of experience, but is the self implied in all experience. The *jīva* or empirical self, on the other hand, is the *ātman* seen under the finite limiting conditions imposed by mind, intellect and body, conditions which do not properly belong to the infinite Self. It is the phenomenal self. It is neither a substance nor simple; rather it is a complex structure. 'It is the systematic unity of the conscious experiences of a particular individual center, which is itself defined or determined at the outset by the bodily organism and other conditions.'[3] It is composed of the witness-self (*sākṣin*), which is the passive observer of the states of the internal organ, and the active, physical internal organ (*antaḥ-karaṇa*), which is the totality of waking-state mental functions.

2. For Vaiśeṣika the self is not essentially conscious; rather, it is the substratum of conscious awareness. Consciousness is a contingent property of the self which arises through the *ātman*'s connection to the body by means of the internal organ. If consciousness were an essential attribute of the self, the series of cognitive experiences would never end and there would be no liberation.

Advaita Vedānta's self, on the other hand, is essentially consciousness itself. In its noumenal state it is not active but the passive witness of everything that transpires. The mere presence of the internal organ[4] is enough to affect the highest Self (*Ātman*) so that it becomes the individual witness-self. In its phenomenal state, the witness-self becomes a part of the psychophysical organism, and due to ignorance the self is taken to be the conscious agent. Its consciousness is manifested in the four states of consciousness: waking, where in directing its attention to the gross elements it takes on the physical body composed of the five elements; dreaming, where being aware of the subtle elements, it takes on the subtle body with its vital, mental and intellectual functions; deep sleep, where in a state of joyous consciousness because of the absence of misery it takes on the causal body; and spiritual consciousness, where in attaining self-realization it is freed from the erroneous identification of the self with the body.

If consciousness is an essential aspect of the self, why is there no consciousness in deep sleep, the Vaiśeṣikas ask? It is this absence of consciousness or intelligence in the deep sleep state to which the Vaiśeṣikas appeal to support their case that the *ātman* is not essentially conscious. Śaṅkara replies that consciousness is present in the deep sleep state. 'The absence of actual intelligising is due to the absence of objects, not to the absence of intelligence.'[5] It must have been there since we can recover consciousness after deep sleep.[6] What this suggests is that there is a difference in the way in which consciousness is understood in the two systems. Vaiśeṣika's consciousness is an intentional consciousness; there is no consciousness unless the self has an object of its knowing. Śaṇkara, on the other hand, distinguishes consciousness as mere presence (the pre-reflective self) from awareness (which takes an intentional object). In deep sleep there is a self as a mere presence, but this self has no awareness, for in deep sleep there is no intentional object.

Since deep sleep is a state without any empirically evidenced consciousness, it is impossible to ascertain whether there is presence in that state. The claim that, upon awakening, I recall that I had no experience in that state, that I did not even know myself, tells me nothing about that state; neither does the claim that I can recover it after I wake up. That is, these claims do not tell me that there was a conscious 'I' in that state which had no experiences. They only inform me about my present relation to that state.

3. For the Vaiśeṣikin, whereas the pure self is a simple substance, the empirical self is a complex formed of at least two substances, *ātman* and *manas*. Similarly for the Advaitin, the empirical self (*jīva*) is a complex, that is, of psychical and physical dimensions. The reason for this, Vedānta argues, is that whereas the noumenal *ātman* is subject only, the *jīva* is both subject (as knower) and object (as the object of self-consciousness), self and not-self, reality (as identical with *ātman*) and appearance (as *ātman*

limited by ignorance, identified with finite, relative conditions).

4. According to Vaiśeṣika, the selves are many. If there were only one self, everyone would be conscious of everyone's experiences and thoughts, and when one person was liberated, all would be.[7] But I know only my own experiences and thoughts, and liberation is an individual achievement. For Advaita, though the highest self (*ātman*) is one, phenomenally there are many selves, because of its connection with distinct limiting adjuncts.

5. For Vaiśeṣika the self is essentially unchanging, though its empirical states change in that the self takes on different properties. Similarly for Vedānta: though the noumenal self is unchanging, the empirical self undergoes changes due to its various cognitive and conative experiences.

6. For both schools the self is infinite. That is, it is eternal and omnipresent. In Vedānta it is the *ātman* which is omnipresent. The empirical self is limited to an atomic form or located in the heart because of its association with the *buddhi*,[8] which along with other mental functions such as memory and the ego-sense, are responsible for our awareness of personal identity.

7. The empirical self must exist after the death of the body (unless liberation has occurred), otherwise the moral order would be subverted. Right acts would not be properly rewarded nor wrong acts punished. That infants in appropriate situations manifest the emotions of joy, fear, sorrow, and have a natural attraction to their mother's breast provide evidence that the self existed prior to birth.[9] One can explain the correctness of the infant's behavioural responses only if the infant remembers the appropriate desire and emotional or physical reaction from previous (before-birth) experiences. The desire manifested in this behaviour cannot be accounted for through the possessed body, for desire can be had only through experience.

In Vaiśeṣika, the *ātman* transmigrates with the *manas*. The karma accumulated by the self is instrumental in shaping the new body. In Vedānta, the *jīva* transmigrates along with its subtle body containing the five organs of perception, five organs of action, the five vitals forms, the mind and the intellect. This subtle body is not only that which makes possible change from one physical body to another, but functions as the repository of karmic residues during both this life and transmigration. The physical body into which it is reincarnated is conditioned by its accumulated karmic residues.

8. According to Vaiśeṣika the self is the non-moving agent of action and the enjoyer of its fruits.[10] Knowing, feeling and willing, as unique, non-physical processes, need an immaterial agent. By its actions it acquires merit and demerit, which determine the bodies in which it is incarnated in subsequent existences. For Śaṅkara also, the empirical self is the agent of all its activities and the enjoyer of their fruits.[11] As such, it is that which both creates karma and experiences its effects. However, when it realizes its true self and achieves liberation (not *qua jīva*, but in its essential identity with *ātman*) it understands that the true self is neither agent nor enjoyer of the fruits of action, for the Self is unchanging, pure consciousness.

There are certain problems which follow from these views. Later in this chapter we will comment on certain aspects of the Vedānta perspective. Here let me note two criticisms of the Vaiśeṣikas' view. The self, they maintain, is pure substance, so that all qualities are accidental to it. As substance, it underlies cognitive qualities, but itself possesses no permanent psychological or other physical properties. Thus, which qualities the individual self has at any given time, including consciousness, is a contingent matter. But if it has no essential qualities, except that of being substance, on what grounds can we distinguish between individual selves? Any differences between individual selves must be accidental rather than essential, for, in essence, all selves are the same. They are the substances which underlie certain qualities. The Vaiśeṣikas' response is to introduce the category of *viśeṣa* or individuator to differentiate or individuate any two selves. However, several problems arise. First, what is there which individuates the individuators? What makes them different, so that one self is individuated from another by its possession of a unique *viśeṣa*? Secondly, since the self is imperceptible, how can *viśeṣas* be discerned? The inability of all but *yogis* to perceive this individuator substantially limits their usefulness to making a logical point. Like Duns Scotus's principle of *haecceitas*, the proposal appears *ad hoc*.

Further, Vaiśeṣikas maintain that the *ātman* is omnipresent. This characteristic is thought necessary to allow *yogis* to inhabit many bodies simultaneously and thus to be able to work off their karma faster than it would take for ordinary individuals.[12] But if each and every self is capable (in principle) of experiencing the internal states of all bodies, there would seem to be only one self. But then the Vaiśeṣikin really does not differ from the Advaitin, who likewise holds that ultimately *Ātman* is one, not many.[13]

In short, for these two schools, as well as for others which we have not developed, there exist persistent selves which undergo transmigration. They are either essentially consciousness or the subject which has conscious experiences. They are in essence or noumenally simple and unchanging, though in their empirical or phenomenal existence they are complex and undergo changes in their cognitive and conative states. They are eternal and omnipresent, though (phenomenally) limited by their association with successive bodies as they transmigrate. As the agent of mental, verbal and physical acts, and the enjoyer of the fruits of its actions, the empirical self is affected by the karma it creates, which in turn helps determine the nature of subsequent bodies and experiences.

EVIDENCE FOR THE PERSISTENT SELF

What reasons can be given for thinking that there is a persistent, transmigrating, immaterial self? Early Vaiśeṣika argued that the self cannot be known directly, for there is always a distinction between knower and known.[14] Even where the self is the object of reflection or intuitive experience, the self as object is different from the self as subject or knower. That is, behind every knowing experience, including self-knowledge, there is a pre-reflective consciousness which eludes being known. In effect, I can never catch myself knowing. That which is known, in being known, becomes other than the knower. Thus, self-consciousness at best provides evidence for the existence of a self as object. The existence of self as subject must be inferred. What arguments are there for this self?

1. First, it is argued that the Self 'cannot be denied . . . for of that very person who might deny it it is the Self'.[15] The very act of knowing implies the existence of a knower. And if this inference be doubted, this act of doubting implies that there is a doubter who is doing the doubting. In short, it is indubitable that there is a self which knows, thinks, wills and doubts.

The response to this argument is that all it establishes is that there are the *events* of knowing and doubting which are indubitable. We cannot doubt that thinking is occurring without at the same time there being the act of doubting. But this is consistent with, for example, a Buddhist denial of a persistent, substantial self. What remains to be shown is that acts of thinking or doubting necessitate a thinker or doubter which is an agent which persists over time or a substantial self. To make this inference, one must invoke the presupposition that every action needs a persistent agent, or that every quality needs a substance to support or 'stand under' it.

2. This, in fact, constitutes the thrust of the second argument. It is argued that the self must exist because all action—mental, physical, and verbal—needs an agent. Seeing and hearing require a seer and hearer; knowing and making judgements necessitate a cognizer.[16] Given this principle about the relation of actions and agents, the previous argument works, for now it is indubitable not only that there are actions or properties such as thinking, doubting and believing, but also that there are (substantial) agents which engage in these actions or have these properties.

However, it is evident that this principle is less argued for than presupposed. That these acts of seeing, hearing and knowing require an agent is precisely what is at issue. To claim that they do and introduce this as evidence for the truth of the principle is to beg the question at issue, for that they do depends upon the truth of the very principle they support. Clearly it is the truth of this central presupposition which is in dispute between the Hindu, who affirms it, and the Buddhist, who denies it.

Further, supposing that one grants the principle, why must the agent be an *immaterial* self? Anthropological materialists could grant both of the above arguments without thereby committing themselves to the existence of an immaterial self. This agent or substance could just as well, if not better, be the psychophysical organism. Before we consider the arguments given to establish the immateriality of the agent, we need to note two other arguments intended to establish the existence of the persisting self.

3. Desires, fears, aversions and attractions would be impossible if there were no persisting subject to experience or know previous pleasures and pains and to utilize what was experienced in its actions.[17] That is, there must be a persistent self to account for the fact that the experiences we are having now have meaning and that we react to the things we encounter in certain ways.

Otherwise every experience would arise for us *de novo*. Unless we experienced or knew in the past that fire burned us, and unless that experience affects us subconsciously or we recall that knowledge, we would not fear fire when we now encounter it. Unless we knew or experienced that the taste of sweets was pleasant in the past, we would not desire them when we pass the sweetshop window. And persons can have this subconscious or conscious recollective knowledge only if there is a persistent self which in the past experienced the event or knew it in some way and now recalls it, consciously or subconsciously.

But why cannot this reaction to fire or desire for sweets be passed causally from one organism or set of components to another? Granted there must be some continuity between the experiencer in the first instance and the one who recalls that experience. But cannot the continuity be causal rather than substantial? The argument establishes that there is continuity, but not the source or ground of that continuity.

Further, even if we grant that our desires, fears, aversions, and remembering establish that there must be a persistent agent, it does not show that this agent is an immaterial rather than a psychophysical being. The self could be the psychophysical organism which persists as a causally continous object. We will return to the continuation of this argument in (5) in the next section.

4. The existence of the self can be inferred from our use of the word I.[18] The 'I' is used in at least two different ways. On the one hand, it is used to refer to the visible, psychophysical agent who is named as the doer of certain actions. For example, 'I went to the bank this morning' or 'He reads much more fluently than I do' or 'I can think about myself'. The 'I' here (or proper name, if so used) is a convention for the psychophysical being. On the other hand, 'I' can be used more strictly to refer to the real person or self. For example, 'I have a young, energetic body'; 'I have a toothache'; 'My facial expression masks the way I truly feel'; 'I wish things were going differently in my life'. Here the 'I' is distinguished from my observable facial characteristics, my particular mental states and my body. It refers to the true self, observed by oneself directly, which is distinct from the psychophysical organism.

But granted that the 'I' in the first usage is referential, why must the 'I' in the second usage be referential also? Cannot it be like the word 'there' in 'There is a difference between carp and trout'? In this case 'there' does not refer to any spatial location, as it does in 'You should see all the people in there'. The point here is that not every usage of a term is referential, and we can be easily misled in our ontology if we think so.

One response is that the second usage is referential because it seems to refer to a subject or substance which is capable of possessing certain properties. That is, it seems to refer to a substance which is characterized by knowledge, volitions caused by desire and aversion, pains and pleasures, and eternity.

However, it might be argued that we cannot trust the appearances in this case. Simply because it appears to be referential does not mean that it is. What this shows is that referentiality or non-referentiality cannot be made the basis of an argument either way, for whether the term is referential or not cannot be decided by the usage, but rather presupposes some prior ontological commitments.

Suppose we grant referentiality in both cases, why cannot the 'I' refer to the psychophysical organism? It cannot, defenders of this view respond, because of the particular properties it can possess. There are several marks of the self, including that it can perceive objects and have knowledge. The body is composed of elements which are devoid of consciousness. Since knowledge cannot reside in these elements or atomic substances, it cannot reside in the body which they compose. Hence, since knowledge is a mark or evidence of the self, the self cannot be identified with the body.[19] The self then must be something other than the body, an eternal substance.[20]

The structure of this argument, however, is unclear. If it is argued that the body cannot be the referent of the 'I' in the second sense (as the possessor of knowledge) because it is composed of insentient constituents, it is obvious that this argument commits the fallacy of composition. If it is argued that this is so because the body is the effect of these insentient constituents, then it presupposes the (perhaps dubious) principle that what does not exist in the cause cannot exist in the effect.

To summarize, it is argued that we have processes and awarenesses which are indubitable. These require an agent or substance. This agent must be something other than those processes, for it provides the continuity which underlies these processes and the selfhood which reflects their ownership. It is a persistent, immaterial self.

THE SELF AND THE BODY

We have seen that there is substantial doubt whether the above arguments make a good case for the existence of a substantial self. But suppose we grant they do, why must the self be immaterial? Why cannot the self be identified with the psychophysical organism of human experience? Each of the Hindu schools provides reasons related to and following from its metaphysical structure. Analysis of these would involve not only unpacking the metaphysics of each system, but passing judgement on their basic presuppositions, a talk suited to a historical survey and much beyond our more modest endeavour. However, Śaṅkara appears willing, at one point, to step to some degree outside the presupposed framework to confront the materialist on his own grounds. He also suggests that his arguments are definitive; he concludes his presentation of the arguments with the statement that 'the view of the Self being something separate from the body is therefore free from all objections'.[21] For these reasons the six arguments he gives to support the immaterialist thesis deserve analysis. Let us consider these in turn.

1. He argues that if there is no immaterial self different from the body, there 'would be no room for injunctions that have the other world for their result'.[22] Though the statement is cryptic, Śaṅkara appears to mean that unless there is a spiritual being which exists after the decease of the physical body, injunctions which, in connection with the law of karma, would say that a person ought or ought not to do such and such in this life because he will be rewarded or punished in the next would have no significance. But moral injunctions of this sort are significant. Therefore, there is an immaterial self different from the body.

First, the truth of the first premise depends on there being no other account of immortality than that provided in terms of a persistent, non-physically embodied self. But there are other accounts. The re-creationist argues that it is possible to re-create the psychophysical organism so that the re-created person is the same as the deceased. The individual, possessing all of the physical characteristics of the deceased, would look identical to the person who died. And since consciousness is a property of physical objects, the person's brain could be programmed so as to have neural and chemical components and structures identical to those of the deceased, such that the person would have the same memories, ideas, perspectives, dispositions and personality traits as the person who died. The re-created person would be the same person as the person who died, beginning again to live where the deceased left off. If this is possible, then the first premise is false, for there are conditions other than those requiring the existence of a persistent immaterial self under which a person can live subsequent to death. And since the person would live after his death, the moral injunctions in question can be satisfied.

Is there any reason to think that such re-creation is not possible? The major argument against it is that personal identity requires some kind of substantial continuity, either immaterial or bodily. And since the re-creationist's position generally implies the possibility of a space and/or time gap between existences, re-creationism is false. But though continuity of a spiritual or physical substance is necessary for most instances of personal identity, there is no reason to think that it is a necessary condition for all cases of personal identity. That it is necessary does not follow from the concept of personal identity. Merely to stipulate this as a condition for personal identity would do little but beg the very question at issue. Further, it might reasonably be contended that re-creationism presents a relevant counter-example providing reason why this condition should not be incorporated into the definition of personal identity. Neither can its truth be established empirically, for not only would the conclusion of the argument lack the universality necessary to require continuity in all cases, but we have few if any experiences with re-created individuals and therefore possess insufficient experiential grounds from which to argue that re-created persons, though immaterially and physically discontinuous with the deceased, are not the same persons as the deceased. It remains possible that the re-created person provides a unique case where the condition of continuity does not apply.

But we need not rest our case solely on an appeal to ignorance. There are numerous cases where we ascribe personal identity to individuals who lack any kind of spatio-temporal continuity. We do this in instances of soap operas, television serials and theatre productions with more than one act. The characters in the serials or plays possess gap-inclusive existences. They exist during the half-hour or hour of the television programme or the time of Act 1, and they disappear until the next programme or

Act 2. There is no possibility of tracing their existence between the instalments or acts; they did not exist during that time span. (One should, of course, be careful not to confuse the actor, whose existence during the show is not gap-inclusive, with the character which the actor is playing and whose existence is gap-inclusive.) Yet on their next appearance, we recognize and identify them as the same individuals we watched in previous instalments of the serial or previous acts, despite their lack of immaterial or physical continuity. In such cases, immaterial or physical continuity is not a necessary condition for personal identity.

It might be objected that these are not real individuals, but merely fictions created by the actors or by us. And since they are not real individuals, they do not constitute a counter-example to the continuity criterion. However, that the characters portrayed on the television screen or stage are not real in the sense that they do not inhabit our world does not mean that they have no reality. Reality is contextual. For you reading this, individuals in television serials and theatrical productions are not real but fictitious individuals. But within the context of television or theatre productions, the characters are real people, as distinguished from, say, persons in these characters' dreams. Within their own particular context, there is no doubt that the characters have a unique personal identity. In short, this shows that absence of immaterial or physical (spatio-temporal) continuity is not a falsifying condition of personal identity. Re-creation of the psychophysical person is possible.

Secondly, if our interpretation of Śaṅkara's argument as applying to karmic results is correct, then his first premise is questionable for a further reason. The injunctions in question can have meaning quite apart from the reward or punishment which might follow from doing or not doing them. The reward or punishment is not a necessary part of the injunction itself. It might be a sanction for obeying the injunction—if you do not do this, then . . .—but the sanction is separable from the injunction. The injunction commands us to do it because it is right; the sanction provides additional incentive for performing it. We will have more to say on this topic in chapter 9.

2. Śaṅkara's second argument is that if the self were the body, it could not 'be taught of anybody that Brahman is his Self'.[23]

This argument invokes the central Advaitic thesis that the Self (*Ātman*) is *Brahman* ('That Thou Art'). The problem here is how to understand the relation between the noumenal *Brahman* and the individual self. One way is to see how the Self, which is purportedly identical with *Brahman*, is related to the phenomenal self (*jīva*). Two models are suggested. One model is of a mirror which reflects the object which is in front of it. The *jīva* is the reflection of *Ātman* on the mirror of ignorance (*avidyā*). The other model is of a physical object which limits something larger than it. As the space in the bowl is the limitation of the infinity of space by the finite bowl, the *jīva* is the limitation of *Ātman* by ignorance (in that it thinks it really is associated with the limiting adjuncts of mind, intellect, and ego).[24] In both models the *jīva* is an illusion, the product of ignorance, and in no case should it be treated as reality.

Though the second interpretation lends more reality to the *jīva* than the first, it faces the difficulty of how, if there is no reality outside of *Ātman/Brahman*, there can be anything which would limit it. If that which limits it is real, reality is not non-dual as Śaṅkara claims. If that which limits it is not real, it is an illusion and it would then be an illusion to think that the self is limited. That is, the illusion of limitation would itself be an illusion and thinking there is illusion is ignorance.

The first interpretation, namely, the mirror model, is faced with similar difficulties. First, the reflector of the *Ātman* cannot exist within the *Ātman*, for this would mean that, since there is a difference between reflector and reflectee (otherwise there can be no such thing as a reflection), reality would not be non-dual. Neither can that which reflects the *Ātman* exist outside the *Ātman*, for then reality is not non-dual. Secondly, the *Ātman* has no definite properties. How then can it cast any reflection?

Perhaps all that can be said is that we cannot know how the phenomenal relates to the noumenal. But such an admission must leave the position considerably, if not fatally, weakened. The relation between the phenomenal and noumenal holds a crucial position in Vedāntic thought. On the one hand the noumenal cannot be known or spoken of, yet to encounter it is true knowledge; on the other hand the phenomenal is what can be known and spoken of, yet knowledge of it is ignorance. Thus, unless some analysis of their relation is presented, enigma resides at the heart of the system. And such an enigma cannot be made the basis of an argument for the existence of a persistent, immaterial self.

3. Śaṅkara's third argument is a refutation of the anthropological materialist's argument to disprove the existence of the immaterial self. The materialist argues that if certain qualities exist where and only where something else exists, the first are properties of the second. They are incapable of a separate existence. Now consciousness, movement and life exist where and only where the body exists. Therefore, consciousness, remembrance, movement, and life—all signs of the self—are only properties of the body. Consciousness arises only when the physical organs and elements are in the proper relationship and functioning. Humans, then, are bodies only, qualified by consciousness.[25]

Śaṅkara's reply is that if certain qualities are not where a thing is, then the qualities are not properties of that thing. Life, movement, remembrance and conscious awareness are not found in corpses. Therefore they are not properties of the body, and the self, of which they are the sign, is other than the body.

Śaṅkara's argument assumes that the materialist is asserting what might be termed the identity thesis, namely, that there is an identity between the thing and certain of its properties. That is, the thing is its properties. And the obvious refutation of this would be to show that the thing exists but not these properties, such that these properties are not identical with the thing. But the anthropological materialist need not be asserting identity, only that these properties are not properties of anything but bodies, because they are found only in conjunction with bodies. Now Śaṅkara's argument shows that bodies can exist and have properties like form, colour and size without having these psychological properties. But this does not show that these are not properties of bodies, only that these qualities are contingent and that certain bodies (corpses) which have form, and so on, do not have these properties. But this the materialist need not deny.

Further, Śaṅkara grants that the materialist is correct when he contends that there is no evidence that these signs of the self exist when the body does not exist. However, he goes on to argue that it is 'possible that even after this body has died the qualities of the Self should continue to exist by passing over into another body'.

One might grant that this is a logical possibility. However, no conclusions concerning what actually is the case can be safely drawn from such a thesis. However, what Śaṅkara's reply does suggest is that there is no final refutation of the immaterialist thesis, for there is no way of knowing what happens to persons after death since we cannot communicate with them (experiences of the *yogi* and the Buddha's accounts of past lives aside). That is, there is no way of establishing that consciousness, memory and life do or do not exist where there is no body.

4. His fourth argument is as follows. If, as the materialist holds, consciousness is a property of physical things (namely, the property of perceiving them) it cannot in turn take those things as its objects. For that which perceives cannot be the product of what it perceives, otherwise the perceived would act on itself, which is contradictory.[26]

But why cannot a thing act on itself? Though it is true, to use Śaṅkara's example, that an acrobat cannot stand on his own shoulders, a surgeon can operate on himself, a boxer can punch himself in the nose, and a person can scratch his own head.

Perhaps we are misled by the analogies, however. Śaṅkara's argument might be more properly restricted to consciousness. Consciousness is subject, and that which is subject cannot at the same time be object, and vice versa. Since the body is object, it cannot then be simultaneously subject. The first premise, of course, works only if consciousness is simple, for if something is complex, there is no reason why it cannot be the object of its own activities. But presupposing that it is simple begs the question at issue. Further, even supposing consciousness is simple, the fact that consciousness (as subject) cannot be both subject and object simultaneously says nothing about whether it is different from the psychophysical organism considered in terms of its cognitive function. Its difference from the psychophysical is not established on the grounds that it can never be an object, for consciousness, along with the psychophysical elements, can be the object of consciousness. It is just that it (as subject) cannot be both subject and object simultaneously. But from this fact, that it cannot know itself knowing, as well as from the subject–object distinction in general, nothing follows about the immaterial or material nature of the subject which can only know itself pre-reflectively.

5. Consciousness has a permanence and continuity which continues irrespective of the activity of the body or its sense organs.[27] When I say, 'I saw this', I must have been present to have experienced it in the first place. My body might have

changed in the meantime or I might have a new one; yet the I or self as a continuous conscious agent has remained for recollection to be possible. Hence, the self cannot be identified with the body.

But why must the 'I' refer in such cases to a non-physical self? Why cannot it refer to the psychophysical organism which persists as a causally continuous object? I can remember what I saw previously, even though my body has changed, because there is a causal continuity between the psychophysical organism which first witnessed the event and that which recalls it now. In having this characteristic, the self is not different from other physical objects. When I say that this softball is the same one that we played with last year, I do not mean that there have been no changes in it in the meantime. It might have additional gouges; it might have even been restitched. What I do mean is that this ball is a physical object possessing certain specified properties, causally continuous with the ball we played with last year.[28] In short, the argument from our experiences of recollection establishes that the agent has permanence and continuity, but it does not establish that the self which remembers is *immaterial.* Additional arguments are necessary to establish this crucial point.

It might be replied that though the appeal to a psychophysical agent which subconsciously applies or remembers past experiences might be adequate to explain this behaviour in children or adults, it will not do with infants. Infants can react with the appropriate emotion, desire or action without having experienced the situation before. Since there must be an underlying agent which had this experience in order to account for the appropriate response, and since this agent in the case of infants had to precede the birth of the psychophysical organism, this agent must be immaterial.

Now, that the infant reacts properly in many cases cannot be denied. But the anthropological materialist argues that this appropriate reaction is due to inherited psychophysical conditions or dispositions, not to any immaterial agent. Its genetic endowment can help explain not only its structure but also its desires, fears and aversions, and the behaviour which stems from these. The evidence in favour of the anthropological materialist is the fact that this kind of appropriate reaction is not unique to humans, but is characteristic of the animal world in general. To use one of Vaiśeṣika's examples, mammalian infants of all kinds know what to do when presented with the breast.

Of course, if souls transmigrate through animals as well as humans, then this evidence will support both views equally, since the anthropological immaterialist could argue that this response was learned in previous lives. In short, it is argued, since the evidence can be explained by either hypothesis, it provides no evidence for one theory of the nature of the self as against the other.

It is also replied that the infant's desire for milk cannot be explained by the unconscious cause-and-effect relations found in physical nature, such as magnets moving iron filings and plants opening and closing with the passage of the sun, for desires are not qualities like those found in physical objects, but the result of previous experiences.[29] That is, a given magnet will move certain iron filings even if that magnet has never done so before or the filings have never before been moved. But if the infant did not have a past pleasant experience with the drinking of milk, it would not desire it soon after birth. Hence something more than physical principles must be invoked to explain this phenomenon.

The issue, then, becomes whether desires can arise instinctively, or whether they can only arise or be formed on the basis of previous experience. In the latter case pain and pleasure become central, for the subconscious or conscious recollection that certain actions resulted in pleasure or pain becomes the basis for the present desire insofar as we naturally desire pleasure and seek to avoid pain.

Further, along a different line, is it really true that the self has in essence the permanence Śaṅkara and other immaterialists ascribe to it? Is not my self really in a state of flux and development? Is it not the continuity of experiences, conceptual structures and perspectives, and the remembrances which I have which constitute my self? Śaṅkara holds that it is the empirical self which experiences change and development, but that it does so is due to its failure to recognize its true identity with the transcendental Self. But do we need to go behind these to some transcendental Self? At this point we again touch fundamental metaphysical assumptions.

6. We can have consciousness even when the sense organ is not in contact with the object.[30] One case appealed to is the case of dreams, where the perceptual apparatus is quiescent and yet

we have various perceptions. Another example concerns memory; we can remember what the moon looked like last evening in its full stage, even though now we do not see the moon.

But though the ordinary sense organs are not functioning in either of these cases, or at least no functioning relevant to what is being perceived or remembered, the brain is still operative. And there is good reason to think that our experiences in remembering and dream states are the product of brain activity.

CONCLUSION

In short, even if one grants the thesis that there exists a persistent self, good arguments to establish that it is an immaterial being and not the psychophysical organism are lacking. Perhaps the strongest argument is not suggested by Śaṅkara, nor have I found it elsewhere in Hindu thought. If the law of causation can be universally applied to material things, then every physical thing has a determining cause. The causal conditions are various. Nonetheless, these causal conditions are individually necessary and jointly sufficient to bring about a particular effect, namely, the psychophysical organism acting in a particular manner. But this would make human choices and actions causally dependent upon prior psychophysical conditions, which in turn find their place in the deterministic causal chain. These conditions would causally determine human choice such that the individual could not have chosen or acted otherwise than he did. Therefore, a freely chosen action (in the indeterminist sense developed in chapter 4) is impossible. But without freedom, humans cannot be held morally accountable for their deeds; neither can there be real and significant moral obligations. Consequently, if, as Hinduism argues, humans are morally responsible for their actions, they must be free, and if they are free (in an indeterminist or libertarian sense), the agent of action must lie outside the deterministic causal chain. This means that either the law of causation does not apply universally (that is, it fails to apply to psychophysical organisms in some of their actions) or else the agent of human action stands outside the material realm governed by the law of causation.[31] The latter option yields the conclusion that there exists a persistent, immaterial self.

On the other hand, the immaterialist view encounters several difficulties. We have already mentioned one.

1. Contemporary scientific evidence indicates that the body is a necessary condition for the existence of human consciousness. How, then, can the human consciousness exist independent of the body?

One reply is that we do not know for certain that the body is necessary for consciousness. The evidence often appealed to, namely, that consciousness is lost upon the decease of the body, is ambiguous. That there is no consciousness might be due to the absence of appropriate organs to communicate that consciousness. And even if consciousness in the sense of awareness of objects is gone, the deceased might 'experience' (in a pre-reflective way) some sort of continued presence. That is, there still might be pure sentience.

We have, then, two differing hypotheses concerning how to explain the fact that we do not experience the consciousness of another after the death of their body. The one hypothesis is that there is no consciousness since the body has ceased to function as a living organism. The other is that there is no apparent consciousness because we have no way to communicate with a being whose relevant psychophysical elements are invisible. The difficulty is to develop evidence which will enable us to decide between these two hypotheses.

A different response to the contention that a body of some sort is necessary for consciousness would be to grant this on the level of the empirical self, and to suggest that this is supplied by the subtle body. As we have seen, it is held that, in addition to the gross, visible body, there is an invisible material body composed of subtle psychological and physical elements which accompanies the self in its transmigrations.

2. Secondly, what is the connection between the immaterial and the material? How does the immaterial self relate to the body and its psychophysical organs in this life, and vice versa?

In Vaiśeṣika the self and the body are connected by the *manas*, which is an atomic, physical substance. These two different kinds of substances, the self and the *manas*, are in contact with each other, even to the point of transmigrating together. What is the nature of the contact? Karl Potter suggests that for Vaiśeṣika 'contact is a quality which inheres in two substances under conditions such that the product of the two individuals is greater than zero but smaller than either of the two . . . . That is, the product of two individuals is the individual (if any) which exhausts their comment content'.[32] But how does this quasi-mathematical analysis of contact help us to understand, for example, how the *manas* functions as the instrument of the self? Further, the self as omnipresent is infinite. How then can one speak of a product 'smaller than either of the two', since the product of infinity and anything else is infinity?

For Śaṅkara, as for Śaṅkhya-Yoga and Jainism, not only is there a gross physical body, there is also a subtle material body which is minute and transparent. It is composed of the subtle or unseen parts of the elements which are the seed elements of the new body. At death this subtle body assumes the functions of the various sense organs and the mind, and in turn envelops the soul and carries it on its journey of transmigration, first to the heavenly bodies (sun or moon), then back to earth via the rain. Here it takes up its abode in plants until they are consumed in the food chain. Once in the semen or blood, in conjunction with the being which it inhabits, it begins to generate a new body commensurate with its accumulated karma.[33]

But how can that which is physical, be it subtle or not, envelop the immaterial? Does the immaterial have location, so that it can be enveloped and exist in the heart or veins on earth? Śaṅkara's discussion concerning the size of the self, whether it is atomic, medium-sized, or infinite, and his answer—that it is in reality infinite but atomic because of the limiting adjuncts of the *buddhi*, and so on—reveals the difficulty of giving size and location to the immaterial. And how does consciousness, as omnipresent, infinite and immaterial, relate to any given set of subtle elements? The relation apparently is not causal but adjunctival. This then raises the problem of the relation of the self to the physical which we found in Vaiśeṣika.

In Jaina thought, there is a concrete connection between the spiritual and the material. 'According to the Jaina philosopher, the worldly existence is impossible without the admission of the relation of the identity-cum-difference between the spiritual and the material, and, therefore, it is maintained that the soul and the matter become somehow identical in the state of worldly existence.'[34] Not only do they causally affect each other, souls possess material form, such that the material can penetrate the immaterial and bring qualitative change to it. Karma, which has both material and spiritual form, is the link between them. It co-ordinates the mutual interactions between spirit and the karmic matter which affects it.

The question of the relation of the immaterial to the material is notoriously difficult to answer. Obviously the fact that a scientifically precise answer has not been provided does not disprove the immaterialist's thesis. Perhaps the relation lies outside the realm of empirical verification. It might be required that the immaterialist, to defend his position, should go beyond the assertion that the spiritual can causally interact with the material and provide some reasonable account of the connection between the immaterial self and the psychophysical organism, both in this life and in the intermediate life.[35] The immaterialist, on the other hand, might reply in *tu quoque* fashion that the materialist has not been overly successful in showing how consciousness can arise from the material either.

3. Finally, how does the immaterial self acquire not only a new but a karmically proper body? How does the transmigrating self discern the time and place for its incarnation and find its way into the womb, family and social setting which accords with its accumulated karma?[36] In the Upaniṣads the workings of karma in relation to acquiring a body seem random. Once the souls occupy or are conjoined with (as 'guests') the plants, rebirth is determined by which animals or humans consume those plants.[37] Since randomness would efface the effect and purpose of the law of karma, some explanation must be given. Either the karmic residues stored in the transmigrating self must be able to cause results in the physical world, so that only certain individuals or animals are attracted to eat certain plants containing specific souls, or else God, as the administrator of karma, must order the reincarnation processes according to the law of karma. Śaṅkara suggests the latter.[38]

Vaiśeṣika, though it gives no detailed account of the process of reincarnation, has the makings of giving an explanation along the lines of the former. As we have seen above, the self is believed to be omnipresent. As such, 'its *adṛṣṭa* can function anywhere and affect all those entities which may become relevant for it in terms of karmic reward and punishment'.[39] That is, as omnipresent, it would then be in contact with all bodies. Thus the causal efficacy of its *adṛṣṭa* can be such as to effect association through the *manas* with a particular, karmically proper body. However, since the law of karma functions without intelligence, later Vaiśeṣikas held that God is necessary to facilitate the appropriate administration of karma.

But as we have seen above, this characteristic of omnipresence proves troublesome to Vaiśeṣika, for if all selves are omnipresent, they can be associated with and directly experience the internal states of all bodies. Consequently, what significance for working off karmic residues has the selection of particular, individual bodies for successive reincarnations? The same property which provides explanation for the karmic appropriateness of particular body selection conflicts with the individuality necessary for successive individual incarnations and ultimate liberation. In short, the difficulties with the explanation of the process by which karma operates persist.

8

Buddhism, Rebirth and the Human Person

Buddhist literature follows in the Vedic tradition of avowing belief in life after death. What is not so clear is the sense in which this belief is to be understood. Even contemporary Buddhist authors give widely differing views. For example, on the one hand immortality is likened to the vital energy which, flowing from time immemorial, is passed on from one organism to the next—from the fruit tree to its seed, on to another tree.[1] On the other hand, all kinds of evidences from parapsychology are adduced to justify the belief that the person survives as a discarnate, non-substantial spirit and returns to human existence.[2] Between these two views there lies an enormous difference; whereas the first substitutes a non-individual, continuing vitality for any persistence of the person, the second presupposes such persistence.

This means that we cannot simply plunge headlong into the topic of the Buddhist view of human immortality. Before we can begin to discuss whether there actually is life after death, we first must discern what Buddhists mean by life after death. And such a discussion requires prior consideration of the view of the human person which is presupposed. With their treatment of the nature of the human person, then, let us begin.

BUDDHISM AND METAPHYSICS

Yet we cannot commence so easily, for how can a question about the nature of the human person be raised when there lurks in Buddhism an alleged metaphysical agnosticism? The Buddha taught that it does not fit the case to say that the truth-seeker exists after death, that it does not fit the case to say that the truth-seeker does not exist after death, that it does not fit the case to say that the truth-seeker both exists and not-exists after death, and that it does not fit the case to say that the truth-seeker neither exists nor not-exists after death.[3] His point was that to advance theories concerning the existence or non-existence of persons after death involves one in the broader speculation concerning the nature of the human person, and worrying over the nature of the human person distracts from the primary concern of freeing the individual from misery. 'Vaccha, the theory that the truth-seeker neither exists nor does not exist after death, is a thicket, a wilderness, a tangle, a bondage and a shackle, and is coupled with ill, distress, perturbation and fever; it conduces not to aversion, passionlessness, tranquility, peace, illumination and Nirvana.'[4]

Granted that the Buddha, as a religous teacher, eschewed becoming embroiled in distracting metaphysical controversies, yet metaphysical questions cannot be so easily avoided. Practical ethics cannot be separated from broader questions of ontology, especially about the nature of human persons. Even in the Buddha's own teaching this is true. For one thing, the Buddha advanced the doctrine of no-self.[5] True, it is advanced with practical concerns foremost in mind. In recognizing the insubstantiality and transitoriness of all things, one can recognize that all is evil, so that the individual who meditates on the non-self, its transitoriness and evil, is free from all desire for the physical and substantial, and thus becomes passionless and understands that his rebirth is exhausted.[6] Yet the theory that there is no self or that the *skandhas* are not the self is a metaphysical theory about the self, even if only about the phenomenal. Secondly, in addressing himself to the question of how to attain freedom from rebirth the Buddha invoked the doctrines of karma and rebirth. But both doctrines are metaphysical as well as moral; both make reference to the workings of 'reality', again even if only phenomenal (which itself reflects a metaphysical distinction between phenomena and noumena). Thirdly, in the passage noted above, the Buddha follows his refusal to take a position on the existence or non-existence of the truth-seeker after death with the assertion that though the Tathagata is free from all theories, he does know the nature of the five aggregates (*skandhas*).[7] But the very presentation and elaboration of the *skandha*-theory raises metaphysical questions: what are the *skandhas*? how are they related to the self? is there any reason to accept the *skandha* doctrine?

In short, in spite of the Buddha's refusal to discuss metaphysical questions, such questions must be raised, for certain views of the self and the world are implicit in his discussions of the self as related to the *skandhas*, karma, rebirth and liberation. Such has been recognized by Buddhists themselves; how else can one explain the *pudgala* controversies over the status and nature of the agent of thought and action?[8] Let us then turn to the question of the nature of the self.

THE BUDDHIST CONCEPT OF THE SELF

From its very outset, Buddhism has attempted to avoid substantialist thinking. Reality is composed of 'an unceasing flow of simple ultimates, called "*dharmas*", which can be defined as (1) multiple, (2) momentary, (3) impersonal, (4) mutually conditioned events'.[9] *Dharmas*, as events or processes, are neither substances nor dependent in the sense of attributes upon substances. With respect to human persons, this means that there is no substantial self which underlies either human experience or human existence. Persons and things are nothing more than the 'conglomeration of elementary dharmic events', an aggregate of certain physical and psychological events.

What are the components of the conglomerate which we term the self? They are five, called *skandhas*. First, there is what is broadly termed the physical. One must be careful here not to consider the physical element in terms of permanent parts of the body or even the body itself. What are referred to here are transitory non-mental events or processes. Secondly, there are feelings; thirdly, perceptions. Fourthly, there are mental dispositions or tendencies which are the bearers of karma or the tendencies caused by karmic acts. Finally, there is consciousness, also a bearer of karma, which consists of three types of events: (1) mental activity (called pure awareness) considered more or less abstractly; (2) mental activity (called thought) considered concretely; (3) mental activity (called mind) considered in terms of function: receiving sense-data, organizing and unifying those data, recalling, making judgements and reasoning, and discriminating the 'internal' from the 'external'.[10]

Yet even here there is a misunderstanding, for the self is not the *skandhas* individually nor their union. Indeed, the unity which is experienced or ascribed to these sets of *skandhas* is apparent only. Just as the 'pole, axle, wheels, chariot-body, banner-staff, yoke, reins and goad unitedly [are not] the chariot', so the five *skandhas* unitedly are not the self. When we identify the self with a given set of *skandhas*, we are creating a fiction. As 'the word "chariot" is but a way of counting, term, appellation, convenient designation, and name for pole, axle, wheels, chariot-body, and banner-staff', so a person's name or 'living being' or 'self' is merely a 'way of counting, term, appellation, or convenient designation'.[11] It is a mode of expression by which we can function in the common-sense world. But at heart it is a fiction; there is no self.

To this doctrine of no-self must be added the doctrine of momentariness. The Buddha contended that all was impermanent: whatever is an arising thing, that is a ceasing thing. Practically, this meant that all persons are subject to old age, sickness and ultimately death. There is nothing that can acclaim its own immortality or lastingness. As Buddhism developed, however, the doctrine of impermanence developed into the doctrine of momentariness: everything is an event, constantly succeeded by other events. All is flux; even the event itself is in flux. Thus each *dharma* arises, persists briefly (how long is a matter of internal dispute[12]), and ceases.

This view of the self (with or without the doctrine of momentariness, which simply exacerbates the problem) has serious implications for such basic Buddhist doctrines as the law of karma, rebirth and liberation. For example, if there is no self, then espousal of rebirth seems nonsense, for it makes no sense to say that the same person would be reborn. That is, there can be no difference between birth and rebirth; we merely choose to call a newborn the reborn. Rebirth, like the doctrine of the self, is a fiction. Similarly with the doctrines of karma and liberation. If the self is a fiction, then that there are subsequent persons who experience the effects of the karma *they* have sown and liberated persons who exhausted their karma is fiction as well.

Buddhists, however, draw back from these implications, which would all but destroy their religious and philosophical perspective. What would remain if both the causation of karma and human liberation were fictions created by us? Their response is that though there is no substantial self, there are identifiable sets of *skandhas*, and though there is no identity between consecutive sets of *skandhas*, neither is there complete difference and discontinuity. The self is both collective—a collection of a certain set of *skandhas*—and recollective—a continuation of successive sets of *skandhas* provided by memory and dispositions.

THE ROLE OF KARMA

Two substantial questions arise with this characterization.

1. In what sense is the self collective? At any given time there are innumerable *skandhas* in existence. The world is a plethora of events. What is it that collects a certain set of events together, bundles them as it were, so that they form the collective feature of human persons? What constitutes the bundling element? What is it that makes a feeling a member of one set rather than another? Or to put it differently, one finds Buddhist writers referring to the person as a psychophysical unit or unity.[13] What is the principle of unity; what is it that makes any given set of dispositions, perceptions, mental acts, feelings and physical events such that it can be termed a person or at least differentiated from another set?

The Buddhist answer is that there is a causal nexus of conditions which allows us to say that one *skandha* goes with another. For example, though there are many feelings and many perceptions occurring at any given time, there is a stronger causal relation between certain perceptions and feelings than between others, or at least we perceive there to be such. Certain perceptual events cause or condition certain feeling events. Similarly certain perceptual events cause certain events of consciousness. Further, it is this causal nexus which explains the unity of the whole. It is karma 'which has brought the five *skandhas* into the present state of co-ordination . . . . As long as the force of karma is thus successively generated, there are the five *skandhas* constantly coming into existence and working co-ordinately as a person'.[14] This causal relation between successive *skandhas*, which is such that when this appears, that follows, constitutes an uninterrupted series.

If this is so, then whether the unity or bundling is a fact about the real world or whether it is merely a subjective imposition (a terming on our part) depends upon the view of karma held. If karma is an objective causal relation between events, then the unity is more than the result of mere naming. There actually is something, that is, the causal action of karma, which bundles the *skandhas* into a set. Consequently, there is not complete difference between successive sets of *skandhas*. On the other hand, if karma is merely the subjective presence of causal continuity, the unity is conventional and fictional at best. Karma may psychologically compel or provide impetus for us to collect various *skandhas* together, but it provides no objective basis for such ascription. In short, the question of the real identity of the person hinges on the question of the ontological status of karma.

Unfortunately it is at this point that Buddhist accounts of the human person lose their consistency. We are frequently given both stories. On the one hand, we are told that there is no real unity between the *skandhas*; the unity found there is merely ascribed to it.[15] The bundling role of karma is subjective only, functioning to (mis)lead us to ascribe unity where there is none. This accounts for the claim that the *skandhas* neither individually nor as a unit are the self. On the other hand, we are assured that the action of karma really causes the human situation. It is because of their karma that people differ in length of life, health, physical characteristics, wealth, and social status.[16] Karma is an objective feature of the world. This accounts for the claim that there is not complete difference between consecutive sets of *skandhas*. As we shall see shortly, this ambiguity as to the status of karma and its relation to personal identity has significant implications for the doctrine of rebirth.

2. How do dispositions and memory provide continuity to persons or *skandhas*? The Buddhist response is that successive *skandhas* are continuous because one set of (momentary) *dharmas* causes subsequent *dharmas*. The latter are functionally dependent upon the first and arise on condition that certain events are present, and in turn they provide some of the conditions for other, subsequent events. As such, it is the causal series of dispositions and events of consciousness which constitutes the continuity.

The argument here is that I am the same person who was born forty years ago, not in the sense that something about me has remained constant, for everything about me has undergone change, but in the sense that one can trace a series of causally related events from birth to the present. Again the functioning of karma proves central, for karma working causally conditions dispositions and consciousness in subsequent sets of *skandhas*, and this causal sequence provides the continuity sufficient to allow us to ascribe both personal continuity and moral responsibility to subsequent persons based upon prior acts, despite the fact that there is no persistent agent.[17]

But what of the recollective feature? This is provided for by memories, which are likewise caused since they are part of consciousness. However, though the recollective functions importantly in this life to provide the individual awareness of his identity, it is not a necessary condition of identity *per se*. That it is not necessary can be seen from the fact that though it might happen that the reborn recalls previous lives, this is not the norm. Its rare occurrence often signals true spiritual insight. In short, both dispositions and memory derive their existence from the action of karma.[18] Thus in the case of rebirth, the weight of continuity in terms of necessary and sufficient conditions falls entirely upon karma.

What then can we conclude about the Buddhist view of the human person? The answer is that there is no substantial self or person. What does exist are (momentary) events of various discrete sorts. When we perceive these discrete events occurring at a particular time and place, we bundle them and label or term that bundle a particular person or thing. Here, however, we get two stories. On the one hand, a name is nothing but a label for any given set of *skandhas*, a label which, when either dispensed with or at the very least recognized for what it is, namely, an arbitrary convention, frees the individual from desires relating to the self and consequently brings the realization that rebirth is exhausted. Yet on the other hand naming is not entirely arbitrary, for, granted that the law of karma has empirical content, that is, that karma is objective, the name reflects the dispositions and consciousness which have arisen upon the prior causal conditions and which provide both the bundling and continuity. Whether these 'two hands' are consistent is problematic at best. In any case, the doctrine of karma functions as the central motif for both views.

APPLICATION TO REBIRTH

It is now time to return to our original issue, the question of the meaning and possibility of life after death. In Buddhism there is a significantly individualistic concept of rebirth, according to which the effects of one person are concentrated in a subsequent existent. There is more than mere birth; otherwise there would not be the round of existence,[19] nor any need for the Four Noble Truths and the Eightfold Path, which have as their objective the cessation of the misery encountered in countless rebirths.

Yet in what sense can this rebirth be understood, for the Buddha affirmed that to say a person is reborn would not fit the case, and to say that a person is not reborn would not fit the case? At the very least it is obvious by now that the same person in the sense of a persistent or substantial self cannot be reborn. That is, this rebirth is not transmigration; there is nothing, including consciousness, which passes from one set of *dharmas* to another. How then does it take place? The answer is in terms of causation. The *skandhas* condition subsequent *skandhas*, which in turn condition others. In particular, the individual's dispositions and consciousness condition subsequent ones, and in this way continuity of the individual is achieved.

Consider the analogy of one lamp lighting another.[20] The light does not pass from one lamp to the other, for it remains in the first; however, there is causal continuity between the two lamps. This being, that arises. Similarly, though nothing passes over between death and rebirth, for all that exists are *dharmas* or events, yet there is a causation so instantaneous that there is a continuity of *skandhas* established through the causal process.

But this analogy fails. Whereas between the original light and the derived light there is spatial–temporal continuity, between death and rebirth no point of contact exists. Even though the rebirth is instantaneous, it occurs in another place. How then can the one condition the other? How can the reborn be functionally dependent on the just deceased?

Dropping the analogy, we might put it more straightforwardly. The Buddhist wants to contend that if karma can account for personal continuity and identity during our present existence, why cannot it likewise suffice to provide the requisite continuity and identity between existences? Since there exist only discrete events in causal relation with each other, there is, in effect, rebirth at every moment. Thus rebirth following death is no different from 'rebirth' between contiguous sets of *skandhas*.

But this is not the case. The continuum of events in this life, the successive states of consciousness, have a certain locus. There is a certain continuity of body, of accumulated experience, of memory and dispositions. But between the death of a person and his rebirth the continuum has been interrupted. The timing of the rebirth—its instantaneousness—is insufficient to establish this fact, for even though there is temporal continuity provided thereby, spatial contiguity and continuity of memory and experiences are absent. That which is the same about this life is not the same between lives.[21] In short, the karmic activity which explains unity and continuity in the present life is insufficient to explain the continuity between lives presupposed by a doctrine of rebirth.

Furthermore, is this conception of rebirth—the causation of the karmic tendencies in some continuous sequence—sufficient to accord with the concept of justice which the law of karma invokes? If there is no self to transmigrate, and if the person who is reborn is not the same person who now exists, 'then is one not freed from one's evil deeds (karma)?' Without a continuous self, can there be moral accountability?

The Buddhist response to this is in the form of an analogy.

> 'Your majesty, it is as if a man were to ascend to the top storey of a house with a light, and eat there; and the light in burning were to set fire to the thatch; and the thatch in burning were to set fire to the house; and the house in burning were to set fire to the village; and the people of the village were to seize him, and say, "Why, O man, did you set fire to the village?" and he were to say, "I did not set fire to the village. The fire of the lamp by whose light I ate was a different one from the one which set fire to the village;" and they, quarreling, were to come to you. Whose cause, your majesty, would you sustain?'
>
> 'That of the people of the village, bhante.'
>
> 'And why?'
>
> 'Because, in spite of what the man might say, the latter fire sprang from the former.'
>
> 'In exactly the same way, your majesty, although the name and form which is born into the next existence is different

from the name and form which is to end at death, nevertheless, it is sprung from it. Therefore is one not freed from one's evil deeds.'[22]

But again, this argument from analogy will not suffice. Suppose that the man borrowed his light from a neighbour before his carelessness burned down the village. Could the village then prosecute the neighbour for setting fire to the village? Why not, given the reasoning above, for the arsonist's fire sprang from or was caused by his neighbour's fire in exactly the same way that the fire which devastated the village sprang from or was caused by his fire? Yet it would be unjust to prosecute the lender of the fire. What this suggests is that, contrary to the Buddhist claim, mere causal continuity is not sufficient to provide a basis for moral responsibility. But the Buddhist doctrine of rebirth places its entire justification for karmic accountability upon the causal relation. Consequently, it follows that there is a fundamental difficulty in accounting for justice given the Buddhist view of the law of karma and rebirth: mere continuity of karma is not sufficient to provide grounds for ascriptions of moral responsibility.

CONCLUSION

To conclude, we have argued that there is an ambiguity in the Buddhist account of the human person. On the one hand, personal identity is merely ascribed; selfhood is a fiction. We are easily misled into thinking that there is personal identity and continuity when in fact there is nothing but series of events. This perspective entails that rebirth is a fiction, as are the doctrines of karma and liberation. On the other hand, the doctrine of karma is held to have empirical content; karma and liberation are experienced realities. This perspective entails that the person is reborn. We have seen that it falls to karma to provide the objective ground for the personal identity and continuity found in rebirth. These two hands are not consistent. Is the self a fiction or not?

Further, the Buddhist has difficulty explaining how on the doctrine of no-self karma can account for rebirth. The model used to explain continuous living existence does not apply to rebirth. And finally, since causal continuity is not sufficient to provide a basis for ascribing moral responsibility, how can the reborn be held morally accountable for and justly experience retribution or reward for the actions of the prior-born? This query, of course, strikes at the heart of the karma doctrine.

9

Karma, Justice and Motives for Right Action

It is reasoned that 'if the law of *Karma* is rejected, the moral law itself will have to be rejected'.[1] To accept the moral law, which affirms that acts are objectively right and wrong, is to accept the law of karma. In other words, acceptance of the moral law is sufficient for accepting the law of karma, whereas acceptance of the law of karma is necessary for accepting the moral law. Given this assertion about acceptance, how are we to understand the connection between the laws themselves?

We have already suggested one connection. As we argued in chapter 1, unless there is a moral law to determine the rightness and wrongness of actions, there can be no proportionate disbursement of pain and pleasure as punishment and reward. This means that to accept the law of karma one must accept that there is a moral law according to which actions can be determined to be right or wrong. But since this is the converse of the relation suggested above, something else is being asserted there.

The answer at its basic level has to do with consequences. The law of karma asserts that moral actions create for the agent experiences of pleasure and pain. On the one hand, these proportionately adjudicated experiences implement cosmic justice: the right will be rewarded and the wrong punished in some determinate measure. The first connection, then, correlates virtue and happiness: justice requires that virtuous actions culminate in pleasure and non-virtuous actions in pain. The law of karma governs that correlation. On the other hand, knowledge of the necessity of universal justice creates the incentive for us to perform right actions and seek the good. We understand that we should perform the right and avoid the wrong and seek to achieve ultimate liberation because if we do not we will suffer, if not now, surely later.[2] We cannot escape accountability and its implementation. The second connection, then, concerns the motive for our moral actions: we should do the right and seek good because they bring pleasant or avoid unpleasant consequences.

Several questions arise concerning these theses. First, does the universe operate according to the dictates of justice? Empirically there is little evidence that the right is always rewarded and the wrong punished. Hence any argument in its defence must be conceptual. One suggested approach follows from the above. It is contended that unless virtue is rewarded with happiness, we have no incentive for doing the right and seeking the good. But this raises the interesting question whether concern for advantage is a proper motivation for doing the right. Secondly, even if virtue is connected with happiness, should this be the reason for us to act virtuously? Is not this an appeal to *self*-interest; and if so, is this kind of appeal consistent with Hindu and Buddhist ethics? Further, what happens to morality when altruistic concerns are justified egoistically? Thirdly, is the principle of universal justice compromised by those who hold that there is such a thing as group karma or that the karmically relevant consequences of actions devolve not only on the doer of the action but on others as well? In arguing that merit can be transferred, have we transcended the boundaries of justice? If merit can be transferred, what about demerit? Finally, the talk about self-interest and justice raises the interesting question whether the law of karma is a juridical rather than a moral law? If the moral is concerned with reform, and if in our subsequent lives we cannot recall what we are being punished for, is reform *vis-à-vis* past behaviour possible? What connection is there between karmic consequences and our own moral improvement? Are we simply being punished or rewarded juridically for our deeds? We shall consider these issues in turn in this and the following chapter.

JUSTICE AS A UNIVERSAL PRINCIPLE

Throughout our study we have noted the connection of the law of karma with the view that the universe necessarily operates according to the dictates of justice. In fact, one might argue that one of the major reasons for subscribing to the law of karma is that it provides (in a pragmatic sense) a defence of universal or cosmic justice by showing us how justice is implemented in human moral experience. According to the law of karma, each gets his due. And what is due a person is established by none other than the person himself. There is nothing arbitrary in the meting out of deserts. This fairness is justice at work.

But why should we think not only that the universe operates according to justice, but that it does so necessarily? Surely there is little empirical evidence to substantiate the claim that it does. In this life it is evident that good persons suffer, often much beyond what their present actions warrant, while evil persons prosper. It is impossible to correlate, for example, the effects of natural disasters upon human persons with their present moral character. Indeed, advocates of the law of karma must concede the lack of empirical evidence, for first, the law of karma is a hypothesis invoked to explain this lack of empirical correlation, and secondly, when they explain how justice is implemented, they appeal to invisible dispositions and qualities of merit and demerit and to indefinitely future lives. Further, even if we could establish empirically that there is cosmic justice, it would not show that events *necessarily* accord with justice.

Any argument, then, to establish the principle of universal justice must be of an *a priori* character. Two arguments might be suggested.

1. The first is that if there is no cosmic justice, there is no explanation for the pain and pleasure that we experience. Since there must be an explanation, there is cosmic justice.[3]

But why must there be an explanation? One response is that if there is no explanation, a significant chunk of human experience, namely, our experience of pleasure and pain and the causes of such, is due to chance, which is contrary to universal justice. But this makes the original argument circular, for in establishing universal justice the arguer appeals to it in an earlier premise. The other response is to invoke some sort of principle of universal rationality, as, for example, there is a sufficient reason for every event. But one might reply that this is only slightly less (or perhaps even more) problematic than the principle of universal justice it is used to support. Nevertheless, it is difficult to argue against the principle of sufficient reason. Even the contrary argument appeals to it, for in giving arguments to show that it does not apply the critic is invoking it on his behalf. One can refuse requests for supporting evidence and simply deny it—but this only terminates the dialogue, and does not advance it. It forms the bulwark of our philosophical and scientific approach to the world. This, of course, does not prove that it is true, but constitutes some (and I think, telling) evidence for its truth.

Suppose we grant the principle of universal rationality, why should we think that there is no explanation for evil (pain and suffering) if there is no cosmic justice? Other explanations can be suggested. For example, it can be argued reasonably that the natural evil we experience is the result of our being part of the natural order.[4] It has nothing to do with justice, but with the structure of our psychophysical being. We experience pain when we are gashed because we are physical beings capable of being cut and conscious beings who experience pain. There is no connection between the pain and the *moral quality* of the previous acts, though of course there is a connection between the pain and previous acts which brought us into contact with the thing that cuts. The argument from natural laws denies that all pleasant and unpleasant experiences are teleological, but why should one think that all such events are teleological?

2. The second argument in defence of cosmic justice goes as follows. Unless right is rewarded and evil punished, there is no reason for us to do right. The benefit which we will receive or the pain and suffering which we will avoid, either in this life or in subsequent lives, is the reason we should act virtuously. It is our very motive for acting rightly. This ties in neatly with the opening contention of this chapter that the rejection of the law of karma implies the rejection of morality, for without the law of karma there would be no motive for doing the right. The law of karma then does more than show how the principle of universal justice functions in the moral sphere; it provides part of an *a priori* argument for its universal truth (though, for reasons stated in footnote 2 of this chapter, not for its necessity).

But this argument raises a fundamental ethical issue: should we do the right because it is right, or should we do it because it is in our best interests and to our benefit? The above argument appeals to the latter. But this, instead of saving moral concerns, destroys morality by reducing moral concerns to considerations of advantage. This can be seen as follows. Suppose there is someone who does the right because it is in his interest. Suppose, further, that though he was once a believer in the law of karma, he is now unconvinced. Though he once thought it paid to do the right and act virtuously, he no longer thinks so. How, then, will he act? If he is consistent in his concern for self-interest and having given up his belief in the necessary connection between virtuous acts and pleasurable consequences, he no longer will always act virtuously; he will do so only in those instances where it is clear that so acting will bring him pleasure or advantage. Compare this person with the individual who believes that she should do the right, no matter what the outcome. Suppose she likewise comes to doubt the law of karma. If she is consistent in her concern for the right, even though she has given up her belief in the connection between virtuous acts and pleasurable consequences, she will continue to act virtuously. Surely there is a crucial difference between the two persons. The first had a concern for advantage which, so long as he believed in the law of karma, meant he did the right, but which, when he gave up believing in the connection between virtue and happiness, affected his doing of the right. The second had a concern for the right which remained, irrespective of her belief in the law of karma. In short, concern for advantage can turn one away from the right; concern for the good for itself cannot.

The objection here is that to motivate doing the right by promising pleasurable results is to reduce moral considerations to considerations of advantage. What is commended is no longer the right, good or virtuous, but the advantage which can be gained from the act. And this, I submit, is to falsify the character of morality.

SELF-INTEREST

This analysis of motivation raises another issue, namely, a concern about *self*-interest. Concern for advantage should not be identified with self-interest. The former is broader, for the advantage sought need not be one's own but could be that of others. Thus we could have constructed our criticism in the previous section using the concept of advantage in general rather than merely self-advantage, and we would have obtained the same conclusion regarding the inadequacy of appealing to advantage as the grounds or motive for doing the right.

The argument regarding motivation given by advocates of the law of karma, however, is formulated, as we have done, specifically in terms of self-advantage. We have seen that the connection between the moral law and the law of karma has to do, among other things, with consequences. Unless our acts have consequences for us, it is claimed, we have no motive for performing right actions. And unless the consequences affect us for good or ill, it would not matter to us whether we did the right or not. But the law of karma affirms that what we do will have consequences of good or ill for us as the agent of the action. Thus, we have an incentive to do that which has good consequences (the right) and avoid doing that which has bad consequences (the wrong). The connection, beyond mere advantage, is self-interest (self-advantage).

The same emphasis on self-interest arises in another way. One might ask why, in our present existence, we should perform meritorious deeds on behalf of others. The answer is that it creates for us good karmic residues. The law of karma by itself neither encourages us to help, nor discourages us from helping, our fellow unfortunates. What it says is that whatever we do will determine the quality of our experiences in this and future lives. Since we do not want to perpetuate our own unhappiness and cycle of sufferings, we should act rightly. If that means that we should do good to another, so be it. But we do good to another, not because that is what we ought to do, but because it will accrue to our benefit. It is the motive of selfishness which drives altruistic actions.

But is this emphasis on self-interest consistent with Hindu and Buddhist ethics? It is interesting that this is one of the central issues in the Mahāyāna rejection of what they termed Hīnayāna thought. For the latter, the individual's goal is to become an *Arahant*. *Arahants* are saints who have overcome the perverted views that there are permanence, ease and a self. Having achieved personal victory by seeing that all is impermanent and ill (in commotion and turmoil), they are now ready to enter by themselves into *Nirvāṇa*). In the meantime, they disassociate themselves from ordinary commerce with others, lest their achievement be jeopardized. They can help others only by showing them the way that they have attained, but there is nothing they can do directly to aid them.

Mahāyāna Buddhists viewed *Arahants* as selfish. Lacking love and compassion, they stood calmly by, secure in their own salvation, while the suffering masses struggled for liberation from the cycle of rebirths. They rejected the Hīnayāna contention that each person's salvation was that person's own business. The true saint models the Bodhisattvas, who refused to seclude themselves in either ascetic retreat or the emptiness of *Nirvāṇa* while others suffered. They postponed their own merited liberation, instead sacrificing the merits of their attainments so that all could benefit. They lived unselfishly for others. They had compassion on others, loving them and seeking their own good without seeking their love in return. Their sacrifice was not done out of their own self-interest, but out of a great, loving heart. This altruistic attitude is found in all persons; it is just that it is fully awakened in the Bodhisattvas.

Psychological egoism, which holds that we are motivated to do the right only out of our own self-interest, is a darkened misunderstanding of our psychological motivation. On the one hand, it contradicts the oneness which Vedāntists and Mahāyāna Buddhists suggest characterizes all persons as manifestations of the non-dual *Brahman* or *Dharmakāya*. As non-dual and yet manifested in everything, it overcomes individuality and selfishness. As love, it seeks the welfare of all, for being in all it understands what they need to obtain liberation. If we are all manifestations of the Non-Dual, we cannot be concerned solely or primarily with our own self-interest. We are dependent on the whole and thus must be motivated to achieve the liberation and realized unity of the whole. There is, then, a fundamental inconsistency between the selfishness invoked as a motive to acquire good karma and the truly altruistic ethics which often are advocated by adherents of the doctrine. The law of karma needs to be expanded to encompass an altruistic dimension. One way of doing this is to expand the concept of karma, so that our actions contribute to others' merit and we in turn draw from them. Of course, it can then be questioned whether we have expanded the law of karma beyond consistency with justice. We shall take up this point in the next chapter when we consider the concept of transfer of merit.

On the other hand—and less tied to a specific metaphysical claim about the structure of reality—psychological egoism confuses the results of our actions with the purpose of or motive for our actions. That we obtain happiness from acting does not mean that our happiness is our only or even a motive or purpose in acting. To make this claim confuses the by-product of an action with its purpose. For example, the fact that my car always burns petrol when I drive it does not imply that the reason I drive it is to burn fuel. I drive it to get somewhere; consuming fuel is merely a by-product. More relevant to ethics, consider the case of a soldier who risks his life to pull his buddy across the firezone. He rushes out and drags him back at great personal risk. Where the risk of death is great or almost certain, the motivation seems not to be his own happiness. Rather, it is to relieve his buddy's distress, and should they both make it, happiness will be a welcome by-product. The achievement of some end outside ourselves can also motivate our action. Indeed, our actions become truly moral when they grow out of love for other persons, seeking their welfare and not simply our own.

Indeed, perhaps the most miserable people are those who seek only their own happiness. That is, making oneself happy, if the sole motivating factor, is almost certainly doomed to failure. To have our every wish and desire satisfied does little but stoke the flames of desire. And desire, in both Hindu and Buddhist ethics, plays a major debilitating role.

This points up a fundamental moral paradox lying at the heart of the karmic doctrine. On the one hand, the appeal is made to consequences to motivate to good karmic action. On the other hand, the law of karma stresses that it is action done without desire for fruits which is the most desirable. How these are to be reconciled is not all that clear, except perhaps to deny that the law of karma is self-referential.

GROUP KARMA

In this book we have emphasized the karma created by the individual. But a few authors—and a distinct minority at that—also refer to group karma. One author writes that 'although man creates his own individual Karma, whatever he does will have its effect on his environment, too. Thus, he at the same time has a common family-Karma, a racial or national Karma, or a group-Karma. The good he does will benefit not only himself but all others who live with and around him, that is, all sentient beings. And vice versa, evil will be not suffered by himself alone'.[5]

Statements concerning group karma, including the quote in the previous paragraph, are subject to conceptual confusion. It is important to distinguish group karma from what might be termed conjunctive karma, that is, the karmic residues which we experience as the result of the actions of everyone or everything operating causally in the situation, but which are justified by our own accumulated karma. In many instances, the pleasure or pain which we experience is caused or occasioned by our environment. As we saw in chapter 6, our dispositions and/or invisible moral qualities manifest themselves in actions in the appropriate circumstances. These acts affect the environment, which in turn mediates the appropriate and just karmic consequences to us. Since we are not alone in the world, the experiences we have are the product of the confluence of the acts of others, many of which arise from those persons' own dispositions and/or invisible moral qualities. That is, the actions of many persons, caused by karmic residues, cause our experiences and mediate our karma to us. But this is not group karma, for the effect which we experience is justified by our own particular acts or pool of karma, and not by the karmic acts or pool of the group, even though it is mediated by the actions of others.

In group karma, on the other hand, the effect we experience is justified in terms of the karma accumulated by the action of the group. The karmic effects are not merely the ripples on the water which toss my boat; the ripples convey responsibility to me as a member of the group. I am held accountable for the group's efforts and experience the just deserts of its actions, to some extent irrespective of my part. This is not to say that all the members are rewarded or punished equally. But it is to say that the karmic residues they accumulate from the group action are not simply the just deserts of their own part in it. They are also deserts received because they are members of the family, political body, group or organization.

This means that insofar as we are members of some group, our actions contribute to the karma of the group, which in turn has group-justified karmic effects for us and other group members. With family karma our actions contribute to good or bad karma for our family. On the receiving end, children experience the karma of their family. National karma moves the principle of group karma to a higher level. Here the actions of the nation or of the ruling authorities have consequences which karmically affect the nation. McDermott discerns three kinds of national karma in the admittedly scarce relevant literature.[6] (i) There is the karma of a nation or group where all act in concert or are participants in the action and thus all partake of its karmic effects. This would be an instance of group karma because each individual justifiably experiences the results of the combined action of the group, and not simply the karma resulting from his own action. (ii) There is the karma which results when the king or other persons in authority act on behalf of the people. If the king or prime ministers act well, the karmic residues of such actions fall on the entire people and they experience peace, prosperity and safety. If the ruler does evil, the people suffer. (iii) There is the karma which the rulers create which allows the karma of the individual to work itself out. Here the rulers, by their actions, make it possible for us to develop our abilities or talents to improve our existence. This latter seems to be less of a case of group karma than a confluence of individual karmas (conjunctive karma).

The notion of group karma introduces some intrinsically interesting philosophical problems.

1. First, can a group be held morally accountable for what it does? We commonly and rightly ascribe moral accountability to individual human persons. But groups are not individual agents and hence seemingly cannot act, except insofar as their members act. How then can groups be morally praise- or blameworthy?

The answer depends on the ontology of moral agents. Individual persons can be held morally accountable because they are intentional agents. They have desires, beliefs and purposes, consider alternative courses of action to realize them, rationally evaluate the options, and act to achieve these goals or purposes. Those who advocate group karma must maintain that the concept of agent need not be restricted to individuals. Organizations or groups can act intentionally because they too are agents with desires, beliefs and purposes, who consider alternative courses of action and act to realize them. But, it might be asked, how can an organization have desires or purposes or perform acts? The answer is that they can do so in ways similar to individual persons. Not every part of the person is involved in goal-setting and decision-making. The digestive system plays no direct role in these, though its activities may influence the process and certainly are necessary for the existence of the person. Rather, the person has an appropriate psychophysical structure which enables him to engage in intentional actions. Similarly with a group. Intentional action is possible because the organization has a structure for corporate or group decision-making. Just as the person's intentional actions incorporate various biological processes, so the group's actions incorporate the actions of biological persons. But the act in both cases is an action of the agent, whether a person or an organization.

When persons act intentionally, they function as basic moral units and we can assign responsibility to them. Similarly, when groups act intentionally, they function as basic moral units and we can assign responsibility to them. For example, they can be treated as persons before the law and held accountable for their actions. As a punishment the organization can be fined or its existence terminated. Even our ordinary language preserves this. We praise a surgical team because of its effort to save a human life in jeopardy or say that a certain corporation lacks a conscience when it overrides the interests of the consumer or rapes the environment.

However, not all groups have this characteristic of acting intentionally and being a basic moral unit; there are different types of groups. Following Peter French, we can distinguish between aggregate collections and conglomerates. The first type of group is simply the sum total of the individual members at any given time.[7] Examples of this type of group would be college teachers, the crowd on the beach, students in the class, the congregation at worship, and those who believe there should be no income tax. Since the identity of this kind of group is defined in terms of its members at any given time, when the membership changes, a new group is created. In this type of group, there is no procedure for collective goal formation, decision-making, or corporate action. The goals and actions of the group are the sum total of the goals and actions of the members of the group. For example, when the audience claps for a performance, the applause is the result of the activities of each person. There is no agent present in the aggregate. The crowd or audience does not act intentionally beyond the intentional actions of the individuals which compose it. Consequently, there is no group accountability over and above the individuals' accountability.

Conglomerates, on the other hand, 'do not consist entirely in or are not exhausted by the identities of the persons that are associated with them'.[8] The membership can change without affecting the identity of the conglomerate. As with the aggregate, the actions of the conglomerate are the results of the actions of all or certain of its members. However, it differs from the aggregate in that it has reasons for doing things over and above the reasons which its individual members have. It incorporates the acts of individuals, but its acts are not reducible to the actions of all its individual members. This is because it has an internal organization which includes a structure for goal-setting, decision-making and action-implementation. Because it has this structure, the conglomerate can have intentions, do things, have reasons for what it does, and ultimately take responsibility for what it did. This type of group can be held responsible as a fully fledged member of the moral community because it is capable of intentional action, and consequently can be considered as a basic moral unit. Accountability falls upon the group or conglomerate for the action it takes. The business is praised for its corporate concern for the environment, the religious organization is chastised for instituting policies which discriminate against women, or the government is responsible for the illegal surveillance of the rival political group.

Of course, responsibility can also fall upon certain members of the group, for example, on the chief executive whose embezzlement of funds caused the investors to lose their money or on the President for ordering that the wiretapping be carried out. But responsibility is corporate as well. The mere fact that the conglomerate is complex and its acts are the results of the acts of its members at any given time does not entail that responsibility must be parcelled out to its members. Persons too are complex psychophysical entities. Yet in ascribing moral responsibility, we do not break them down into their psychophysical components. It is not the case that the hand is held accountable for the murder while the heart is not. The entire psychophysical organism is treated as a basic moral unit to which is assigned praise or blame.

In sum, the concept of moral agent can, without violence, be broadened to include groups or organizations (conglomerates) which are capable of intentional action. Consequently, it makes sense to claim that conglomerates are capable of karmic action and of experiencing karmic effects.

2. This leads to a second question; is group karma consistent with justice? Can a member be held accountable for the actions of the group? Specifically, is it just for responsibility to fall upon the individual members of the group in ways which might exceed the extent to which they participated as individuals? Further, is

it just for a person to experience group consequences or karmic residues which exceed that which result from his own contribution to the group act? In the case of mere aggregates this does not seem to be just. Since the identity of an aggregate is defined in terms of the individual members, they would be accountable for their own actions and their deserts should accord with their acts alone. But conglomerates are different. In some cases it would seem that additional (or sometimes less) praise or blame beyond that warranted by a person's acts can fall on the individual, even though the person played what might be termed a minor role in the group action. For example, if a gang of thieves conspires to hold up a bank, but in the process one of them kills the guard, all—including the getaway driver—are guilty of the murder and liable to the murder charge. Or if a surgical team performs a successful operation to save the life of an infant with a congenital heart defect, all receive high praise, irrespective of whether they wielded the scalpel or simply passed the needed instruments. The glow, as it were, falls even on the assistants.

However, though all might be held accountable, often we do make differences in rewarding and punishing. Here we reintroduce considerations of individual contributions to the act. In an amoral context, the football team might have a 'most valuable player' or 'goat'. The surgeon receives a higher salary than her assistant. The person who actually pulled the trigger is given a longer sentence than the driver of the getaway car. That is, distinctions in dispensing deserts are made in terms of the degree to which persons performed, or to the degree of their responsibility. This means that the degree of merit or demerit depends both upon the action of the group and the action of the individual participant. There is no simple calculation.

Further, there are other times when we are not willing to accord any responsibility and impose punishment on or give a reward to particular members, despite their affiliation with the group. Sometimes we are participants in an act only in the sense that we are members of the group or organization which acted. We might not have done anything to contribute to bringing about the result. Indeed, we even might not have known anything about what was transpiring. This can be true of family karma, where children might neither participate in nor know of the family's action. It is frequently true in corporations and businesses. Most workers have little idea of the overall corporate activity.

And it is certainly true of most instances of national action. Rarely does the ordinary person know what the decision-making body or government is doing or participate in the action itself. In such cases, is it reasonable to hold individuals accountable for more than what they knew or did?

3. This raises the third issue. Though we can concede that individuals can be held accountable to some degree beyond their particular contributions for a conglomerate's actions to which they willingly and knowingly contributed, it is not so clear that we can hold them accountable when they either did not act or had no knowledge of the action or intention so to act. It is generally held that blame can be assessed only when a person can be held morally accountable for the action, and there is no moral accountability without knowledge of the action, intent to perform it, and a part in the performance.[9] If persons did not know of or agree to what was done by the group, or if they had no voice in the decision or part in the group's action, it would be unjust to hold them accountable for the action. Since in most instances of alleged family, organizational or national karma many members of the group either have no knowledge of the intended outcome or make no direct contribution to achieving it, group karma generally would conflict with justice. Consequently, to hold the individual member accountable in such cases means a rejection of the contention that intentional action is a necessary condition for ascribing moral responsibility and administering deserts.

Suppose that you work for a large firm which, among its legitimate actions of producing electrical equipment, is engaged in dumping pollutants (for example PCBs) into a local river. You might be an engineer engaged in equipment design or a secretary who does the typing, filing and correspondence, but you are unaware of the polluting activity. Though you through your actions are contributing to the company's existence and business activity, if you are ignorant of what is transpiring, even though the company is guilty of breaking certain environmental laws, does that culpability fall upon you? Do we agree that knowledge and intentional action are not necessary conditions for assessing moral accountability?

Here, I think, we encounter a dilemma. On the one hand, it is difficult to see how an agent can be culpable when he neither acts, knows of nor intends the action. To assign moral accountability without these seems unjust. On the other hand, advocates of group accountability claim that persons can be held accountable simply by virtue of being a member of the group, quite apart from their knowledge of and/or participation in the action. How are we to resolve this dilemma?

Perhaps one way is by making accountability and deserts in regard to group actions depend upon something other than or in addition to individual intentional acts, namely, upon group membership itself. I am accountable and must experience just deserts simply because I am a member of a particular group. Membership means that I share in some measure in every aspect of the group, including its experiences, decisions, actions, accountability and deserts. As such, my accountability extends beyond (or possibly at times is less than[10]) what I individually merit. As an individual I might not be accountable for a group's action where I had no intention regarding its performance, but as a group member I am accountable for and merit the effects of its actions.

To put it another way, though individual knowledge, intent, and participation in some manner are necessary conditions for assessing the moral accountability of individuals in cases of individual acts, they are not necessary conditions of moral accountability of persons in cases of group acts of conglomerates. And the reason they do not apply is due to the dynamic of conglomerates. For example, when I injure myself, it is not just the injured arm which aches. If the injury is serious enough, the entire body aches. We do not question the 'justice' of this. We explain the fact that other, uninjured parts of the body 'suffer' on the grounds that they are intrinsically connected to the injured part, and as intrinsic parts of the whole, suffer with the whole. Similarly, conglomerates are not simply the sums of their members. There is a group dynamic which holds, such that the trespass of the group can bring blame or praise both on the group and on its members. And we do not question the justice of this; it is part of what it is to be a member of this kind of group. Just as you share in the profits and rewards of the company or organization, so you share in its moral and immoral acts and the responsibilities, praise and blame which arise from them.

One must, however, be careful with this type of argument. Though the analogy of the body helps us understand how consequences can affect the entire body, it is not entirely applicable here, for we are dealing not simply with the effects experienced by one member of a group, but with *just* deserts. It is true that the actions of the group affect its members; the analogy illustrates this. What the analogy does not and cannot show is whether the effects are just. But this is what is central to the question, for we are concerned with accountability and just deserts. The dimension of justice means that even if one grants the thesis that membership *per se* conveys accountability because of the nature of group dynamics or integrity, this would hold only insofar as I am morally accountable for joining and continuing as a member of the group.

This, of course, places a heavy burden, not only on membership *per se*, but on accountability for membership. For one thing, I must have freely joined or continue in the organization. If I am a member only by virtue of circumstance, if I was compelled to join, if there is no escape from the membership, or if I joined or continue to participate not knowing the full scope of the group's activities or under significant delusion, then my membership is such that it would be unjust to say that I am accountable for and deserve the consequences of all the group's acts. It is true that despite all these I might experience the consequences of the group's actions. But I *deserve* to experience these consequences of the group only if I am accountable for my group membership (or, of course, if I knowingly and willingly participated in the action even if I was compelled to join). If accountability requires both relevant knowledge and intentional action, then there must be some knowledge of what the group is, stands for and does, and intentional action in joining or maintaining membership in the group. This means that, even with the above resolution of the dilemma, the way is not entirely clear to ascribe such things as organizational, family or national karma to individuals. Though we might consciously join a business organization and have some choice about where we work, we are often ignorant of its activities or do not intend that it should engage in certain immoral actions. Lacking this relevant knowledge, as in the example of the firm producing electrical equipment given above, though we continue to work there, our association with the group is not relevantly informed and hence we cannot justly be held accountable for its polluting activities.

Regarding family and national karma, we have no choice as to the family we were born into or often the nation or society in which we live. Of course, it might be responded, as it was to Socrates, that we can always leave our country. Yet in most cases this is not an option. And even in those cases in which it is, group karma would be inapplicable until this becomes a realistic option.

In sum, group karma seems to accord with justice only when the person is knowingly and intentionally a participant to some degree in the group action in question, or intentionally and actively a member of a group about whose activities he has significant, relevant, and generally accurate knowledge.

4. Finally, is group karma possible? The answer to this question depends upon (a) being able to give an account of how group karma works, and (b) showing that transfer of merit from one person to another is possible. With respect to the former [(a)], since karma understood naturalistically is a causal notion, what kind of causal account is to be given of the workings of group karma? How is group karma causally transmitted to the individual group members? The defender of group karma cannot appeal solely to dispositions to transmit karmic residues, for not only can the effects of the group karma exceed the intention with which I participated or was involved in the given action, but in individual cases the group to which I consciously and willingly belong could act without my knowledge, consent or involvement. For example, the king might sign a peace treaty which creates good karma for the country, but more than likely he does this unbeknown to me and quite apart from my input. How then could the king's action become part of my dispositions and tendencies? Or if the group conspired to sabotage a train, and I played only a minor functionary role in the group and did not know the extent of the act, though I am an accountable member of the group, how could the karmic residues become part of my dispositions? It would seem that any *causal* account of how group karma operates would generally proceed through the intermediary of insentient nature. But as we saw in chapter 6, that insentient nature would preserve the precise karmic influences and administer them appropriately is difficult if not impossible to believe. If group karma is to be rescued, a causal account in terms of dispositions must be supplemented by an account which includes a conscious agent who both knows the merit of the acts performed by the individual and the group, and who has the power and wisdom to bring about consequences which accord with that

merit. In short, group karma would work best in a theistic system. A non-theistic account of group karma would again stumble on the difficulty of being able to give a reasonable causal account of how group karma operates.

The other thing [(b)] that must be shown in order for there to be group merit is that transfer of merit is possible. We shall take this up in the next chapter.

10

Transfer of Merit and the Law as Juridical

In the previous chapter we raised the question of the relation of the law of karma to justice. Two issues—whether transfer of merit is possible and consistent with justice, and whether the law of karma is a juridical or moral law—remain outstanding. We shall take them up in this chapter, which is a continuation of chapter 9.

TRANSFER OF MERIT

Let us begin with the issue raised at the end of the last chapter, namely, the question of the possibility of merit transfer. That merit could be transferred from one person to another is an old concept in India. It can be found in the Vedic literature, where it applies to the merit which is transferred from the gods to the person who offers the sacrifice or to the person on behalf of whom the sacrifice is made.[1] The same theme is continued in the Purāṇas and *Mahābhārata*, where transfer of merit between the gods and mankind, members of the same family, and the king and his subjects is affirmed.

With the emergence of Buddhism and Jainism, however, individualism develops, and along with it comes the denial that merit can be transferred. Each individual reaps in accord with what he sows. Generally there is no transfer of merit in early Buddhism,[2] and Jainism rejects it outright.[3] Likewise the doctrine is absent from Vaiśeṣika-Nyāya,[4] Yoga, and Advaita Vedānta.[5] It is with the development of Mahāyāna Buddhism—in which the Bodhisattva postpones his entrance into *Nirvāṇa* so that he can share his accumulated merit with the unenlightened or unliberated and thus facilitate their liberation[6]—and the *bhakti* religions of Hinduism that the concept is again introduced.

But is the transfer of merit possible?

1. First of all, how can transfer of merit occur? What kind of causal account can be given of it? As before, it is difficult to conceive how merit could causally pass, this time from one agent to another, via insentient nature. Likewise it is difficult to see how merit (and correspondingly, demerit) embodied as dispositions (*saṃskāras*) could be transmitted. Dispositions and tendencies we create for ourselves; we only provide the opportunity for others to exercise theirs. Transfer of merit seems to be possible only in a system where there is some powerful being who both is conscious of the merit of the acts we perform and can act upon other people in ways which accord with the merit earned. That is, transfer of merit seems possible only within some kind of theistic system.

It might be replied that if merit exists as an invisible quality (*adṛṣṭa*) it could be passed from one person to another. Just as we can transfer physical things to other persons, as, for example, we can give them our money or our suitcase, so we can transfer invisible, non-physical moral qualities. There are numerous examples of the transfer of non-physical things or qualities from one person to another. For example, dynamic leaders can transfer their vision of the future or of the possibilities which are present in a project to their associates. Similarly, charisma can 'rub off' from one person to another simply by the latter living or working with the former. Or again, suppose that I am being applauded for some public performance. I might call the programme director to the podium and transfer to her the audience's approbation because of her part in setting up the programme which made my performance possible. In some analogous or parallel way invisible qualities of merit might also be transmitted, either consciously or unconsciously.

2. But this raises several important issues. First, if merit can be transferred as an invisible quality, can demerit likewise be transferred? If my wife can share in my merit, can I also involve her, simply by virtue of her position as my wife, in my demerit? On the one hand, the traditional answer is that only good karma can be transferred. King Milinda inquired of Nāgasena why the merit of sacrifices could be transferred to the departed but not any demerit. After a bit of verbal jousting, in which Nāgasena asserted that this is a question which should not be asked because, like the question why space is boundless or why the Ganges does not flow upstream, it is impossible to answer, he

replied, 'An evil deed, O king, cannot be shared with one who has not done it, and has not consented to it. . . . Vice, O king, is a mean thing, virtue is great and grand. By its meanness evil affects only the doer, but virtue by its grandeur overspreads the whole world of gods and men'.[7] Evil and vice are compared to a raindrop, which does not spread on the earth when it lands, whereas good and virtue are like the downpour from a thunderstorm which fills all the crevices and gullies. But if evil is so insignificant, one might wonder why evil or demerit can be transmitted at all, that is, from one set of *skandhas* to another or to the agent from one existence to another. Further, degree considerations do not constitute an important difference, for there are petty as well as significant goods, and momentous evils as well as trifling ones. If a small or negligible merit can be transmitted, surely also a great evil. Finally, since in a non-karmic sense we can affect others for good and evil, it seems we would be able to do likewise in a karmic sense.

D.T. Suzuki, on the other hand, contends that both evil and good can be transmitted. For example, children can inherit the evil karma of their parents. Even a person's more remote lineage is affected by his karma. Doing good actions causes good karmic residues for our descendants, whereas 'if some [have] left a black record behind them, the evil karma will tenaciously cling to the history of the family, and the descendants will have to suffer the curse as long as its vitality is kept up, no matter how innocent they themselves are'.[8] This need not always be for the bad, he notes, for it might be an incentive to good deeds. Inherited evil karma might be a condition or stimulus which encourages the descendants to overcome it and remove the spot from their heritage. Whatever the case, for him both merit and demerit can be transferred.

This occasions some serious questions. For one thing, in transferring merit and demerit, does the donor in the transfer give up some of that which he already possesses? This not only would properly parallel cases where we transfer physical properties to others, but seems to be the case in descriptions of how Bodhisattvas operate when they dedicate their merit to others. But if so, this becomes a handy and efficient method by which we can work off our demerit. By transferring our demerit to another we can free ourselves from its burden and speed up our entrance into *Nirvāṇa*. The inconsistency of this with justice makes such an idea morally repugnant.

It might be replied that transferring merit does not diminish the merit of the donor. For example, leaders with charisma and vision do not have any less of these after they transfer them to others. As a lamp is not diminished by lighting others, so the merit of the donor is not diminished in its sharing. Similarly, then, transferring demerit would not diminish one's demerit. It provides no short cut to liberation. Some have gone further to suggest that the donor actually acquires merit by transferring merit to others.[9] This seems implied by Nāgasena when he likens the goodness which is transferred to the pool which, even when it overflows, is filled again, so that the more merit persons give away, the more they have.[10] This would seem an attractive solution, for then by parallel persons who transfer demerit actually thereby add to their own demerit and consequently delay rather than facilitate their liberation.

For another, is there any limit on *who* can transfer evil to another, or *to whom* we can transfer it? If merit can be transferred to complete strangers, can one likewise transfer demerit to them? Surely this contradicts justice, according to which it would be grossly unfair to transfer our evil karma to other, unsuspecting, possibly innocent persons.[11] This possibility of getting others to suffer for our deeds without their consent makes a mockery of justice, which holds that *we* must suffer for what we do. But in the general system of the operation of the law of karma employing invisible moral qualities, what would prevent demerit as well as merit from being transferred? Again, some sort of good, knowledgeable, theistic administrator who distinguishes between good and bad karma and allows transfer only of the former seems required.

3. The mention of justice raises a final issue. Is transfer of merit consistent with justice? We have already raised questions concerning the justice of transferring demerit. What about that of transferring merit? With justice, we are to treat persons fairly. With respect to retributive justice, this means, among other things, giving them what they deserve. But in transferring merit, another person in mercy either declares less punishment than we deserve, helps to relieve the pain and suffering which are ours as the recompense for our actions, or removes impediments to and thus facilitates our liberation. The issue, simply put, is whether grace or mercy is compatible with justice.

There is a conflict between mercy and justice only if all obligations are equally binding. But not all obligations have equal force; they are ordered. That is, certain ones take precedence over others in situations where they come in conflict. For example, in the textbook example where the Nazi soldier comes to your house while you are hiding a Jew and inquires of you if you are doing so, you are faced with two moral duties: not to lie and not to betray an innocent person to death. But there is an absolute conflict between them only if these two obligations are equally obligatory. If the duty not to betray an innocent person to death is more binding, then it takes precedence, and you are justified in breaking the obligation not to lie. Your lie, though undesirable, is justified by the precedence of the other obligation.

Similarly we might order the obligations to show mercy and dispense justice. But how are they related? On the one hand, if justice takes precedence, the question arises as to when and how we can show mercy without compromising the punishment due offenders. In giving grace or mercy instead of proportionate punishment we have not done what we ought, for we have not given them what they deserve. On the other hand, if compassion and mercy take precedence, it would seem that justice is infringed, for showing mercy might well mean giving persons less than their due or perhaps no punishment at all. In both cases there arise legitimate worries over leniency and 'soft justice'.

The point is that in the case of secreting the Jew we were justified in abandoning truth-telling altogether in favour of protecting the life of the innocent. But to abandon either justice or mercy seems more problematic. On the one hand, if justice is dispensed with, mercy can become tyranny. Mercy, to be effective, is not administered willy-nilly, but with the laudable goal of the other's benefit or good. But without justice important controls over selecting whom we seek to benefit or how we do it are lost. For example, without justice the primary purpose of punishment becomes the reformation of the person. But the basis on which people are chosen for reform has nothing to do with deserts for deeds done, but with analyses of personal and social past and present behaviour and tendencies. Thus in seeking the other's good, actions directed toward reform might well be extended not only to those who have done wrong but also to those who have not done wrong, but in whom the tendency to act in certain anti-social or non-beneficial ways is deemed to lie. Intervention to bring about their reform would be justified on the grounds that it would be for their ultimate benefit. Likewise with the means employed for reform. Without justice we cannot ask the critical question, 'Did they deserve that type of punishment or degree of intervention?' The question now is not one of oughts, but of facts; is there reasonable evidence that doing such and such will reform or benefit the person subjected to it, or that this method is more successful than another? Without justice, the restrictions on what is done are ends, rather than means, oriented. In short, justice and the concept of deserts are necessary to protect the individual, and hence to make punishment humanitarian.[12]

On the other hand, if mercy is removed, dispensing justice possesses no teleological aspect. Punishment and reward are administered according to what is due the person, without thought for the person's reform or improvement. The judicial machinery marches to its own drummer.

Thus, the integrity of both justice and mercy must be maintained. We cannot dispense with either: mercy and justice, on the highest level, must kiss. Consequently, their ordering will differ from the lying/betraying case. Where mercy takes precedence justice continues to play a major part, but its role is partially curbed. Justice calls to our attention that a wrong has been committed and that the perpetrator deserves to be punished. It requires us to discern *who* it is that did the wrong. It does not allow us to 'punish' for their benefit persons who have done no wrong or to punish an innocent as, for example, a deterrent to others who might consider doing the wrong. It also dictates that the methods of punishment be just and appropriate. The change occurs in that it leaves open the degree of punishment to be administered to be determined by factors other than due deserts, that is, factors having to do with the person's own good and that of affected members of the community. However, justice in regard to determining the penalty is not abandoned. Otherwise there is no limit to what is imposed to achieve the end of reform, apart from the successful outcome of the reform effort. But this might mean punishing or interfering with the freedom of recalcitrant learners far beyond what is due them or just. The standard of dispensing due recompense for deeds done delineates the maximum penalty that can be imposed, whereas the actual punishment is meted out (in part or in large measure) in order to achieve other ends. Offenders might get less than their due, but never more.

Does this partial restriction of justice constitute a violation of the law of karma? In the strict understanding of the law of karma portrayed in the opening chapters, I think it does. As we have understood the law of karma, karmic actions have consequences which affect the agent in this and subsequent lives, such that *each* gets the appropriately proportioned deserts from his *own* actions. What happens to me is due me because of what I and not another have done. Further, there is a strict accounting between agents' karmic actions and the results they experience. The results of agents' actions cannot be obviated except by the present and future deeds of the agents themselves. But the introduction of the concept of grace, where some deserts are ameliorated by the actions of others, means that there are some karmic consequences which neither affect the agent nor are ameliorated by the agent's own later acts. We do not reap what we have sown, but benefit from the actions of others.

But perhaps this statement of the law of karma, as we have worked with it, can be broadened. By the standard account, not only can we draw from our pool of karmic residues, by our actions in this life we can affect the *sañcita* karma we have stored up. These acts counter or enhance the accumulated karma. But the fact that we can, by our actions now, affect the accumulated karma does not mean that the law of karma is broken. The law that what we reap we have sown still holds. It is just that we are sowing additional seeds which alter the character of that which must be lived out. If we modify the law of karma to assert that our karmic pool can be affected by the actions of others as well, transferring merit does not violate the law of karma. The merit of another, which is transferred to us, is capable of counteracting or augmenting what we have sown in the same way as our present acts counteract or augment what we have sown.

In short, the advocate of the law of karma might abandon the notion of individual karma in favour of pools of karmic residues to which the agent and others can contribute, but from which the agent alone draws. Further, to comport with the claims of justice, it must be stipulated that others can only add merit to a pool characterized by demerit.[13] But these two broadening stipulations have several important consequences.

First, they imply that a completely naturalistic, causal account of the operations of karma is no longer adequate. Good and bad dispositions are both dispositions; good and bad invisible moral qualities are both invisible moral qualities. A strictly causal account could not allow one (that is, good) to be transferred but not the other (that is, bad). Hence, if we can transfer merit but not demerit to another, the explanation of how karma operates can no longer be put simply in terms of dispositions and tendencies or invisible moral qualities which adhere to the agent of the action. It implies the existence of some kind of theistic administrator who is aware of the karma accumulated and who can transfer merits as accounts kept from one person to another.

Secondly, this broadening weakens the karmic preoccupation with the principle of universal justice. It means that the principle of universal justice is subservient to a higher ideal of mercy and benevolence. Doing an action does not mean that we necessarily will experience the deserts of it, though it does have consequences. The deserts might be forgiven as the person is led to his own liberation. The goal is no longer the preservation of justice, but the good of the person, for example, in developing his character, attaining moral virtue, acquiring self-knowledge, and ultimately achieving liberation. This, of course, is more in line with the overall teaching of Hinduism and Buddhism, for the point of their teachings is to free us from the karmic and bring us to liberation. This alteration makes the connection between the karmic and salvific more visible and consistent.

Thirdly, it returns us to the dilemma posed at the end of chapter 6. It means that the law of karma no longer provides the neat moral explanation of good and bad experiences, for my experiences are no longer the deserts of my own actions, but the products of the actions of many who have contributed to my pool of karma. When I experience happiness, it is not necessarily the reward for my own virtuous actions; it could be the gracious gift of another. And when I experience unhappiness, it is not necessarily the punishment for my own wrongdoings; it could be imposed by another, not as the result of my actions, but to bring me to my senses, that is, for my soul-building. But then the problem of evil arises anew, for if what I receive is the result of the contributions of others, why do they not contribute more to me? Why do the meritorious not share more of their merit to help me avoid the diseases, illnesses and misfortunes which plague my present existence? Why is not more grace given to speed up my liberation from *saṃsāra*? If some wrong acts are forgiven, why not others? If some penalties are lessened, why not others? Explanations for the good and evil experienced other than the law of karma are called for. For example, one might appeal to a soul-building explanation to account for why the Bodhisattvas do not share more merit. That is, they share only that which is beneficial to our spiritual growth leading to liberation. But then the justification for the evil we suffer is no longer given in terms of our past acts, as with the law of karma, but in terms of what it does for us in the future as it helps build and mould our character and prepare us for liberation. The law of karma, then, becomes insufficient as an explanation of our experiences of pain and pleasure, misfortune and fortune. Since mercy takes precedence over justice, other explanations take precedence over the law of karma.

IS THE LAW OF KARMA A JURIDICAL RATHER THAN A MORAL LAW?

Throughout our presentation we have assumed that the law of karma is the application of the law of universal causation to certain aspects of *moral* experience. We also have assumed that the universal justice presupposed by the law of karma is moral justice. In effect, as the quotation—'if the law of karma is rejected, the moral law itself will have to be rejected'—at the beginning of chapter 9 makes plain, the law of karma is the bulwark of Hindu and Buddhist ethical systems. But this claim can be seriously questioned. Perhaps the law of karma, contrary to initial appearances or subsequent claims, is not a moral but a juridical law. This contention is supported by a number of arguments.

First, the law of karma applies regardless of whether we know what we have done or, for some, whether we are morally accountable for the action (recall the example in chapter 2 of the mixed karma obtained by accidentally killing ants while pounding out rice). Our reward or punishment hinges, not on any recollection of past experiences, but on an objective consideration of the accumulated karmic residues. Everything proceeds as if there were no recollection. Contrast this with the moral. Moral reformation is impossible unless we have some way of knowing what our wrong deeds were so that we might alter our attitudes, intentions and behaviour in the proper way.

Second, since it is generally admitted that in our future lives most of us have no recollection of our previous lives and their constituent actions, the doctrine of karma cannot affect our present moral attitude toward the past beyond, for example, a general regret that whatever we did landed us in our present predicament. Hence it neither encourages nor discourages us to feel sorry or repent for our deeds. Contrition will not remove the penalty; we will receive the appropriate punishment regardless of our acknowledgement of or penitence for our wrongdoing.

Indeed, it is not the intent of the law of karma, in its specific formulation, that we change. It governs change but does not command or commend it. Change of character does not alter the karma that is affecting us now (*prārabdha* karma). It can only affect our future in that this change of character as manifested in our actions might ameliorate the further punishment (or reward) that is due us by creating good effects to counteract the already established bad ones (or vice versa). Note that this change of character covered by the law of karma works equally well, whether we change from bad to good or from good to bad. As such, the law of karma *per se* does not look to our reformation. What the law of karma stresses is that we are appropriately rewarded or punished for our actions. Right actions bring their proportionate, pleasurable experiences, wrong actions unpleasurable. But this has the flavour of the juridical, not the moral.

On the other side, the moral is concerned less with our punishment than with our becoming virtuous. With respect to our deeds, this involves remembrance of them, acknowledgement of moral accountability for what we have done, repentance for our wrongdoings, and reformation. Punishment is present, but it stands in the background. It is not the purpose for introducing moral considerations. Rather, what is in focus is creation of a moral character through right actions.

That the law of karma is juridical rather than moral can be seen from a third perspective. Suppose, for example, that you live in a society which invokes capital punishment and that the executioner is determined by chance. You draw the lot to be the executioner in a particular case. From the juridical point of view, it does not matter whether you or another person carry out the sentence. If you do not, then another will be selected. As such, from this perspective you are as good as another for the task. You are simply an agent of the courts. What is looked for is the efficient and correct implementation of the sentence so that justice might be properly served.

Contrast this with a moral perspective on whether you should serve as the executioner. Here other questions are central. What moral obligations do I have? Is this a humane or moral action? Am I benefiting others and myself? True, considerations of justice are present—for example, you might ponder whether intentionally taking the life of another person is ever just—but it is moral, not legal, justice. Moreover, considerations of justice constitute only one factor in deliberating how to act, not the entire purpose of the action. You act not merely to serve justice. You are no longer the agent of another—the courts of law—but your own agent, carrying out actions which can be morally evaluated and which ultimately impinge on your quality of character.

The law of karma best fits the first perspective. Belief in the law of karma does not prevent or discourage us from lending help or aid to a fellow-sufferer. Indeed, it is through our freely chosen actions that the law of karma, in part, operates. By doing the right action of lending aid we lessen our negative karma. But the pain or pleasure that we bring to others is already determined for them by their respective karmas. With respect to others we function merely as agents of that pain or pleasure, such that were we not to render it, they would derive that which is due them from another source. Thus, our motive for helping others is not true altruism or genuine concern for their pleasure, but rather our own avoidance of future pains. But this suggests that the law of karma, with respect to our attitude toward others, works juridically rather than morally. It forces us to see ourselves as agents of the karmic law rather than as genuinely altruistic agents of the other's good.

These hints are supported by the most telling fact, namely, that the law of karma does not lead to salvation. The law of karma simply regulates our endless reincarnations. According to it our acts, whether good or bad, when done for their fruits have good or bad consequences. A system of salvation had to be superimposed on the karmic system governing *saṃsāra*. What Hinduism and Buddhism present to us are two systems. On the one hand we have a phenomenal emphasis on a juridical system, where all is regulated according to universal justice. Justice becomes the order of business. Right is rewarded, evil punished; each experiences his just deserts. On the other hand, there is a system of salvation which links the phenomenal and noumenal. Its purpose is to enable us to escape the endless, karmically regulated *saṃsāra*. Here the order of business is no longer justice, but salvation and liberation.

Evidence for this dualism can be drawn from several areas. Let me note three.

1. In Hinduism three paths or ways of life lead to liberation. *Jñānayoga* is the way of knowledge. It involves, for example in Vedānta, knowing what *Brahman* is or, better, is not, what our relation to it is (that *Ātman* is *Brahman*), and that the cause of our actions is not the self but the attributes of nature (*guṇas*). It results in contemplative union with Brahman. *Karmayoga* is the way of action. To live is to act; there is no inaction in the world. But what is important is how we act. Liberative action is performed, not to obtain an end, but for the work's sake. The will is single-mindedly directed toward an ideal. We are to act out of self-control, disinterestedly, without any kind of attachment to the action or its results, to do our duty out of a tranquil mind. *Bhaktiyoga* is the way of devotion. It involves worshipping Krishna, surrendering ourselves to him, loving him and having faith in him.

What points to the dual systems is the claim in several of the orthodox schools, most notably Vedānta, both that *jñānayoga* by itself is capable of bringing liberation and that this way is superior to the others. Knowledge alone suffices to liberate since it is ignorance which enslaves us. There is a place for *karmayoga* and *bhaktiyoga*, but they are strictly preparatory. They purify the mind so that it is not distracted by the world in its higher, meditative functions, but by themselves are insufficient to bring about *mokṣa*. In short, concerns with action are secondary in importance. In fact, ultimately action is to be dispensed with in favour of the contemplative life.

This thesis is likewise evident in Buddhism. Wisdom (*prajñā*) gives us insight into the nature of reality—that it is impermanent, ill and empty of self—and dispels all delusions which lead to craving. 'It is regarded as the highest virtue because ignorance, and not sin, is the root evil.'[14] Cultivation of the moral virtues, such as love, compassion and sympathy, are not unimportant, but they do not bring deliverance from the world. 'They are concerned with the social world and with living beings, who represent a deceptive, diminished, and alienated reality, and the final effect of the Brahma-vihāras [prescribed meditations] is to push them out of the way and to allow the yogin to peacefully withdraw from them. . . . Wisdom alone can set us free.'[15]

It might be objected that the substantial emphasis, especially in Mīmāṃsā and the Epics (including the *Bhagavad-Gītā*), on *karmayoga* refutes the charge of dualism. *Karmayoga*, like *jñāna-yoga*, is a way to bring about liberation. This is true, but does not alter the significance of the evidence. First, in early *Mīmāṃsā*, fulfilling our obligations and avoiding what was prohibited did not bring liberation or salvation. In fact, the Mīmāṃsakas did not seek liberation but perfect enjoyment and bliss in heaven. We perform actions; these create fruits; we transmigrate and experience these fruits in subsequent lives. This cycle continues endlessly. Salvation, conceived as escape from individual conscious existence, was impossible, for life is essentially incessant activity. Thus, the duties enjoined on humans never enabled transcendence of *saṃsāra* and karma. Only much later does Mīmāmsā see *karmayoga* as leading to liberation. Secondly, even where action is recommended as leading to salvation, there is the distinction made between actions which have fruits and which can lead to acquiring a zero-balance of karmic residues, and actions which have no fruits and hence which can be performed without fear of creating further karma. In *karmayoga* it is only actions performed solely for the sake of duty which bring salvation and which can be performed by one in the salvation-mode. That is, there is a distinction between the kind of actions performed which continue the phenomenal realm, and the kind which bridge the phenomenal and noumenal in salvation. The former actions do not bring liberation; they only cancel or add to karma already accumulated. The latter create no karmic residues and hence are incapable of affecting the accumulated karma. Consequently they do nothing to resolve the karmic predicament of *saṃsāra*, except that they do not exacerbate it. Their true function is salvific.

2. This leads to the second point: the centrality of meditation in Hindu, Buddhist and Jaina thought. The path to salvation involves renunciation and meditation. The goal of the former is detachment from everything related to the world, so that in meditation we are not easily distracted. That of the latter is the cessation of all mental activity, so as to bring release. In all ordinary forms of consciousness, from perception to self-consciousness, the mind is active. By the proper use of yogic

methods we can terminate all mental modifications and achieve a state of inner calm and tranquillity. The first five stages of Yoga's eightfold path—abstention (for example, from injury through thought, word or deed), self-culture, attaining a steady and comfortable posture, breath control, and withdrawal of the senses—are mere external aids. They are preparatory to the higher stages, in which the *yogin* engages in concentration (*dhāraṇa*), meditation (*dhyāna*) and contemplation (*samādhi*). In the latter the mind is completely absorbed in contemplation of the object of meditation until even the object disappears and only pure consciousness remains. All normal psychological processes cease; the *yogin* has achieved the state of complete mental tranquillity.

In Buddhism there are two qualitatively different kinds of persons, ordinary people, who still operate within the karmic system, and saints, who function on the supramundane plane of existence. 'A person becomes "supramundane" on "entering the Path", i.e. when he has detached himself from conditioned things to such an extent that he can effectively turn to the Path which leads to Nirvana.'[16] This involves, among other things, progressive detachment from receiving sense impressions. The goal is to attain a state of neither perception nor non-perception. At the higher stages saints engage in meditation. They are disinterested onlookers of the world. They turn inward in meditative contemplation, mindful of anything that might disturb their tranquillity. They concentrate on the emptiness of everything, their own wishlessness or volitionlessness, and signlessness, which is a withdrawal from all perception and cognitive thinking, until they reach the state of non-discrimination.[17]

This emphasis on meditation as central to the liberative process is a far cry from the kind of behaviour which invokes morality. *Yogis* or *Arahants* withdraw from the world and society. They turn inward, mastering their mental functions, overcoming ignorance and eliminating any desires or cravings. They engage in a minimum of activity. In particular, they avoid any activity which could possibly have moral valuation and hence karmic results. The social life, with its moral involvements, evaluations and judgements, is abandoned to those who live on the ordinary, karmic level.

3. One can see this dualism in the Vedāntic claim 'that Brahman transcends all moral distinctions and that man, being essentially not-different from Brahman, is likewise in his essence "beyond

good and evil." . . . "Morality," if it has any enduring spiritual meaning, is simply a quality of the man who realizes his self as "not-different" from Brahman.'[18] Vedānta does not deny that there are ethical principles, moral laws, duties and moral judgements. But these function at the appropriate, phenomenal, karmic level. 'The Advaitin does hold that one who has not yet attained self-realization is very much bound up in the moral consequences of his action: he is subject to ethical judgment, and he must accept a scale of values by which his own judgment may be informed.' But once he has attained self-knowledge, he realizes the true phenomenal status of the moral prescriptions and duties. They can now be transcended. 'But what about the man who has realized the highest value, who has gone beyond good and evil? Is he justified in committing any kind of act whatsoever? The logical answer to this is yes; but the psychological answer is no.'[19] That is, as a liberated person (*jīvanmukta*), he is no longer subject to any moral judgements. However, though logically he could perform any act and it would transcend moral evaluation, psychologically he cannot perform wrong acts, since these are performed out of egoistic desires and the false identification of himself with the *jīva*. He no longer has these desires since he possesses proper knowledge of his true being.[20]

This means that liberation is freedom from karma and *saṃsāra*. The phenomenal realm of karma, the realm of duty and the moral law, of retribution and reward, no longer applies nor is binding upon such persons. But this is not held to mean that liberated persons are free to negate the ethical. Freedom from is freedom to. They have the freedom to realize themselves fully and in doing so have attained the true ethical perspective of self-attainment.[21]

There are, then, two systems, the karmic and the salvific. That the second system both is needed and differs from the first is evidence that, though the law of karma can be coupled with various moral systems of determining the rightness or wrongness of actions, its own focus is on dispensing proportionate justice. And it is this which suggests that the law of karma is less a moral than juridical law, for in a moral order justice is presupposed, not its business. In the moral order justice is an instrument in the ultimate salvation of mankind; in the juridical system it is an end in itself.[22]

To summarize, on the one hand, the law of karma operates phenomenally, invoking as its central principle universal justice. On the other hand, liberation from the phenomenal is the final goal of all persons. There is, then, a tension between the juridical which emphasizes assessment and just deserts, and the salvific, which emphasizes world-transcendence and liberation. It is only when the latter is stressed that the extreme focus on juridical assessment can be overcome.

This emphasis on the juridical in effect negates one of the claimed strengths of the law of karma, namely, its alleged intrinsic connection with and support of the objective moral law. It is, as we have seen, intrinsically linked with the principle of universal justice. Yet that principle as invoked by the law of karma is more juridical than moral. In asserting the certainty that actions of a particular moral character will have appropriate consequences its end is itself. That is, it is concerned with seeing to it that justice is carried out, not that the wrongdoer is reformed. On the other hand, the connection of the law of karma to the moral law is not intrinsic but associative. That is, it is associated with moral laws or principles which claim that certain acts are morally right and others morally wrong. Given whatever the moral law is, the law of karma then implements it in terms of the reward or punishment which follows from the performance of the act. But the content of the particular moral law is irrelevant to the law of karma. Whatever the moral law decides is right or wrong is what is rewarded or punished. In short, it implements the moral law, but neither justifies it nor is conceptually connected to it.[23]

CONCLUSION

We have, at various points in this and the preceding chapter, raised serious ethical questions regarding the law of karma. We have questioned its use in motivating moral conduct on the grounds that it appeals to advantage rather than moral concerns for the good in itself. We have questioned its apparent appeal to self-interest rather than genuinely altruistic concerns and asked whether this is consistent with Hindu and Buddhist ethics. We have also questioned whether it is a properly moral law or whether it is a fundamental juridical law which only implements associated moral laws. Evidence for the latter, most notably, is found in the appeal to two systems, the karmic one to explain the operation of the phenomenal realm, and the salvific one, which brings us liberation.

But what is the significance of our thesis, if correct? The significance has to do with the matter of moral character. Does the law of karma have, as its purpose, the development of virtue and self-realization? Is its function character-building and character-changing? Does it provide a moral incentive to right action? If the answers to these are no, then though it has an explanatory role in accounting for good and bad experiences, and though it attempts to provide the description of how moral causation works, it can only be associated with morality. The moral law and the development of moral character stand or fall independently of it. And this means that there is good reason why Hinduism and Buddhism develop their self-realization ethics primarily in connection with that which brings us liberation rather than with the karmic. Consequently, the role that the law of karma plays in the respective systems and the claims as to its centrality must be reassessed. The law of karma does not cease to be important. The value of justice must be preserved and its workings explained. But more emphasis must be placed on the moral law and moral principles, on moral motivation, and most important of all on the development of moral character, and less on the juridically operative law of karma. Human existence goes beyond assessment of rewards and penalties for right and wrong doings; its end is the development of a virtuous character, self-realization, and salvation.

This, of course, takes us into the whole question of liberation and its relation to both the law of karma and the karmic. To this topic we shall turn in our next chapter.

11

Karma and Liberation

Our discussion of the law of karma would be incomplete without consideration of the relation of the law of karma to human liberation. Our current existence, governed by the law of karma, must be transcended into something higher. The goal of life is liberation from the misery and suffering which accompany the cycle of rebirths. This can only occur when we have exhausted our accumulated karma and have terminated that with which we are afflicted: ignorance (which takes the non-eternal, impure, painful and not-self to be eternal, pure, pleasurable and the self), egoism, attachment to pleasure, aversion to pain, and love of life.[1] Termination of these occurs by removing ignorance[2] (attaining knowledge of ourselves in regard to our true nature and knowledge of the causes of birth, becoming, grasping, craving, feeling, consciousness[3]), attaining freedom from desires, cravings, and passions, and eliminating egoism and self-concern. Karma, then, is not the final word, only the preliminary word, the word characterizing conscious existence apart from or prior to final liberation. What more can be said about the relation of the law of karma to liberation? The answer to this will occupy our attention in this chapter.

THE RELATION BETWEEN THE KARMIC AND SALVIFIC

As we noted at the end of the previous chapter, there are two systems, the karmic[4] (having to do with our saṃsāric or phenomenal existence) and the salvific (having to do specifically with liberation). There we noted that there are important differences between them. They have, at least in significant part, different concerns, methods, and intrinsic qualities or characteristics. The karmic, though ultimately directed toward preparing us for freedom from *saṃsāra*, more immediately is concerned with bringing about better rebirth. We attempt to acquire merit to counteract our accumulated demerit. It alone does not lead to deliverance because it is concerned with active involvement with and by living persons in a social world, replete with distinctions, self-affirmation, and concern with that which, for many, is deceptive and unreal. The salvific is concerned with ending rebirths. Actions are to be done without attachment to the fruits so that neither merit nor demerit is acquired. External actions are only preparatory. Deliverance comes by overcoming ignorance and ending our cravings, and this is accomplished by renouncing everything which binds us and realizing inner tranquillity. In particular, we gradually extricate ourselves from the social world and from inter-personal relations so as to turn inward in meditative contemplation.

But some have suggested a stronger thesis, namely, that these are antithetical systems, modes of living, or ethics,[5] that between them there is a tension which is fraught with intellectual and practical difficulties. The karmic and salvific are a two-tiered, self-conflicting structure. Others have responded that though they are distinguishable, they are not antithetical but complementary. The karmic previews and prepares for, indeed underlies, the salvific, whereas the salvific interpenetrates and dialogically informs the karmic. Clearly this disagreement must be addressed.

What, more specifically, is the evidence for the contention that these two are disparate? Five arguments might be suggested. First, there is a difference in the goods which are aimed at. The karmic is concerned for interpersonal goods, whereas the salvific is concerned for intrapersonal goods. For example, in Buddhism, in going from the karmic to the salvific we move from the realm of social interaction, the realm of good deeds and active concern for other persons, where we develop our virtue through non-injury and delight in open-handed charity,[6] to the realm of 'mystical realization', the higher, internalized experience of the no-self. We go from 'the virtue of vigorous affirmative preference for the ethically good over the ethically evil, to the language of non-preference or detachment; we rise in the scale from loving-kindness, compassion, and sympathetic joy to neutrality or equanimity'.[7] Indifference, seeing nothing as significant or desirable, negation of the world and all its disgusting features, having neither perception nor non-perception, freedom from mental disturbance, inner calm and tranquillity, emptiness and silence, become the goods aimed at.

It might be responded that Mahāyāna Buddhism corrected this deficiency by stressing the importance of loving-kindness and compassion. The Bodhisattvas are beings of infinite compassion who dedicate their superabundant merit for the good of others. Out of compassion they postpone their own entrance into Nirvāṇa to bring others to liberation as well. Yet even here there is a progression from personal and interpersonal to the apersonal. In the lower stages Bodhisattvas 'who have raised their hearts to enlightenment' take persons as the objects of their compassion; in the later stages, however, out of their equanimity and indifference their compassion 'has no object at all', but is given or overflows impartially out of the proper attitude (it simply 'radiates outward').[8]

Secondly, related to the first, there is a difference in the directedness of action. The karmic is concerned with attitudes toward others and with ethico-social action in the community or society. In Buddhism there is emphasis on the Five Virtues: restraint from taking life, taking what is not given, wrong indulgence in sense pleasures, falsehood, and alcohol which causes intoxication and indolence,[9] and the Ten Virtues: the first four above, plus abstention from slander, harsh speech, frivolous chatter or trivial conversation, covetousness, malevolence, and false and heretical views.[10] Though they have the character of personal virtues, they are actualized in a social setting and clearly govern social interaction. Similarly in Yoga, the first two steps of the yogic path (*yama*, which involves non-injury, truth-speaking, abstinence from stealing, celibacy, and abstinence from avarice, and *niyama*, which involves cleanliness, contentment, purificatory action, study, and giving all the fruits of action to God), which are referred to as the outer disciplines, have this social character.[11] This is particularly evident in the central role which non-injury plays in the restraints (*yamas*).

The salvific, on the other hand, is concerned with the development and proper employment of our mental powers of concentration and contemplation. The path involves, of course, a gradual process. In Buddhism, for example, it proceeds from progressive detachment from the world. The person entering the path detaches himself from the conditioned, which is the object of the senses.[12] In this state, he cultivates the realization that all is ill, impermanent, and that there is no self. He realizes that the attractiveness of the world is deluding, and thus achieves disgust with it. He loses interest in and no longer desires the world which his senses presented to him. He understands that all is void (alien, empty of self), signless (seeing everything as limited and conditioned, without significance and hence not a worthy object of attention or recognition), and desireless.[13] There is, then, a progressive movement inward. We detach ourselves from our emotions and anything which would bind us to the world and create in us cravings and desires. We cut off or circumscribe perception by mindfulness and thus prevent it from reaching the stage of recognition, achieving the state of neither perception nor non-perception, that is, equanimity found in meditation.

The highest ideal is meditation, in which we abstain from vigorous bodily or mental activity, 'unswayed, unhankering and aloof'.[14] We restrain and eventually cease all mental modifications.[15] The mediator has lost interest in the world and becomes one who has 'so mastered the powers of his mind, and developed them, that he can at will put himself in a state of complete absorption wherein nibbanic factors, if not the realization itself, may be experienced. The moment of nibbanic realization, in which the saint is "dead" to the outside world, i.e. totally unconscious of it and perhaps to all appearances dead physically, is the perfect life arrived at its perfect moment'.[16]

Thirdly, within the recommended paths to liberation there are important distinctions made. For example, in Yoga there is the contrast between the external or outer disciplines (*yama* and *niyama*) and the internal or inner disciplines [concentration (*dhāraṇā*), meditation (*dhyāna*), and contemplation (*samādhi*)]. The first have decided ethical and social concerns. When we abstain from injury, we do not injure others with whom we are in social interaction. When we abstain from falsehood or theft, we again do this in a social context. These constitute the yoga of action (*karmayoga*).[17] But meditation and concentration are done by turning inward.[18] The senses have been withdrawn from contact with physical objects, and the objects of concentration gradually change from gross objects inward. Action is abandoned, along with the afflictions which arise from it.[19] Likewise in Buddhist ethics, a distinction is made between the moralities (*sīla*), which particularly involve the middle directives of the Eightfold Path, right speech, right action and right employment; *samādhi*, which involves right effort, right mindfulness and right concentration; and *prajñā*, which involves right understanding and right thought. *Sīla* is more external in nature, whereas the others are internal or mental.[20] And even if *prajñā* be understood as involving the karmic, three stages are noted, the last of which is meditational, which 'requires the aid of transic concentration'.[21]

Fourthly, whereas karmic action is individualized action, liberation is to trans-personal existence. Buddhist salvific action, consistent with the emphasis on no-self, aims at not only overcoming the personalized self-consciousness, but (particularly in Vijñānavāda) also attaining supra-personal consciousness. But though 'the individual loses his individuality when he reaches Nibbana he does not thereby gain sociality, nor does he join in a heavenly communion of the saints. As a personal existent he becomes "extinct" and therefore his personal essence cannot contribute to any society whatsoever'.[22] Likewise the *yogi*, by *saṁyama* (the last three, meditative stages) achieves inaction and eventually disappears.[23] The *puruṣa* (self) wins its liberation from the *buddhi*, and the *guṇas*, which are responsible for change and experience, are submerged in the *manas*, and this into *prakṛti*. And with this separation of *puruṣa* from *prakṛti*, neither action nor conscious experience is any more possible.

Fifthly, the karmic is concerned with actions which have consequences. We can diminish our accumulated bad karma by performing deeds which have good karma. But the actions which will eventually aid our liberation and which are done by the liberated are undertaken with no attachment to the result. Here again, there is the movement from the karmic concern for values of a social quality to disinterested, desireless action.

Given these differences, how serious are they? Do the karmic and salvific present two incompatible ethics?[24] Can we properly conclude that they are antithetical? There is good reason to suggest that they are not completely antithetical. First, the karmic is held to be preparatory for the Nirvāṇic. For example, though in Buddhism the four Illimitables—loving-kindness, compassion, sympathetic joy and equanimity—cannot bring deliverance, they are important means of self-extinction. These same virtues play the similar, preparatory role of purification in Yoga.[25]

Secondly, though the karmic and salvific can be viewed in terms of a two-level approach, they are not entirely separate. Temporally they are intermingled, occurring in some respects simultaneously. Ethical discipline continues to the end, while equanimity is commended as a goal from the start. Even in the early stages techniques generally directed to salvific ends are encouraged. Meditation and concentration, usually thought of in connection with the salvific, are also proper techniques to achieve the karmic end of a better rebirth.[26] For example, loving-kindness, which is the positive statement of non-injury, is a proper object of meditation, where the beginner repeats: 'May I be free from enmity; may I be free from ill-will; may I be free from distress; may I keep myself happy'.[27]

The Eightfold Path is not to be taken as containing consecutive, mutually exclusive steps. Though the general order of the Buddha's ethical teachings is morality (*sīla*), concentration (*samādhi*) and wisdom (*prajñā*), [28] in the Eightfold Path the aspects associated with *prajñā*—namely Right Understanding and Right Thought—come first, for the moralities (*sīlas*) cannot be practised rightly without wisdom (*prajñā*). 'The interrelation of the components is inevitable, and recognizing this one comes again to the strength of the Buddhist teaching, namely, that the Moralities are never an end in themselves; they are inextricably bound up with all the other components which form the path to final release from suffering.'[29]

A similar thesis is advocated in Yoga. The purificatory acts of *Yama* and *Niyama* can be practised at all stages of Yoga, though of course in degrees of increasing perfection as the mind attains maturity of insight. This means that some form of the external disciplines are practised even in the higher states where meditation is the predominant method. They are the negative side of making the mind steady.

Thirdly, ethical values are never abandoned, even in the salvific. Saints transcend the struggle between right and wrong and do good spontaneously. But they never transcend the moral good in the sense that they dispense with it. They would not do wrong because they have discerned the cause of suffering and transcended self-concern. The salvific is not exclusive of moral goodness; progress toward salvation presupposes moral virtue in the saint. Moral virtue is an indispensable precondition for wisdom. Here, then, is the dialectic: wisdom is necessary for proper actualization of moral virtue, and moral virtue is necessary for wisdom.

Fourthly, karma itself is associated with the liberative path. Though black, white, and black-and-white karma are performed by persons still subject to karma, the liberated person is said to perform karma which is neither black nor white.[30] However, performance of this karma is not limited to liberated persons, but can be performed by others. Indeed, the whole karmic process is geared to eventually performing only this kind of karma.

Fifthly, the religious life is not merely asceticism. In response to Ānanda's comment that half of the religious life is friendship and intimacy with that which is lovely, the Buddha replied: 'It is the whole, not the half, of the holy life,—this friendship, this association, this intimacy with what is lovely. Of a monk who is a friend, an associate, an intimate of what is lovely we may expect this,—that he will develop the Ariyan eightfold way.'[31]

Yet that there is incompatibility between the two cannot be denied. Liberation cannot be attained until all karmic residues are used up. This is one reason why saints (*yogis* or *arahants*), in later stages, have the power to speed up their elimination of karma by passing it in review and promptly taking appropriate measures to exhaust it.[32]

Perhaps the point of greatest contrast, especially in Buddhism, is that the karmic leads one to consider persons as both important and real. The salvific, on the other hand, brings us to the knowledge that there is no self, that only *dharmas* are real (and in Mahāyāna that not even these are real). This is evident from several things.

1. The karmic attitudes of love, compassion, sympathetic joy and equanimity (the Four Illimitables) are held to govern our social relations. But in contrast with the Buddhist emphasis on the no-self, these presuppose that reality includes both one's own self and that of others with whom one is in social contact.[33] For example, when we have compassion on others in their suffering or sympathetic joy in their happiness, we are sensitive to the existence of others and consider their suffering and happiness as important, attach ourselves to them emotionally, and deal with them in a differentiated manner.

2. Love or friendliness initially, on the karmic level, grows out of selfishness. 'Concentration and wisdom are necessary to transmute "friendliness" into "selfless love".'[34]

3. The karmic process is held to be a long process covering thousands of reincarnations. But this long process of character formation emphasizes the continuity and integrity of the self.

4. In seeking to acquire better rebirths, the karmic aims at qualitative enrichment of the self (ethical self-culture), which is antithetical to the doctrine of no-self.

Yet even here, the salvific represents not so much the complete antithesis of the karmic as its transformation. It is true that the self-concern which underlies the attitudes must be changed into selflessness. But though the attitude is altered, the values themselves are not denied, only raised to a higher level characterized by non-discrimination. For example, love for family and friends is transformed into non-discriminative love for all, for after having achieved wisdom one can see that all beings are essentially the same, that there is no difference.

In sum, there are indeed two different levels of concern: the karmic concern with improving our karmic destiny, and the salvific concern with escaping further rebirths by achieving liberation from *saṃsāra*. They differ in the role which actions play. For the karmic, further action is critical to overcoming the accumulated bad karma, whereas saints move from the active to the contemplative mode. Initially they perform only white karma, which involves strictly mental actions (since physical actions can always bring about some harm), and then neither white nor black karma. Actions improve our rebirth position, but only knowledge or wisdom, which brings liberation from desires, can save. Karmic actions (in general) are done for their fruits, whereas salvific ones are done without any attachment to the fruits of the action. They differ on the amount and quality of social involvement. On the karmic level rules and principles guide our social interaction, so that we do not cause each other harm, whereas on the salvific level saints transcend all moral rules and withdraw from society into themselves to meditate. Though meditation is important on the karmic level, it is central to the salvific. Yet granted these (and other) differences, the two must not be seen as strictly antithetical. There is a unity in that the character values themselves do not change. Though saints transcend moral categories, they do not destroy them, but expand or transmute them into non-discriminatory fullness. The methods of concentration and meditation are useful even on the karmic level. And there is a continuity. The karmic is preparatory to salvific realization in that it begins the process of self-renunciation and self-control. Indeed, deeper than this, the two interpenetrate, the karmic underlying the liberative, and the liberative providing the understanding necessary for the karmic.

ZERO ACCUMULATION OF KARMA AND LIBERATION

The goal of human striving is to achieve liberation from the constant round of rebirths which is driven by karma. The cycle can be broken and liberation achieved only when our karma is exhausted and there is nothing more to cause subsequent rebirths. This means that the ideal karmic state occurs when the sum total of karmic residues is zero.

From the outset, this is counter-intuitive. This goal of realizing a zero pool is *reasonable* so long as we are attempting to make good some deficit. In such a case, acquired merit compensates for acquired demerit, and the recommendations or commands to act morally properly fit. But it is *less reasonable* when we have achieved the balance, for then the performance of meritorious deeds no longer can be recommended. To engage in them links us to further existence. Two replies might be suggested. First, it might be contended that though persons who have achieved the balance do not engage in actions which produce merit, they still can do right actions insofar as they do their duty for duty's sake and act not to realize any end or out of any desire for the fruits thereof. They simply act out of a loving or compassionate heart, but not for any gain, praise, recognition or desire to benefit particular persons. Theirs is neither black nor white karma. The acceptability of this response hinges on the moral acceptability of actions which are done out of no desires or to achieve no purposes (for example, to benefit particular persons, which in effect creates an a- or impersonal compassion). The other reply, related to the first, is that the person can engage in meritorious action, but that the merit thereby acquired is donated or transferred to others and does not accumulate to the donor. This reply rests on the feasibility of merit transfer, which we discussed in the previous chapter.

This goal is *unreasonable* when we have to deplete a surplus of merit, for as long as there is merit there is karma. Auspicious merit works no differently from inauspicious merit in driving the cycle of rebirths. Do we deplete the store of merit simply by using up our merit, that is, by doing nothing more to create merit? But this constitutes a recommendation not to act meritoriously. Do we do this by creating demerit, so as to more quickly exhaust our merit? But this constitutes an unacceptable recommendation to act immorally. The traditional view that the supremely meritorious go to heaven (a *deva*-world) for an extended period of time, there to enjoy abundant health, pleasures, prestige, good fortune and power for millions of years, is also out of character with the Buddhist ethical precept to avoid sensuality which leads to craving.[35] To the contrary, it would seem that we should seek to acquire additional merit by good deeds rather than to achieve a state of neither positive nor negative karma.[36] Liberation should grow out of meritorious existence, not karmic emptiness.

Three replies to this last objection might be suggested. First, good deeds are generally recommended because most of us have acquired over the years a substantial pool of negative karmic residues. Thus, though logically this doctrine of the zero pool could allow for the doing of evil deeds to counterbalance acquired positive merit, empirically this is not the case due to the human condition. The logical possibility must be balanced by an appeal to human experience. This reply will not work, however, for if recommendations to act immorally or unmeritoriously are even logically possible, it contradicts sound moral theory and should be rejected.

Secondly, it might be suggested that the person could transfer his surplus of merit to another. That which is in excess of what he needs to achieve the zero-balance and liberation would be an appropriate donation to others who need merit. This becomes feasible on a schema which allows merit transfer, and is consistent with the Mahāyāna schema of Bodhisattvas who have infinite compassion and so continue to benefit others even at the cost of delaying their *parinirvāṇa*. Whether this is acceptable depends on the dynamics of merit (and demerit) transfer which we discussed in chapter 10. That is, does one actually lose merits (and demerits) in the transfer, or to the contrary, does transfer actually accumulate merit (and demerit)?

Thirdly, it might be argued that this particular aspect of the doctrine is not intrinsic to the law of karma itself. Rather, it is the result of other doctrines of salvation which are linked with the law of karma. That is, one could be a believer in karma and not be committed to the doctrine of the zero pool.

How would this work? On the karmic level, it is necessary that we have experiences which use up the negative karma which we have accumulated. Thus we must be punished for our wrong acts. But this only affirms the justice of punishment as applied to the agent. We also must seek to achieve liberation, and this might be done, at least in part, that is, in respect to our overt ethical behaviour, by acting in ways which do good to others and which for us create merit. In this schema, the more merit we acquire (in addition to the other necessities such as overcoming ignorance and our desires, and concern for our individuality), the more quickly we move to the stage where complete liberation is possible. In this sense, *Nirvāṇa* or *mokṣa* becomes a reward for a meritorious, desireless life lived with knowledge and mindfulness.[37]

It might be wondered why this direction has not been taken. One possible reason is that it poses a fundamental practical problem: how much merit must be accumulated before liberation becomes possible? What amount is enough? Another perhaps more fundamental reason is that the acquisition of merit is incompatible with the no-self or selflessness doctrine. If the source of our misery and continual rebirths is concern with and doing that which attempts to preserve the self, then that which brings liberation must seek to eliminate that self. But in seeking to acquire and accumulate merit, we are accumulating it for ourselves. It is my merit, and the more merit I have, the closer I get to liberation. But all of this places emphasis on the wrong thing, namely, it aggrandizes the self, whereas the doctrine of zero-accumulation does not have this problem. Where there is no accumulation, there can be no self-concern or aggrandizement. Ultimately I have and am nothing, and consequently am properly prepared to enter into *Nirvāṇa,* into emptiness. Whether the doctrine of merit could be accommodated to the no-self or selflessness doctrine is an interesting question.

ASCERTAINING OUR KARMIC STATUS

Supposing one must acquire a zero pool of karmic residues, how does one know when one has attained it? At least three responses have been given to this query. First, in Hinduism we know our general karmic status by noting the caste into which we are born. Caste ranks are believed to be determined by our merit or demerit. Again this linkage between karma and the caste doctrine is not logical or necessary; rather, it follows from other doctrines associated with the law of karma, in particular, doctrines about the structure of society and social theory.

Secondly, in popular religion it is believed that though we cannot know our own karma directly, there are helpful intermediaries. For some Hindus, our karma is written, as it were, on our forehead.[38] As we need a mirror to see our forehead, so we need the mirror of divination to ascertain our karma.[39] For others, 'birth-time and its associated planetary configurations fulfill the karmic process which links the person's present lifetime to his previous lifetime. A person is born at a particular nexus of time, place, and familial and social position through which planetary configurations and their ongoing permutations intimate and actually effect the unfolding of his karma.' As such, astrology becomes a medium of ascertaining our karma.[40]

Thirdly, it is often held that as we progress toward liberation, we can achieve insight into our previous lives and into the nature of the karmic pool itself. Just as the common person can perceive physical qualities, so the enlightened can perceive moral qualities. This special knowledge can assist us in achieving our liberation from the round of rebirth.

Unfortunately this last type of perception is available only to a select few, and only after a long, strenuous process of renunciation and meditation. This has several implications. First, it means that ordinary persons who take caste status to be simply a social convention and have no truck with divination or astrology lack a means of ascertaining their karmic situation. They might, of course, attempt an introspective analysis of their dispositions and tendencies, but not only is introspection notoriously fickle, but it would proceed properly only with correct understanding, which presumably the ordinary person or stream-enterer lacks. Secondly, it means that there is no way the philosopher can intellectually resolve the question whether there are such things as invisible moral qualities or properties (unless such entail a contradiction, which does not seem to be the case). The intuitive manner of their apperception short-circuits the kind of discussions of moral properties which is present in twentieth-century Western ethical theory.

To make the karmic doctrine more practical, some more reliable way of ascertaining karmic status is necessary. Otherwise, since the process is long and gradual, and since one's present status is unclear, there would be little motivation to undertake the strenuous efforts needed for improvement of karmic status. Perhaps this is why in practice more attention is paid to worship, with its anticipated immediate benefits, than to the doctrine of karma.

LIBERATION AND IMMORTALITY

In chapters 7 and 8 we analyzed the relation of karma to rebirth. Here something must be said about the implications of karma for immortality in a broader sense, that is, which extends beyond the cycle of rebirths. We shall restrict our discussion to the Buddhist view, since it is a particular problem for them. For Buddhists, in liberation the karma of saints is exhausted, while the acts which they perform produce no fruits. Since there is no karma, there is no ground for unity of sets of *skandhas* or for continuity between death and rebirth, and as such there is no reason to ascribe rebirth to the saints. They are free from the cycle of rebirths. Furthermore, according to the Buddhist doctrine of causation, if the cause is removed, so is the effect. And since where there is no cause there is no existence, without the causal conditions of karma there is no existence.[41] Thus, for the finally liberated one in *Nirvāṇa*, there is no longer any karma and consequently no unity, continuity or existence. What this means, in effect, is that though Buddhists believe in rebirth or life after death, they do not believe that this process necessarily continues indefinitely. Upon a person's (final) liberation, all causation and consequently all existence ceases. It would seem, in effect, that for the liberated there is no immortality.

But have Buddhists given up belief in immortality? Is there a sense other than invoking individual existence in which it is to be understood? The answer to this question depends, in part, upon their view of *Nirvāṇa* or *Parinirvāṇa*. We have already noted in chapter 8 that the Buddha, in responding to the question of a wandering ascetic named Vaccha concerning the state of the liberated truth-finder, said that it would not fit the case to say he is reborn, neither would it fit the case to say that he would not be reborn. Just as one cannot say where the extinguished flame has gone because the question is illicit, so one cannot say what has happened to the truth-finder.[42] 'Profound, measureless, unfathomable, is the truth-finder, even as a mighty ocean; reborn does not apply to him nor not reborn nor any combination of such terms; everything by which the truth-finder might be denoted, has passed away for him, utterly and forever.'[43]

Two interpretations of this are suggested. Some have argued that the Buddha simply refuses to commit himself to anything for which there is no empirical evidence. For *Nirvāṇa* there is no such evidence. Hence, concerning its metaphysical status or the metaphysical status of the person who has attained it one must be agnostic.[44] In fact, discourse concerning its metaphysical status is irrelevant; what is significant is that when the truth-finder attains *Nirvāṇa* he has ended his cravings and hence broken the chain of dependent origination. *Nirvāṇa* has a distinctly soteriological role. Concerning immortality in any sense stronger than rebirth we must be silent.

Others have attempted to provide some ontological structure for this soteriological concept. *Nirvāṇa* exists in contrast to *saṃsāra*, to everything that characterizes our present, conditioned existence. Its character as an unconditioned, permanent, unending, changeless, transcendental reality means that it stands beyond all predication and can only be approached *via negativa*. It is a reality which neither exists nor does not exist, but transcends existence; which neither is caused nor uncaused, but transcends causation; and so on with respect to whatever predicates one chooses.[45] With respect to immortality in an enduring sense, this means that one cannot say anything about individuals who attain *Parinirvāṇa*—that they are immortal or not-immortal or that they are both or neither. Human language breaks down at this point. Yet some state has been attained, for there exists transcendental reality unpenetrated by language, concepts and distinctions.

Where does this leave us with respect to the question of human immortality? Since karma provides for the individual both collectivity and continuity, and since *Nirvāṇa* transcends karma, it is hard to see what sense can be made of the claim that on attaining *Parinirvāṇa* at final liberation the individual has transmuted to a transcendental reality. If *Nirvāṇa* is truly transcendent to all categories, then it is transcendent to categories having to do both with individual and corporate existence and with immortality. In the transmutation the entire conception of the individual has changed. Of course, if the individual is unreal, both as a self or as a collection of *dharmas* which are themselves unreal, then perhaps nothing has been lost in this conceptual change. To the response that little has been gained as well, the Mahāyānist would reply that at least the illusion of selfhood and the reality of individuality have been overcome in the realization that all reality is eternally non-dual.

In short, two things conspire to cast a cloud over Nirvāṇic immortality: the karmic and hence conditioned nature of the self and the unpredictable, unconditioned nature of *Nirvāṇa*. Buddhists who affirm the reality of *Nirvāṇa* and some sort of transmutation of the individual affirm that there is more than the cycle of rebirths, but in both denying that *Nirvāṇa* can be predicated of and asserting that it transcends karma, they deny any means of incorporating it within any meaningful metaphysical perspective which would enable us to speak of human immortality. To put it another way, tension exists in any account of immortality as transmutation at the time of final liberation into the inconceivable. The tension lies between the conditioned self and unconditioned *Parinirvāṇa*. Since karma provides the collectivity and continuity of the individual, while *Parinirvāṇa* transcends karma, some account of the transmutation of the individual into the Nirvāṇic state is necessary in order to lend intelligibility to any claim of enduring immortality. Since such an account is barred from the outset by the nature of the transcendent, concerning immortality, as about all true Reality, there can properly be only silence.

We have touched the Transcendent and have reached only silence. The gates marking the end of intelligibility limit further advance. Analysis ceases at this point, a fact which the Buddha, Mahāyāna Buddhists, Advaita Vedāntists, among others, long ago affirmed. But the role of karma has also ceased. Metaphysically there is pure Transcendence; soteriologically there is liberation from the karmic; epistemologically there are no distinctions; logically there are paradoxes. In the end, analysis and the law of karma terminate at the same point.

Epilogue

Several years ago I presented a draft of one of the chapters of this book at an academic meeting. After the presentation, questions and comments, one of my colleagues asked, 'What have you found of value in the law of karma?' A good question deserves an answer. In this epilogue I intend to give just that.

What truths and insights can be gleaned from our philosophical study?

1. The connection of the law of karma with an objective ethic is important. It is true that the connection is not as tight as some advocates of the law of karma have proposed. As we suggested in chapter 9, the arguments for thinking that accepting the law of karma is a necessary condition for accepting the moral law are flawed. Neither is the law of karma part of the explication of the moral law. As we argued in chapter 10, the relation between the law of karma and the moral law is associative rather than necessary. However, by its claim that doers of wrong actions will be punished and doers of right actions rewarded, it presupposes that there is a moral law or set of moral principles by which the rightness or wrongness of actions can be ascertained. Accordingly it leaves no room for conceptual moral relativism.

2. It rightly draws our attention to the significance of the principle of universal justice. It is important to emphasize that our moral actions have appropriate consequences, not only in general, but for us and our own welfare. In chapter 9 we argued that it is overstating the case to affirm that the principle of universal justice—when formulated as stating that all rightdoers will be duly rewarded and all wrongdoers punished—is necessarily true or even true. There is, I think, too much empirical evidence to the contrary (though it is one of the functions of the law of karma to explain this evidence consistent with the principle of justice). Yet if we formulate it in terms of an 'ought'—all rightdoers ought to be rewarded and all wrongdoers punished—the principle is more plausible, especially for wrong actions.

According to *retributive* justice, if we break the moral law, we deserve to be punished. This applies even when we do wrong for a good cause, for example, when we engage in acts of civil disobedience to draw attention to or change what we perceive to be an immoral law or unjust situation. However, acceptance of this aspect of retributive justice—that wrongdoers deserve punishment—does not commit us to accepting a thesis detailing a particular degree, severity or proportionateness of punishment. Though deserts of some fair dispensing should follow immoral actions, the punishments inflicted need not always follow the strict rule of proportionality generally affirmed by defenders of universal justice and the law of karma. The reason for this is that they can be appropriately ameliorated by grace, so that what is imposed can be for the benefit or reform of the wrongdoer. Yet even where grace alters the amount due, justice plays a role. For one thing, in giving just deserts for wrong actions there is a maximum penalty that justice allows and which should not be exceeded, even on the teleological grounds that it will benefit the offender. Further, it is agreed that when we punish, we should punish the guilty, not the innocent. We demur from punishing innocent persons even in cases where punishing them might benefit society by acting as a deterrent. The reason, I suggest, is our strong sense of justice which requires that punishment only be imposed on the guilty.

Undoubtedly the more controversial side of the principle of universal justice concerns rewards. According to the law of karma, if we keep the moral law, we deserve to be rewarded. In effect, the law of karma makes no distinction between retributive and distributive justice. Both are put on the same footing. In both cases, it claims, what we get or experience correlates with what we have done. Meritorious acts bring pleasure and happiness which are channelled through others and our environment; wrong acts similarly bring pain, suffering and misfortune.

In contrast with this karmic approach, contemporary discussions of *distributive* justice generally exhibit little sympathy with correlating distribution with merit. Rather, the grounds for distribution are equality of treatment or, where there are relevant differences, need. For example, it is argued that the 'only kinds of reasons one could give for using [the criteria of merit or desert for distributing benefits] would be in the utilitarian terms of public interest, such as stimulating production'.[1] Indeed, even using the criterion of absolute equality in distribution is often looked at askance. For example, when the government distributes surplus cheese, many of us do not think that all should have a chunk or the same size piece, but that it should go to those who cannot purchase it because of their poverty. In short, it is need rather than merit which often determines our distribution.[2]

Yet one might argue that we should not so easily overlook considerations of merit in distributive justice. This is not simply for teleological reasons (as in, 'if we offer bonuses to our employees, they will produce more'), but because of the nature of justice and deserts. In contrast to 'equal pay for equal job descriptions', one might argue that the productive worker deserves better pay than the unproductive one doing the same job; to pay equally is an affront to justice. In place of an educational structure that, in the name of democratization of education, provides the same educational package to all students equally, or which maximizes benefits for the disadvantaged or slower learners to the neglect of the gifted, justice might demand that we construct advanced curricula to reward students who put out more effort or achieve high results. Where there are scarce medical resources to be distributed, are randomness and need the sole just considerations? Does contribution to society, past and potential, deserve special consideration? It is not simply a matter of social stimulus; it is a matter of justice.[3] The law of karma, at the very least, gives a reasoned voice to this other dimension.

3. The law of karma affirms that it is not simply the fact that actions affect the agent which is significant. It is the *kind* of effects which demand our attention. Doing right brings good effects; doing wrong brings the unpleasant. That is, it importantly stresses that there is a connection in kind between the moral quality of the act or the way the act was performed and the kind of effects which the act has on the agent. We improve ourselves by doing right, while doing wrong actions destroys our desire to do good. Or to put it another way, right actions feed on right actions, and wrong on wrong. There is a consistency in quality between cause and effect.

4. The law of karma helpfully focuses on the primary locus of these effects. In its naturalistic form, it emphasizes the causal connection between the karmic action and the good and bad experienced later. The connection, in part, occurs through

the *saṃskāras*, the dispositions and tendencies which our performance of the act creates in us. The insight preserved here is that our actions, to a large part, issue from our character, desires, dispositions and tendencies, and contribute to the same, either in reinforcing those out of which we have acted, or helping us to develop contrary character traits, desires and dispositions (when we act contrary to certain dispositions and tendencies).

This means that in performing actions, we should consider not only what action we are going to perform and not only the moral quality of the action, but also from what motives we are acting and what our doing it will do to us. If we are acting greedily, do we want to reinforce our greedy tendencies? If we are acting jealously, do we want to create or augment this character trait? If we are acting out of love, can this be reinforced by other actions? This dimension asks us to consider not merely the moral quality of the action, but our motives and states of character (virtues and vices) out of which we act and how this comports with the kind of individual we want to be.

This emphasis on the virtues is a necessary antidote to the almost total emphasis in contemporary Western ethical theory on the moral quality of the act itself. Until recently,[4] almost nowhere in modern ethical theory was the character of the person considered a relevant factor in assessing moral actions. And yet it is this insight which Aristotle had over 2300 years ago and which is found in non-Western philosophy in the doctrine of karma. As Aristotle argued, a good action is one which is done by a virtuous person.[5] The character of the person is important not only in determining the moral quality of the act, but also in determining how the act will affect the agent. And if we are serious about ethics, we not only want to do good acts, we want to become good or virtuous people. The doctrine of *saṃskāras* addresses this. We are what we do, why we do it, and how we do it.

5. In introducing the notion of *adṛṣṭa*, advocates of the law of karma have raised the important issue of the status of moral qualities. As invisible, non-physical qualities, possessing the character of merit and demerit, they might be described as non-natural properties of selves. Since they persist over time, they help explain how merit and demerit can be preserved from one time and one incarnation to another. As properties of agents, they are conditions of their causal actions and thus provide

grounds for ascribing causal efficacy to moral qualities. In Western ethical theory, the view that goodness is a non-natural property succumbed to positivist dogma about what things were real. Even G.E. Moore, who in *Principia Ethica* strongly defended the concept of good as a non-natural property, accusing those who reduced good to natural or supernatural properties of being guilty of the naturalistic fallacy, was later hesitantly swayed by the emotivist challenge.[6] With the demise of positivism, however, it is time to rethink the question of the (possibly unique) status of moral qualities. Is there any reason to think that goodness is not a non-natural property of agents? If agents can have powers of intellect or insight, charisma, fortitude or self-control, cannot they also possess *adṛṣṭa* as well? When we characterize persons as good or meritorious, might we not be saying something objective about those persons, that is, doing something more than merely praising, lauding or expressing our approval of them? It might be replied that these are merely functional properties describing a person's behaviour. Yet one might argue that they are more than this. Persons might have fortitude or merit even when they are not acting in ways which demonstrate it. And even if it be argued, in a behaviourist sense, that this simply means that they possess the power, ability or tendency to act in a certain way, this power, ability or tendency must lie in or depend upon certain properties. Just as one explains, for example, the brittleness of a glass vase by noting certain of its properties, such as its composition and the strength of the bond between its particles, so one can explain persons' fortitude by noting certain of their non-physical (or physical) properties. And if moral qualities have real existence, it seems reasonable to hold that persons are meritorious by virtue of possessing certain non-natural properties.

Of course, much more needs to be said about *adṛṣṭa* as a non-natural property. For example, what are non-natural properties, and how do they differ from natural properties? What kinds of evidence does one adduce to show they exist? How are we to understand the causal relation between non-natural properties and natural properties? At the same time, there is something to be learned by listening to the proposal that moral qualities are objective and causal in character.

6. The law of karma asserts that karmic actions have a cumulative effect. Acts not only have individual effects; they also can

contribute to our character by emphasizing or strengthening the qualities we already have. Thus it is true that the more evil we do, the harder it is to escape the pull to do evil. Doing wrong augments the disposition to do wrong; it makes doing it easier. Similarly with doing right; doing right creates a tendency to do right and makes doing it easier. Deep down we already know this. Yet we camouflage it by pretending to believe that 'just one more won't hurt'. We are persistent believers in atomistic causes and effects.

7. According to the law of karma, though we are continually forming our dispositions, we are not slaves to these dispositions. We can work to counteract them, either for good or evil. Dispositions do not coerce, though they become stronger the more we act in accord with their dictates. But the law of karma emphasizes that no matter what karma we have built up, we can change. What we do now also builds up karma, which contributes to or counteracts what we have done. The next moment is the first moment in the rest of our lives, and what we do now can alter who we are, what we will be, and what will happen to us. Thus, there always is the promise that we can change if we really want to. Of course, advocates of the law of karma recognize that we will not change overnight, that change of character takes time and effort. This is evidenced by their emphasis on renunciation as achieved through a gradual process of training. Yet change is possible—and this is the hope held out.

Believers in the law of karma, then, are believers both in human freedom and in hope. As we saw in chapter 4, it is a misunderstanding of the doctrine to interpret it fatalistically. Only if we are truly free, only if freedom is not an illusion, can we ever hope to escape the human predicament. And liberation from that predicament is the ultimate goal of human action, no matter how far in the distance it seems.

8. We saw in chapter 6 that attempts to explain the operations of the law of karma completely naturalistically fail. The weak link is the connection between the dispositions and tendencies or moral qualities created by karmic actions, and the environment which affects us for good or ill, whether it be through other persons or natural events. To make this connection some sort of theistic administrator of karma is necessary. This God must have knowledge of our actions and the attitudes from which they were performed. He must know what merit and demerit we have

accumulated. He must also have power to use nature to punish us for our evil and reward us for our good. And he must be good himself, for he is the custodian of the principle of justice which the law of karma implements. In short, if the law of karma is to operate, there must be a god or gods who are responsible for remembering, accounting, and administering the karma created.

9. It is an insight of certain schools of Hindu and Buddhist thought that merit can be transferred. Applied in a theistic context, not only can we share our merit by showing mercy and compassion to others, but God himself can act graciously on our behalf. Again, this is not to deny that God acts justly. As the administrator of the law of karma, he punishes us for our evil deeds and rewards us for our good. But justice does not utter the final word. God out of mercy intends that we become better persons, and so employs his mercy justly.

10. If, as we have suggested, the law of karma describes the justice of God's actions, and if justice qualifies mercy at God's own initiative, then the law of karma (in its strict sense that each reaps in accord with what he sows) is not an absolute law, but a principle used by God in his administration of the world. But if the law of karma is not the final word, if it is simply one among many tools or principles used by God to achieve his purpose of human liberation, it no longer provides a complete explanation for the good and evil we experience. True, it does explain some of the pain and suffering as well as the pleasure and happiness which we experience. Because we do good to others, we receive good in return. Likewise with evil. It also explains some natural evil we experience. In particular, it explains the evil and good we experience which comes as God's punishment or reward. But it does not explain all natural evil, or even a great deal of it. If God is involved in graciously removing obstacles to our liberation, there is, at the very least, some end in view which characterizes God's acts. But if so, the description of this end becomes significant in providing an adequate account of the good and evil which we experience. Another explanation for evil is needed to supplement the law of karma. This, I believe, is provided by a free-will theodicy. I have articulated this in substantial detail elsewhere.[7]

11. Finally, and perhaps most intriguingly, in presupposing a doctrine of rebirth the doctrine of karma asserts that one lifetime

is not sufficient to build up the kind of character necessary as the proper propaedeutic to liberation or which God desires. This is obviously true of those who die in infancy and childhood. But it is also true of those who survive to be adults! If God wants us to be persons of virtue, and if virtue cannot be imposed on us but only achieved by our free actions, then life after death is required. It need not be a succession of rebirths and redeaths, though this is not excluded. But it must be the kind of life where the virtues can continue to be developed.

This, however, need not entail a pessimistic, saṃsāric view of human existence. We need not be condemned to seemingly endless or practically countless numbers of miserable incarnations. Liberation need not be for the few who can undergo the rigours of purification and renunciation and the severe disciplines of meditation. Where a doctrine of karma is coupled with the significant intervention by God who not only is interested and concerned with human liberation, but significantly intervenes in nature and human affairs to bring it about, optimism about the future can replace the pessimism of life seen as a cycle of misery, of old age, sickness, and death, where every experience is ill.

Here I think of C.S. Lewis, who, when he gets to describing the end of our lives, sees God calling us to 'Come farther in! Come farther up!' 'All our life in this world . . . is only the cover and title page.' There is more to life than suffering. Life provides opportunity for significant growth, and through its moments courses the divine, vicarious mercy which, even in punishment, aids the maturation and perfection of the wrongdoer and finally ends the predicament with true forgiveness. In this light the challenge of existence continues after death. As the phoenix, we rise again to begin 'Chapter One of the Great Story which no one on earth has read: which goes on forever: in which every chapter is better than before'.[8]

Appendix

THE LAW OF KARMA IN THE UPANIṢADS

11. 'Yājñavalkya,' said Jāratkārava Ārtabhāga, 'when such a person (a liberated sage) dies, do the vital breaths move up from him or do they not?' 'No,' replied Yājñavalkya. 'They are gathered together in him. He (the body) swells up, he is inflated and thus inflated the dead man (body) lies.'
12. 'Yājñavalkya,' said he, 'when such a person dies, what is it that does not leave him?' 'The name. The name is infinite and infinite are the *Viśve-devās*. Thereby he (who knows this) wins an infinite world.'
13. 'Yājñavalkya,' said he, 'when the speech (voice) of this dead person enters into fire, the breath into air, the eye into the sun, the mind into the moon, hearing into the quarters, the self into the ether, the hairs of the body into the herbs, the hairs on the head into the trees and the blood and the semen are deposited in water, what then becomes of this person?' 'Ārtabhaga, my dear, take my hand. We two alone shall know of this, this is not for us two (to speak of) in public.' The two went away and deliberated. What they said was karman and what they praised was karman. Verily one becomes good by good action, bad by bad action. Therefore, Ārtabhāga of the line of Jāratkaru kept silent.

Bṛhad–āraṇyaka Upaniṣad III, 2, 11–13.

* * * * *

3. Just as a leech (or caterpillar) when it has come to the end of a blade of grass, after having made another approach (to another blade) draws itself together towards it, so does this self, after having thrown away this body, and dispelled

ignorance, after having another approach (to another body) draw itself together (for making the transition to another body).

4. And as a goldsmith, taking a piece of gold turns it into another, newer and more beautiful shape, even so does this self, after having thrown away this body and dispelled its ignorance, make unto himself another, newer and more beautiful shape like that of the fathers or of the *gandharvas*, or of the gods or of *Prajā-pati* or of *Brahmā* or of other beings.

Bṛhad-āraṇyaka Upaniṣad IV, 4, 3–4.

* * * * *

1. So those who know this, and those who in the forest meditate with faith and austerity go to light and from light to day, from day to the bright half of the month, from the bright half of the month to those six months during which the sun moves northward.
2. From these months to the year, from the year to the sun, from the sun to the moon, from the moon to the lightning. There, there is a person who is non-human. He leads them on to Brahmā. This is the path leading to the gods.
3. But those, who in the village practise (a life of) sacrifices, (and perform) works of public utility and almsgiving they pass into smoke, from smoke to night, from night to the latter (dark) half of the month, from the latter (dark) half of the month to the six months in which the sun moves southwards, but they do not reach the year.
4. From those months to the world of the fathers, from the world of the fathers to space, from space to the moon. That is the king Soma. That is the food of the gods. That the gods eat.
5. Having dwelt there as long as there is residue (of good works) they return again by that course by which they came to space, from space into air; and after having become the air they become the smoke; after having become smoke, they become mist.
6. After having become mist they become cloud, after having become cloud he rains down. They are born here as rice and barley, herbs and trees, as sesamum plants and beans. From

thence the release becomes extremely difficult for whoever eats the food and sows the seed he becomes like unto him.

7. Those whose conduct here has been good will quickly attain a good birth (literally womb), the birth of a Brāhmin, the birth of a Kṣatriya or the birth of a Vaiśya. But those whose conduct here has been evil, will quickly attain an evil birth, the birth of a dog, the birth of a hog or the birth of a Caṇḍāla [outcast].
8. But on neither of these ways are those small creatures (which are) continually revolving (those of whom it is said), be born and die. Their's is a third state. By this (it comes about) that that world becomes full. Therefore let one seek to guard himself. To this end, there is this verse.

   If we pursue wisdom, we travel by the path of the gods. If we perform good works we travel by the path of the fathers. If we do neither, we will continually revolve like little creatures.
9. He who steals gold, he who drinks wine, he who dishonours the teacher's bed, he who kills a Brāhmaṇa, these four do fall as also the fifth who consorts with them.

Chāndogya Upaniṣad, V, 10, 1–9.

* * * * *

1. (Know that) all this, whatever moves in this moving world, is enveloped by God. Therefore find your enjoyment in renunciation; do not covet what belongs to others.
2. Always performing works here one should wish to live a hundred years. If you live thus as a man, there is no way other than this by which karma (deed) does not adhere to you.

Īśa Upaniṣad, 1–2.

* * * * *

4. When the embodied self that dwells within the body slips off and is released from the body, what is there that remains? This, verily, is that.

5. Not by any outbreath or inbreath does any mortal whatever live. But by another do they live on which these (lifebreaths) both depend.
6. Look (here). I shall explain to you the mystery of *Brahman*, the eternal, and also how the soul fares, after reaching death, O Gautama.
7. Some souls enter into a womb for embodiment; others enter stationary objects according to their deeds and according to their thoughts.

Kaṭha Upaniṣad, II, 2, 6–7.

* * * * *

11. By means of thought, touch, sight and passions and by the abundance of food and drink there are the birth and development of the (embodied) self. According to his deeds, the embodied self assumes successively various forms in various conditions.
12. The embodied self, according to his own qualities, chooses (assumes) many shapes, gross and subtle. Having himself caused his union with them, through the qualities of his acts and through the qualities of his body, he is seen as another.

Śvetāśvatara Upaniṣad, V, 11–12.[1]

Notes

Chapter 1

1. Sarvepalli Radhakrishnan puts the metaphor slightly differently: 'We reap what we sow.' *Indian Philosophy* I (London: George Allen and Unwin, 1923), p. 245. This way of putting it, though popular, can be misleadingly deterministic. The Buddha is described as making the following distinction which helpfully avoids begging the question of the deterministic character of the law. 'O Priests, if any one were to say that a man must reap according to his deeds, in that case, O priests, there is no religious life, nor is any opportunity afforded for the entire extinction of misery. But if any one says, O priests, that the reward a man reaps accords with his deeds, in that case, O priests, there is a religious life, and opportunity is afforded for the entire extinction of misery.' *Aṅguttara-Nikāya*, III, 10, 99; quoted in Henry Clarke Warren (ed.), *Buddhism in Translations* (New York: Atheneum Pub., 1962), p. 221.
2. Though the most common orientation is that what each person experiences is justified in terms of his own prior actions, some authors speak of the transfer of merit from one person to another, while others expand individual karma to include family, caste, city, national and cosmic karma which affects large numbers of individuals. The question of transfer of merit is raised in the *Milindapañha* (IV, 8, 29–31), where the suggestion is made that merit but not demerit can be transferred. More recently, writing in the Mahāyāna tradition, D.T. Suzuki expands the notion even further. 'Buddhism, however, does not advocate this individualistic interpretation of karmaic law. . . . Deeds once committed, good or evil, leave permanent effects on the general system of sentient beings, of which the actor is merely a component part; and it is not the actor himself only, but everybody constituting a grand psychic community called "Dharmadhātu" (spiritual universe), that suffers or enjoys the outcome of a moral deed.' *Outlines of Mahayana Buddhism* (New York: Schocken Books, 1963, pp. 192–3. Examples of group karma in contemporary Theravāda Buddhism are found in James P. McDermott, 'Is There Group Karma in Theravāda Buddhism?' *Numen* 23 (1976), pp. 67–73. This expansion of the usual individualistic interpretation of karma raises some interesting and important questions concerning the nature of justice and moral responsibility for actions. Followed consistently, it suggests that there can be group responsibility for moral actions, and that

the individual can experience just deserts apportioned beyond what his individual acts merit. If I receive the karmic effects of others in ways not wholly connected with the principle of justice as applied to the actions I performed in previous lives, then moral responsibility is shared. But then has the character of the doctrine of karma substantially changed? It is no longer the case that what I reap accords with what I sow, but rather what the members of that group reap accords with what the community or group sows. The issue of group karma and transfer of merit is taken up in Chapters 9 and 10 respectively.

3. A defence of this thesis is given by David J. Kalupahana, *Causality: the Central Philosophy of Buddhism* (Honolulu: The University Press of Hawaii, 1975).
4. *Majjhima-Nikāya,* sutta 63.

Chapter 2

1. 'The threat of repeated deaths, in the case of heretics incapable of performing the sacrificial rites, as seen from the *Śatapatha-Brāhmaṇa,* though indicating the possibility of one more rebirth, is far from being identical with the theory of transmigration as current in the Hindu belief.' A.N. Upadhye, 'Jainism and Karma Doctrine', *The Jaina Antiquary* 2 (1936), pp. 8–9. Wendy Doniger O'Flaherty refers to this as the theory of re-death. 'Karma and Rebirth in the Vedas and Puranas', in Wendy Doniger O'Flaherty (ed.), *Karma and Rebirth in Classical Indian Traditions* (Berkeley, Ca.: University of California Press, 1980), p. 3.
2. Originally 'karma', stemming from the root *kṛ*, meant what was done, a deed or action. Subsequently it came to be understood more broadly to refer both to actions and their consequences. Though 'karma' was used to refer to the Vedic sacrifice, in the Upaniṣads its meaning was broadened to refer to actions which determined the conditions of human rebirth.
3. David M. Knipe, '*Sapiṇḍīkarana*: The Hindu Rite of Entry into Heaven', in Frank Reynolds and Earle H. Waugh (eds.), *Religious Encounters with Death, Insights from the History and Anthropology of Religions* (University Park, Pa.: Pennsylvania State University Press, 1977), p. 112.
4. Sarvepalli Radhakrishnan, *Indian Philosophy* I (London: George Allen and Unwin, 1923), p. 109.
5. Arthur B. Keith, *Religion and Philosophy of the Vedas and Upaniṣads* I (Boston: Harvard University Press, 1925), p. 250.
6. The Upaniṣads themselves contain this mixture, where one's accumulated karma is worked off both by retribution in another world and by rebirth in this world. (*Chāndogya Upaniṣad* V, 10, 5). In Buddhist literature, the accumulated karma can be worked off in hell (purgatory) (*Milindapañha,* IV, 4, 17, where Devadatta suffered for an extensive period in hell for the schism he created in the Order, but then was made a Pakkeka-Buddha because at the moment

of his death he took refuge in the Buddha) or by retribution both in another and in this world (*Saṃyutta-Nikāya*, III, 2, 10).

7. Knipe, p. 115.
8. O'Flaherty, pp. xv–xvi, 6–8. 'Thus a word whose primary meaning is seed-food for the dead ancestors comes to mean the unshaped embryo, made out of ingested food transformed into seed, or, by extension, the womb that receives the embryo and the testicles that contain seed, and finally the body which develops from seed, womb, and embryo.' p. 8.
9. For the Upaniṣadic sources which refer to the law of karma, see the Appendix.
10. Charles Johnston, 'Karma and Liberation', *The Hibbert Journal*, 21 (1922–3), p. 98. A.N. Upadhye writes, 'With regard to the doctrine of transmigration there is a decided advance in [the] Upaniṣads.' 'Jainism and Karma Doctrine', *The Jaina Antiquary* 2 (June 1936), p. 12.
11. The Upaniṣads do not 'formulate any universal law of causation. . . . The Greater Upaniṣads do not develop the doctrines of karma and transmigration much beyond the stage they had reached in the Brāhmaṇas.' P.D. Mehta, *Early Indian Religious Thought*, (London: Luzac and Co., 1956), p. 143.
12. George L. Hart, III, 'The Theory of Reincarnation among the Tamils', in *Karma and Rebirth*, pp. 116–33.
13. O'Flaherty, pp. xvi–xvii.
14. Gananath Obeyesekere, 'The Rebirth Eschatology and Its Transformations: A Contribution to the Sociology of Early Buddhism', in *Karma and Rebirth*, pp. 137–64.
15. Johnston argues that, since in the *Bṛhad-āraṇyaka* and *Chāndogya Upaniṣads* the young Brahmin, Śvetaketu, when questioned by his king, did not know the answers to questions to which karma was the answer, and since his Brahmin father subsequently went to a Kṣatriya to be taught the answer and since Yājñavalkya taught him the doctrine only in secret, the doctrine was a product of Kṣatriyan thought, known only esoterically by the Kṣatriyan caste during this early Upaniṣadic period. Only subsequently was it adopted by the more sacrificially oriented Brahmins (pp. 98–100). V.P. Varma rejects this conflict theory on the ground that the widespread acceptance of the doctrine in post-Upaniṣadic times implies either that a period of several centuries must have elapsed between the introduction of the doctrine and the post-Upaniṣadic period for this doctrine to have developed and been successfully propagated (which, he claims, is not historically tenable), or else 'Yājñavalkya was not expressing something novel, unique, and unheard of by the people and that his desire for communicating this doctrine in secret was only in the general Upaniṣadic fashion.' 'The Origins and Sociology of the Early Buddhist Philosophy of Moral Determinism', *Philosophy East and West*, 13 (Apr. 1963), pp. 33–5.
16. Radhakrishnan writes, '[A]ll deeds have their fruits in the world and effects on the mind.' (p. 247).

17. 'Work alone is your proper business, never the fruits [it may produce]; let not your motive be the fruit of works nor your attachment to [mere] worklessness.' *Bhagavad-Gītā*, II, 47. 'But even these works (sacrifice, giving alms, penance) should be done [in the spirit of self-surrender], for [all] attachment [to what you do] and [all] fruits [of what you do] must be surrendered.' XVIII, 6.
18. 'To those who have not yet renounced the ego and its desires, action bears three kinds of fruit—pleasant, unpleasant, and a mixture of both. They will be reaped in due season. But those who have renounced ego and desire will reap no fruit at all, either in this world or in the next.' *Bhagavad-Gītā*, XVIII, 12.
19. *Aṅguttara-Nikāya*, III, 4, 33, translation from Henry Clarke Warren, *Buddhism in Translations* (New York: Atheneum, 1973), pp. 216–7.
20. As with much else, one can find exceptions to this. For example, Nāgasena puzzles King Milindi with his assertion that the person who sins *unconsciously* acquires greater demerit than he who sins *consciously*. The reason, he argues, is that the one who does not know what he is doing and is unaware of the resulting effects can inadvertently sin more grievously and thus experience more severe karmic effects. *Milindapañha*, III, 7, 8.
21. That the effect pre-exists in the cause was held by Advaita Vedānta and Sāṅkhya; that it exists independent of the cause was advocated by Buddhism, Mīmāṃsā, and Nyāya-Vaiśeṣika.
22. Since in most cases, i.e., in non-theistic systems, karma is not deliberately or consciously imposed but is rather the natural consequence or outworking of a person's moral actions, it might be claimed that this theory technically is not a theory of punishment and hence not a theory of retribution. For example, Stanley Benn writes, 'Characteristically punishment . . . is deliberately imposed, not just the natural consequence of a person's action (like a hangover), and the unpleasantness is essential to it, not an accidental accompaniment to some other treatment (like the pain of the dentist's drill).' 'Punishment', *Encyclopedia of Philosophy*, VII (New York: Macmillan, 1967), p. 29. This characterization, however, might be held to impose too narrow a view on the way punishment is administered. What might be requisite is that the requiting be done according to strict laws or rules, not that the meting-out be done naturally or by conscious volition. If so, then a doctrine of natural retribution could still be considered to constitute a retributive theory of punishment.
23. One can find such a view in contemporary restatements of the law of karma. For example, Christmas Humphreys suggests that karma is consistent with compensation, though precisely how is left ambiguous. *Karma and Rebirth* (London: John Murray, 1942), p. 69.
24. The Buddha speaks of these two kinds of karma in terms of punishments meted out in this life and those meted out in future lives. *Aṅguttara-Nikāya*, II, 1, 1.
25. Padmanabh S. Jaini, 'Karma and the Problem of Rebirth in Jainism', in *Karma and Rebirth*, pp. 231–2. For a more detailed breakdown of

these types into sub- and sub-sub-types, see Nathmal Tatia, *Studies in Jaina Philosophy* (Benares: Jain Cultural Research Society, 1951), pp. 332–43.

26. Patañjali, *Yoga-sūtra*, IV, 7. This classification is also found in early Buddhism. For references see McDermott, pp. 180–1.
27. It might be thought that designating a category of 'neither-black-nor-white karma' contradicts our above contention that actions done out of no desire for their fruits produce no karma, for here we have such karma. However, to produce neither-black-nor-white karma is equivalent to producing no fruit or karmic consequences. See Vāchaspati-Micra's explanation of *Yoga-sūtra* IV, 7, in *The Yoga-System of Patañjali*, translated by James H. Woods (Delhi: Motilal Banarsidass, 1966), p. 306.
28. Satischandra Chatterjee and Dhirendramohan Datta, *An Introduction to Indian Philosophy* (Calcutta: University of Calcutta, 1950), p. 414.
29. 'It is not, for instance, the case that a certain act *x* in some past life specifically determines a certain event of experiencing, *y*, in this one; at best, *x* generates a determination on the agent's part to pursue a life-plan or -style which leads him to develop a desire to do something which will produce *y* if nothing interferes.' Karl Potter, 'The Karma Theory and its Interpretation in Some Indian Philosophical Systems', in *Karma and Rebirth*, p. 257.
30. For example, in Advaita when the *saṃskāras* mature, they co-operate with the *vāsanās*, which are the decisions of the internal organs, to determine how these tendencies are to be manifested. The maturing of the tendencies in accord with the *vāsanās* creates desires. See Potter, p. 249.
31. Yoga uses the example of the farmer who removes parts of the waterway to direct the flow of water. Similarly, merit removes the obstructions raised by demerit, and vice versa. Vyāsa's commentary on *Yoga-sūtra*, IV, 3.
32. Buddhaghosa's commentary on stanza 137 of the *Dhammapada*, in Warren, pp. 222–5.
33. *Saṃyutta-Nikāya*, III,2,10.
34. See Ludo Rocher, 'Karma and Rebirth in the Dharmaśāstras', in *Karma and Rebirth*, pp. 61–89.
35. O'Flaherty, 'Karma and Rebirth in the Vedas and Purāṇas', p. 22; McDermott, pp. 177–8.
36. Wilhelm Halbfass, 'Karma, *Apūrva*, and 'Natural' Causes: Observations on the Growth and Limits of the Theory of *Saṃsāra*', in *Karma and Rebirth*, pp. 289–90.

Chapter 3

1. Actions have 'a double effect—one physical and visible and another moral and invisible. . . . The physical effect follows the law of instantaneous succession, but the moral effect (which is often compared to a seed) may remain in abeyance and fructify at a much later time when maturing conditions are present. Again, while the

physical effect is mainly, if not wholly, produced on others, the moral effect comes to rest upon the head of the doer himself. . . .' H.D. Bhattacharyya, 'The Doctrine of Karma', *The Philosophical Quarterly* (Amalner) 3 (1927), p. 239. Mysore Hiriyanna, treating *phala* somewhat differently, makes a similar distinction. '. . . [E]very deed that we do leads to a double result. It not only produces what may be termed its direct result—the pain or pleasure following from it according to the karma theory, but it also establishes in us a tendency to repeat the same deed in the future. This tendency is termed saṁskāra; and the direct fruit of the karma is known as its phala. Every deed is bound to yield its phala; even the gods cannot prevent it from doing so. . . . As regards the saṁskāras, on the other hand, we have within us the full power of control, so that we may regulate them as they tend to express themselves in action.' *Outlines of Indian Philosophy* (London: George Allen and Unwin, 1932), pp. 129–30.

2. *Aṅguttara-Nikāya*, VI,VI,63. See James P. McDermott, 'Karma and Rebirth in Early Buddhism', in Wendy D. O'Flaherty (ed.), *Karma and Rebirth in Classical Indian Traditions* (Berkeley: University of California Press, 1980), p. 181. ('Karma' is termed 'kamma' in Pāli, the dialect of the Buddhist scriptures, which has become the religious language of Buddhism. To maintain uniformity, however, we shall use 'karma' throughout our book, irrespective of whether we are dealing with Hindu or Buddhist thought.)
3. For example, 'Superficial appearances to the contrary notwithstanding, Buddhist ethics is essentially an ethics of intention. Actions themselves are neither good nor bad: for the Buddhist even more than for Shakespeare, "thinking makes them so." *Kuśala* and *akuśala*, literally skill and unskill, the more precise Buddhist expressions for what is morally good and morally bad, are terms applicable only to karma-producing volitions and their associated mental phenomena. By the figure of speech according to which qualities belonging to the cause are attributed to the effect, an action is termed immoral when it springs from a mental state . . . dominated by the three unskilful or "unwholesome" roots of greed, hatred, and delusion, and moral when it proceeds from mental states characterized by the opposites of these.' Bhikshu Sangharakshita, *A Survey of Buddhism* (Bangalore: Indian Institute of World Culture, 1959), pp. 142–3.
4. McDermott, p. 182.
5. Again we can illustrate this through Sangharakshita, 'It is not possible to commit murder with a good heart because the deliberate taking of life is simply the outward expression of a state of mind dominated by hate. Deeds are condensations of thought just as water is a condensation of air. They are thoughts made manifest, and proclaim from the housetops of action only what has already been committed in the silent and secret chambers of the heart. One who commits an act of immorality thereby declares that he is not free from unwholesome states of mind.' p. 143.

6. For a discussion of this perspective with respect to the question whether old age and death are the result of karma, see James McDermott, 'The *Kathāvatthu* Kamma Debates', *Journal of the American Oriental Society* 95 (1975), pp. 426–7.
7. Vyāsa, *Yoga-bhāṣya*, on *Yoga-sūtra*, IV, 11.
8. We will say more about this presupposition in Chapter 9.
9. Patañjali, *Yoga-sūtra*, II, 3–17.
10. Aṅguttara-Nikāya, IV, XX, 197; *Milindapañha*, III,4,2. That karma conditions our rebirth bodies and our environment is also clearly asserted in Hinduism. *Chāndogya Upaniṣad*, V, 7–9; *Śvetāśvatara Upaniṣad*, V, 11–12. *Manu*, 11, 49–52 lists actions of various sorts and their correlative diseases, while 12, 74–80 not only emphasizes the state of rebirth but also lists such things as the heat of scorching sand, afflictions of heat and cold, imprisonment, separations from loved ones, being enslaved, gaining wealth and its loss, old age and death.
11. Patañjali, II, 13.
12. Jainism has an extensive (what might be termed mythological) explanation of what happens in the fourteen stages of spiritual development leading to liberation. In the seventh stage the soul gains self-control and freedom from spiritual inertia to continue its progress. In the eleventh stage the passions (deluding karma) are suppressed, while in the twelfth they are eliminated, though the karma resulting from activity remains. In the thirteenth stage the threefold activity of the body, the sense-organ of speech, and mind remains, though this activity does not create any further bondage (its bondage does not last longer than an instant and hence is technically non-affecting). In preparation for entering the fourteenth stage, the soul ends this activity. Thus both sources of karmic attraction—passions and activity—are eliminated. However, the karma which determines the body formation, social status, and production of feelings is longer than that which determines length of life. Hence, the soul in eight instants expands to the size of the universe, and then contracts again. This equalizes the length of all the other karma with that which determines the length of life in any incarnation (*āyuh* karma). That is, it assures premature fruition and complete exhaustion of all karma which is of longer length than the *āyuh* karma and would require a longer existence. The fourteenth stage is an extremely brief period ('the period of time required to pronounce five short syllables at the ordinary speed') of non-activity, immediately followed by liberation. For a detailed description of this process, see Nathmal Tatia, *Studies in Jaina Philosophy* (Benares: Jain Cultural Research Society, 1951), pp. 276–80.
13. 'There the meditation-born mind is devoid of the vehicle.' Patañjali, IV, 6.
14. The conflict between the role of the parent and the role of the persistent self (*ātman* or *jīva*) in determining the characteristics of the newborn can be found in classical Indian philosophy. On the

one hand, some held that it is the parents who are responsible for the sex and physical characteristics of the newborn. In one account, the mother contributed the hair, nails, skin and flesh, and the father the bone, sinew and marrow. In a different account the mother contributed the blood, flesh, fat, heart, lungs, liver and other internal organs, whereas the father contributed the hair, beard, nails, teeth, bones, etc. From the transmigrating *ātman* came the life span, self-knowledge, *manas* (mind), senses, desires, pleasure and pain, consciousness, *buddhi* (intellect), etc. On the other hand, others restricted the influence of the parent on the new gross body to environmental input. The food which they ate interacted with the subtle elements in the transmigrating self to produce certain physical characteristics, or the behaviour of the expectant mother influenced both mental and physical characteristics of the fetus she carried. For details, see *Karma and Rebirth*, pp. 22–3, 97–8, 103–5, 254.

15. We will take up the question of the consistency of merit transfer with justice in Chapter 10.
16. Some classical Indian traditions maintain that the embryo is active and can accumulate karma even while inside the womb. See Wendy D. O'Flaherty, 'Karma and Rebirth in the Vedas and Purāṇas', in *Karma and Rebirth*, pp. 20–1.
17. '"Fiction," in this context, does not mean a concept or theory that is necessarily false; rather a concept or theory may be called a fiction when it is undemonstrable, when it is impossible to determine its truth or falsehood, or when . . . it cannot be established by any of the *pramāṇas*.' Eliot Deutsch, *Advaita Vedānta: A Philosophical Reconstruction* (Honolulu: The University Press of Hawaii, 1973), p. 76.
18. Deutsch, pp. 71, 73, 76.
19. Our argument will not turn on whether we have correctly interpreted Deutsch; it is the thesis that the law of karma is merely an interpretative concept and not literally true about our experience which will interest us in what follows.
20. Deutsch, p. 77. It is interesting to note that, on the basis of a sociological study done in a Himachal Pradesh village, Ursala Sharma contends that the doctrine of karma fails to fulfil this purpose. For one thing, the Hindu villager was primarily concerned with this life and not the next. For another, there are other things that he believed he could do to avert trouble and suffering, including doing good acts, engaging in proper rituals, and placating the deities. 'Theodicy and the Doctrine of Karma', *Man* 8 (1973), p. 357.
21. Deutsch, p. 78.
22. Deutsch, p. 70.
23. Deutsch, p. 72.
24. Deutsch, p. 75.
25. Mysore Hiriyanna, *Outlines of Indian Philosophy* (London: George Allen and Unwin, 1932), p. 359.
26. Hiriyanna, p. 181. Deutsch himself writes, 'It is the rare Advaitin indeed who would hold to a scriptural utterance if it directly

contradicted empirical or rational experience' (p. 75).

27. Deutsch, p. 71.
28. Karl H. Potter, 'The Naturalistic Principle of Karma', *Philosophy East and West* 14 (April 1964), pp. 39–40. Donald Walhout, in a subsequent article, has correctly pointed out that the law of karma serves another function besides the cause-searching function, namely, the moral-reminder function, which 'points us directly to the deliberating subject existing in the present and looking to the future'. 'A Critical Note on Potter's Interpretation of Karma', *Philosophy East and West* 16 (July 1966), p. 236.
29. This is illustrated by the discourse concerning the apparently inexplicable death of Moggāllana the Great, who met with such an untimely death, considering the kind of person he was. The Buddha's knowledge of prior existences provides the explanation to the puzzled disciples in terms of Moggāllana's past deeds and accumulated karma. Buddaghosa's commentary on the *Dhammapada*, stanza 137, in Henry Clarke Warren (ed.), *Buddhism in Translations* (New York: Atheneum, 1962), pp. 222–6.
30. For an analysis and defence of *de re* necessity, see Alvin Plantinga, *The Nature of Necessity* (Oxford: Oxford University Press, 1974), chs 1–3.
31. This view, interestingly enough, accords with Karl Potter's view that the doctrines of karma and rebirth appear as a theory. 'A *theory*, as I shall use the term, is a set of connected hypotheses, involving postulation of unobservable or uncommonsensical items, that purports to predict, postdict, or otherwise explain processes in the world. ... To criticize a theory ... one may produce counterexamples, ... demonstrate inconsistency, ... show that the theoretical constructs introduced are redundant, or that the theory is empty, without explanatory force.' 'The Karma Theory and Its Interpretation in Some Indian Philosophical Systems', in *Karma and Rebirth*, pp. 241–2.

Chapter 4

1. Sarvepalli Radhakrishnan, *The Hindu View of Life* (New York: The Macmillan Co., 1927), p. 76. Radhakrishnan goes on to deny that the doctrine of karma is either deterministic or fatalistic, however.
2. S.S. Suryanarayanan, 'Karma and Fatalism', *The Philosophical Quarterly* (India) 16 (April 1940), p. 82.
3. A.B. Keith, *The Religion and Philosophy of the Vedas and the Upaniṣads* I (Boston: Harvard University Press, 1925), p. 232.
4. It is important to distinguish our question whether the law of karma entails fatalism from the question whether the law of karma is associated with fatalism. That it has been and often is associated with fatalism is not disputed. See Wendy D. O'Flaherty, 'Karma and Rebirth in the Vedas and Purāṇas', and J. Bruce Long, 'The Concepts of Human Action and Rebirth in the *Mahābhārata*', in Wendy D. O'Flaherty (ed.), *Karma and Rebirth in Classical Indian*

Traditions (Berkeley: University of California Press, 1980), pp. 23–7, 44–5.

5. *Daiva* or fate can be traced etymologically to that which pertains to the gods (*devas*), though even the gods are at times under fate's sway.
6. *Bṛhad-āraṇyaka Upaniṣad*, III, 2, 13.
7. *Bhagavad-Gītā*, XVIII, 59–60.
8. Sarvepalli Radhakrishnan, *Indian Philosophy* I (New York: Macmillan and Co., 1923), p. 246.
9. Swami Abhedananda, *Doctrine of Karma* (Calcutta: Ramakrishna Vedanta Math, 1944), pp. 16–17, 79–80. 'That which we are doing today is the result of the dormant powers with which we were born; and the cause of these powers lies in the activity of some previous state of existence. We have not received any of these latent powers from outside; . . . *Our* present is the result of our past, and our future must be the result of our present.' p. 81.
10. *Majjhima-Nikāya*, II, 32; *Saṃyutta-Nikāya*, XII, 7, 61. 'Neither self-made the [human form or individual] is, nor are its misfortunes made by another. By reason of a cause [the human form or individual] came to be; by destruction of its causes it ceases.' *Saṃyutta-Nikāya*, V, 9.
11. *Brhad-āraṇyaka Upaniṣad*, IV, 4, 5.
12. *Bhagavad-Gītā*, XVIII, 63 & 65.
13. Radhakrishnan, *Indian Philosophy* I, p. 246.
14. Abhedananda, pp. 16–19.
15. 'The doctrine runs that the sum of each man's inheritance—his body, character, capacity, temperament, birth, belongings, and social position—and the whole of his experience in life, whether of happiness or of sorrow, together form the just recompense for his deeds, good and bad, done in former existences.' J.N. Farquhar, 'Karma: Its Value as a Doctrine of Life', *Hibbert Journal* 20 (1921–22), p. 20.
16. *Milindapañha*, III, 14, 2.
17. *Manu*, 11, 53–54.
18. 'Pray, lord, what is the reason, what is the cause why in this world some women are ill-favored, deformed, of mean appearance, [or lovely to look upon, amiable, and possessed of greatest beauty of complexion], and poor, having little of their own, of small possessions and are of small account [or wealthy, of great riches, of great possessions and of great account]?' *Aṅguttara-Nikāya*, IV, XX, 197.
19. 'Those whose conduct here has been good will quickly attain a good birth, the birth of a Brahmin, Kṣatriya or Vaiśya. Those whose conduct here has been evil, will quickly attain an evil birth, the birth of a dog, hog, or outcast.' *Chāndogya Upaniṣad*, V,10,7. For this in Buddhism, see *Digha-Nikāya*, XXXIII,5,4; *Aṅguttara-Nikāya*, IX, VII, 68.
20. Śaṅkara, *The Vedānta Sūtras of Bādarāyaṇa with the commentary by Śaṅkara*, trans. by George Thibaut (New York: Dover Pub. Inc., 1962), II,3,30.

21. Śaṅkara, II,3,33–40.
22. Śaṅkara, II,3,37.
23. Eliot Deutsch, *Advaita Vedānta: A Philosophical Reconstruction* (Honolulu: The University Press of Hawaii, 1973), pp. 61–3. The other two states of consciousness are the waking and dream states.
24. In response to the contention that the Naiyāyikas were concerned with logic and grammar and that their attention to liberation was mere 'lip service', Karl Potter writes, '[L]iberation is always on their minds even if not always uppermost in the question of the moment.' *Indian Metaphysics and Epistemology: The Tradition of Nyāya-Vaiśeṣika up to Gaṅgeśa* (Princeton: Princeton University Press, 1977), p. 24.
25. Praśastapāda, *Padārthadharmasaṃgraha*, 44.
26. Īśvara Kṛṣṇa, *Sāṅkhya-kārikā*, xix.
27. 'Of a certainty, therefore, not any spirit is bound or liberated, nor does any migrate; it is *prakṛti*, abiding in manifold forms, that is bound, is liberated, and migrates.' Īśvara Kṛṣṇa, lxii.
28. The fundamental problem with Sāṅkhya-Yoga's view of the self is the failure to establish any ground for a relation between the *puruṣa* and *buddhi*, for on the one hand only when the empirical self is the reflective juncture of them is the conscious self possible. On the other hand, as absolute within their own spheres any relation between them can be apparent only; to think there is a real relation is a product of ignorance which must be removed if liberation is to be attained.
29. In Sāṅkhya-Yoga, of course, it is the reflection which acts as agent, but its consciousness which is essential for intentional action arises because it reflects the *puruṣa*. The *puruṣa* then is involved in intentional action in a more indirect way than in the other two systems.
30. According to David Kalupahana, early Buddhism only emphasized the impermanence of the self: momentariness is a later feature introduced by Buddhist scholars of the Abhidharma tradition. *Buddhist Philosophy: a Historical Analysis* (Honolulu: University of Hawaii, 1976), p. 36.
31. There is much more to be said about the Buddhist concept of the human person. We shall explore this in detail in Chapter 8.
32. As one Buddhist author puts it, 'Indeed, one might also gather that even the active side, or choice, of the present is largely determined by the past kamma. In *this* sense, the Dhamma teaches that "free-will" is an illusion. But the Blessed One has declared that a being can mould kamma itself. *One can modify or alter, in the present, a past inherited kamma. . . .* The Dhamma, the Middle Doctrine, therefore steers clear of both "determinism" and "libertarianism".' Cassius Pereira, 'An Elucidation of Kamma', *The Buddhist Review* 9 (1917), p. 61. Unfortunately this author says nothing more about this middle way between determinism and indeterminism. His attempt to avoid both determinism and libertarianism sounds very much like an attempt to arrive at a compatibilist theory. Yet his

'largely determined' renders this interpretation uncertain and perhaps somewhat indeterministic.

33. F. Th. Stcherbatsky, *Buddhist Logic* I (New York: Dover Publications, 1962), pp. 124–5.
34. *Aṅguttara-Nikāya,* III, 99.
35. D.T. Suzuki, *Outlines of Mahayana Buddhism* (New York: Schocken Books, 1963), pp. 196, 198.
36. *Saṃyutta-Nikāya,* XXXVI,II,3,21; *Aṅguttara-Nikāya,* IV,IX, 87.
37. Sheryl Daniel notes that Tamil villagers use the perspective of fatalism or indeterminism to account for events according to which is most advantageous to them. This often means that they switch between these explanations with no apparent recognition of the inconsistency. 'They rarely choose to consistently favor one perspective to the exclusion of the other. Rather, the choice of perspective is a context-sensitive one determined by needs and biases, among other factors. . . . The result is not only what appears to be conflicting perspectives of reality but conflicting judgments concerning the moral responsibility of the individual in question.' 'The Tool Box Approach of the Tamil to the Issues of Moral Responsibility and Human Destiny', in Charles F. Keyes and E. Valentine Daniel (eds.), *Karma: An Anthropological Inquiry* (Berkeley: University of California Press, 1983), p. 41. She also ties the perspective taken to the person's sense of self. A positive sense of self leads to adopting an indeterminist viewpoint that one can change one's fate or headwriting. A negative sense leads one to acquiesce to what one conceives to be one's fate (p. 49).
38. For a thorough discussion of the roots and role of fatalism in Indian thought see Sukumari Bhattacharji, 'Fatalism—Its Roots and Effects', *Journal of Indian Philosophy* 10 (1982), pp. 135–54.

Chapter 5

1. As I have argued elsewhere, in order to establish a logical inconsistency between God's existence and possession of certain properties and the existence of pain and suffering, another proposition is required, namely, that God can eliminate every evil state of affairs without losing a greater good or producing a greater evil. Unfortunately, there is no good reason for thinking this last claim is true. Indeed, to the contrary, there is good reason to think it is false, for there are cases in which it is logically impossible to remove an evil without removing a greater good. This is the case with respect to many human virtues. For example, the virtue of courage cannot be maintained without the evil of fear or an evil which is feared. Further, the removal of all moral evils would entail the removal of human freedom and of the moral good which it makes possible. For a more extensive defence of this thesis, see Bruce R. Reichenbach, *Evil and a Good God* (New York: Fordham University Press, 1982), ch. 1.

2. For the analysis and critique of the inductive argument from evil, see Reichenbach, ch. 2.
3. The distinction between a defence and a theodicy is this. A defence attempts to establish that there is no incompatibility between God's existence and possession of certain characteristics and the existence of evil, or that the quantity, quality and intensity of evil in the world does not make improbable God's existence. That is, a defence attempts to refute the claim that evil counts decisively or probably against God's existence. However, it makes no pretension to suggesting what morally sufficient reason God might have for allowing pain and suffering. The creation of plausible morally sufficient reasons is the task of a theodicy.
4. Arthur Herman, *The Problem of Evil and Indian Thought* (Delhi: Motilal Banarsidass, 1976), pp. 235, 251. Herman argues that in the exceptional cases where the theological problem is taken up, it is done so only as a side issue in the defence of the thesis that Brahma created the world. An example of this is found in an argument by Aśvaghosa attacking theism. 'Lord Buddha is said to have argued thus with one Anāthapiṇḍika and attacked the idea of an all-powerful God: "If the world had been made by Īśvara there should be no such thing as sorrow or calamity, as right or wrong, seeing that all things, pure and impure, must come from him. If sorrow and joy, love and hate, which spring up in all conscious beings, be the work of Īśvara, he himself must be capable of sorrow and joy, love and hatred, and if he has these, how can he be said to be perfect?"' *Buddhacarita*, quoted in Herman, p. 245. A second example confirming Herman's thesis is provided by the context of Śaṅkara's and Rāmānuja's discussion of the issue. Śaṅkara, *The Vedānta Sūtras of Bādarāyana, with the commentary by Śaṅkara*, vol. I, tr. George Thibaut (New York: Dover Publications, 1960), II,1,34. Rāmānuja, *The Vedānta Sūtras of Bādarāyaṇa with the Commentary by Rāmānuja*, tr. George Thibaut (Delhi: Motilal Banarsidass, 1962), II 1,32–6.
5. Karl Potter (ed.), *Indian Metaphysics and Epistemology: The Tradition of Nyāya-Vaiśeṣika up to Gaṅgeśa* (Princeton: Princeton University Press, 1977), p. 100.
6. Bhāsarvajña, *Nyāyasāra*, 3,42. See Potter, p. 34.
7. *Bṛhad-āranyaka Upaniṣad*, III,9,1–24.
8. 'The fact is that we cannot properly look for any theistic view in the Upaniṣads whose main concern is with the philosophic Absolute, except where that Absolute itself is personified and spoken of as God.' Mysore Hiriyanna, *Outlines of Indian Philosophy* (London: George Allen and Unwin, 1932), p. 82.
9. '*Brahman*, indeed, was this in the beginning. It knew itself only as "I am *Brahman*." . . . Whoever knows thus, "I am *Brahman*," becomes this all. Even the gods cannot prevent his becoming thus, for he becomes their self. So whoever worships another divinity (than his self) thinking that he is one and (*Brahman*) another, he knows not.' *Bṛhad-āranyaka Upaniṣad*, I,4,10.
10. *Taittirīya Upaniṣad*, II,4; *Kena Upaniṣad*, I, 1–9.

11. *Chāndogya Upaniṣad*, III, 14, 1–4.
12. 'He is to be seen as beyond the three kinds of time (past, present and future), and as without parts after having worshipped first that adorable God who has many forms, the origin of all being, who abides in one's own thought. Higher and other than the forms of the world-tree and time is he from whom this world revolves, who brings good and removes evil, the lord of prosperity, having known Him as in one's own self, the immortal, the support of all (he attains *Brahman*). He in whom is the Supreme Lord of lords, who is the highest deity of deities, . . . let us know as God, the lord of the world, the adorable. . . . The wise who perceive Him as abiding in their self, to them belongs eternal happiness, not to others. . . . That cause which is to be apprehended by discrimination and discipline (*yoga*)—by knowing God, one is freed from all fetters.' *Śvetāśvatara Upaniṣad*, VI, 5–7, 12–13.
13. Hiriyanna, pp. 366–7.
14. Eliot Deutsch, *Advaita Vedānta* (Honolulu: The University Press of Hawaii, 1973), p. 13.
15. Hiriyanna, p. 367.
16. Śaṅkara, II,1,14.
17. Śaṅkara, I,2,13.
18. Śaṅkara, II,1,33.
19. Śaṅkara, II,1,34.
20. *Bhagavad-Gītā*, VII, 24; X, 12.
21. 'On Me all this universe is strung, like heaps of pearls on a string.' *Bhagavad-Gītā*, VII, 6–7. Also IX, 7–8.
22. He makes 'all beings go around by his mysterious power (*māyā*), as if they were fixed on a revolving machine.' *Bhagavad-Gītā*, XVIII, 61. Also XV, 12–15.
23. *Bhagavad-Gītā*, VII, 12.
24. *Bhagavad-Gītā*, X, 4–5. See also X, 36–38.
25. One such attempt is found in this same context in the *Bhagavad-Gītā*. 'Might of the almighty am I, too, such as is free from desire and passion; so far as it is not inconsistent with right, in creatures I am desire.' VII, 11.
26. *Bhagavad-Gītā*, VII, 16, 19; VIII, 13; IX, 22, 25; XVIII, 65–6.
27. *Bhagavad-Gītā*, IV, 7–8.
28. *Bhagavad-Gītā*, IX, 30–31.
29. Similar concerns can be found in Mahāyāna Buddhism, with its emphasis on Buddhas and Bodhisatvas bestowing grace.
30. Patañjali, *Yoga-sūtra* I, 23. Actually, none of the *puruṣas* really suffer the afflictions, but all but God appear to do so and hence (appear to) need liberation.
31. Patañjali, II, 1,32,45. This is listed as one of the observances (*niyamas*) of the accessories or yogic path.
32. Patañjali, I, 27–31.
33. Patañjali, I, 26. How this accords with the inactivity of God is difficult to fathom.

34. 'God has the fulfilment of the purpose of the purusha as His own purpose, for which He behaves as the prime mover.' Vācaspati, *Tattravaiśāradī*, IV, 3. Quoted in Surendranath Dasgupta, *Yoga as Philosophy and Religion* (Delhi: Motilal Banarsidass, 1978), pp. 89–90. The question, of course, is whether one can have purposes without desires.
35. For example, Tatia writes of the Jaina view of God, 'It is only those rare souls, who have acquired the potency of revealing the truth and establishing a religious community by their moral and virtuous activities of the past life, that are capable of revealing the truth and preaching it to the world at large on their attainment of omniscience. Such souls become the founders of religion, who are the embodiment of the best and highest virtues that the human mind can conceive of, the fullest expression of the potentialities of embodied existence. This is the Jaina conception of Godhead. God, according to the Jainas, is the symbol of all that is good and great, moral and virtuous. But he is not the creator or the preserver or the destroyer. He is not in any sense responsible for the destiny of the universe or the individual. Nor is he capable of granting grace to any individual. Nor is he himself eternally free, but has worked out his own freedom exactly in the same way as the others do.' In short, each and every special person who, as enlightened, is qualified to preach the truth to others is a god. Nathmal Tatia, *Studies in Jaina Philosophy* (Benares: Jain Cultural Research Society, 1951), p. 268.
36. In what follows, we shall treat Śaṅkara and Rāmānuja more as theists interested in resolving the theistic problem of evil than they really were. Our purpose is to use them to construct how a Hindu theist in this general tradition might use the law of karma to resolve the theistic problem of evil.
37. Śaṅkara, II,1,34. Rāmānuja agrees (II,1,34).
38. Moral evil may be defined as all the instances of pain and suffering—physical and mental—and all states of affairs significantly disadvantageous to the organism which are caused by actions for which human agents can be held morally blameworthy. Natural evil is all similar instances for which human agents cannot be held morally blameworthy. Examples of this latter kind are pain and suffering caused by creatures of nature, natural forces such as wind, hail, lightning and movements of the earth, and painful diseases, dysfunction and premature death caused by natural organisms such as viruses or by genetic defects. See Reichenbach, pp. xi–xii.
39. For a more detailed analysis of omnipotence, see Reichenbach, ch. 8.
40. Śaṅkara and Rāmānuja, II,1,33.
41. Śaṅkara, II,1,32.
42. Contemporary popular Hinduism preserves the thesis that the gods act out of sport. Though this divine sport is viewed as senseless from the human perspective, it is also seen as suprarational and possessing the purpose of balancing the disequilibrium in the world created by desire. That it has a purpose, even in a transcendent

sense, is inconsistent with its exculpatory use in Śaṅkara. However, it supports our contention that engaging in sport is a purposeful activity. See Sheryl B. Daniel, 'The Tool Box Approach of the Tamil to the Issues of Moral Responsibility and Human Destiny', in Charles F. Keyes and E. Valentine Daniel (eds.), *Karma: An Anthropological Inquiry* (Berkeley: University of California Press, 1983), pp. 51–60.

43. It is interesting to note that in the passage where Śaṅkara speaks only of Brahman modifying himself in the causative process, Rāmānuja speaks of Brahman who is 'desirous of creating' the world. I,4,26.
44. Śaṅkara and Rāmānuja, II,1,35. For a discussion of this, see Herman, pp. 278–83.
45. Rāmānuja, II,1,35.
46. Rāmānuja, I,4,26 & 27.
47. For the significance of this distinction in Western theistic thought, see Reichenbach, pp. 130–8.
48. This applies not only to any first creation, but to the re-creation after the periodic dissolutions.

Chapter 6

1. For a detailed description, see Wilhelm Halbfass, 'Karma, *Apūrva*, and "Natural" Causes: Observations on the Growth and Limits of the Theory of *Saṃsāra*' in Wendy D. O'Flaherty (ed.), *Karma and Rebirth in Classical Indian Traditions* (Berkeley: University of California Press, 1980), pp. 273–84.
2. Kaṇāda, *Vaiśeṣikā Sūtra*, V,2,7 & 13 & 17.
3. Kaṇāda, VI,2,11–15; see Halbfass, pp. 284–90.
4. For a discussion of the various degrees of units of intensity of karmic matter, see Nathmal Tatia, *Studies in Jaina Philosophy* (Benares: Jain Cultural Research Society, 1951), pp. 235–8. The classification is strictly a priori, without any empirical evidence. Indeed, there can be none, since material karma is invisible.
5. Sarvepalli Radhakrishnan, *Indian Philosophy* I (New York: Macmillan and Co., 1923), p. 319. This is similar to the subtle body in Vedānta, which we shall discuss in Chapter 7.
6. Their description of the operations of the self and karma makes abundant use of metaphor and analogy. 'Even as a lamp by its temperature draws up the oil with its wick and, after drawing up, converts the oil into its body (viz. glow), exactly so does a soul-lamp, with the attributes of attachment and the like, attract the material aggregates by the wick of its activities and, after attracting, transforms them into *karman*.' *Tattvārthasūtra-Bhāṣya with Siddhaseṇaganin's Ṭikā*, quoted in Tatia, p. 232.
7. The examples are taken from Tatia, ch. 4.
8. Tatia, p. 252.
9. *Saṃyutta-Nikāya*, XII,2,20; quoted in David Kalupahana, *Causality: The Central Philosophy of Buddhism* (Honolulu: The University Press of Hawaii, 1975), p. 55. That is, causation is an objective relationship

between events, not a subjective imposition.

10. 'Because of the epistemological standpoint he adopted, the Buddha was able to formulate an empiricist theory of causality without getting involved in either of these [Sāṅkhya and Sarvāstivāda vs. Vaiśeṣika and Sautrāntika] metaphysical doctrines.' The former emphasized the identity of cause and effect, while the latter held to their difference. David Kalupahana, *Buddhist Philosophy: A Historical Analysis* (Honolulu: University of Hawaii Press, 1976), p. 29.
11. T.W. Rhys Davids, 'On Nirvāna, and on the Buddhist Doctrines of the "Groups," the Saṅskāras, Karma and the "Paths,"' *Contemporary Review* 29 (1877), p. 258.
12. Edward Conze [*Buddhist Thought in India* (Ann Arbor: The University of Michigan Press, 1967), p. 149] argues that the concept of productivity is absent in Buddhaghosa's analysis of causation. 'There is no real production; there is only interdependence.' On the other hand, David Kalupahana (*Causality*, pp. 73, 75, 81–2) contends that it is found in the Sarvāstivādins, the Sautrāntikas and the later Theravādins. The former held that the static moment during which an event existed had causal efficacy, whereas the latter two assigned causal efficacy to the preceding event (*dharma*).
13. Some speak of a consciousness which carries over from one set of *skandhas* to another. (Kalupahana, *Buddhist Philosophy*, p. 32.) But this seems contrary to Buddhist metaphysics, where there is nothing permanent to carry over between events. Others speak of the consciousness which arises as functionally dependent upon prior consciousness. For example, Buddhaghosa speaks of a rebirth-linking consciousness. This is not a consciousness which is carried over from one birth to another, but newly arises in the reborn, though as causally conditioned. (See James P. McDermott, 'Karma and Rebirth in Early Buddhism', in *Karma and Rebirth*, pp. 169–70.) But the Buddha also denied that things newly arise. This reflects the tension in the Buddhist attempt to find a middle ground between eternalism and annihilationism.
14. The *avijñapti* was also introduced to resolve another problem. In particular, it was invoked to explain how an act which had results which were separated in time and space from the agent's volition (for example, where person A willed the murder of another and commanded it, but where it was carried out later by person B) affected the agent. It was held that an *avijñapti* was created when the volition of the agent culminated in the act and that this caused the appropriate disposition in the agent of the volition. See Surama Dasgupta, *Development of Moral Philosophy in India* (New York: Frederick Ungar Publishing Co., 1961), pp. 153–4, 167–71.
15. 'Over and above the stream of thought which proceeds from moment to moment the Sautrāntikas introduce a "substratum", again a polite word for the "person", in which they anchor all the possibilities of this continuity. The "substratum" is the psychophysical organism, or the body endowed with organs, and

it is the support of thought and its concomitants.' Conze, p. 142.

16. *The Pali Jātaka*, 222; quoted in D.T. Suzuki, *Outlines of Mahayana Buddhism* (New York: Schocken Books, 1963), p. 184.
17. Suzuki, p. 212. The agricultural metaphor is also used in Hinduism, perhaps through Buddhist influence. For example, it is found in the *Yoga-bhāṣya* of Vyāsa (II, 4). Śaṅkara employs the seed metaphor [*The Vedānta Sūtras of Bādarāyaṇa with the commentary by Śaṅkara*, tr. George Thibaut (New York: Dover Publications, Inc., 1962), III,1,1], as do contemporary Hindu philosophers. For example, G.R. Malkani writes, 'Every moral action . . . produces its own *apūrva* [unperceived potency linking the action and result] or *adṛṣṭa* [unseen sum total of merit and demerit], something that is subtle and invisible and therefore not empirically knowable, but potent like a well-kept seed.' 'Some Criticisms of the Karmic Law by Prof. Warren E. Steinkraus Answered', *The Philosophical Quarterly* (India) 38 (Oct. 1965), p. 160.
18. Suzuki, pp. 204–5.
19. Suzuki, p. 42.
20. 'The Dharmakāya, which literally means "body or system of being", is the ultimate reality which underlies all particular phenomena; it is that which makes the existence of individuals possible; it is the *raison d'être* of the universe; it is the norm of being, which regulates the course of events and thoughts. . . . It does not stand transcendentally above the universe, which . . . is a manifestation of the Dharmakāya himself. It . . . is not absolutely impersonal, [but] is capable of willing and reflecting; . . . it is love and intelligence, and not the mere state of being.' Suzuki, pp. 45–6.
21. 'Potential karma stored from time out of mind is saturated in every fibre of . . . the *Ālayavijñāna*.' Suzuki, p. 201.
22. Suzuki, pp. 66–7.
23. Suzuki, p. 165.
24. Suzuki says that the Ālayavijñana is "indifferent to" that which occurs in its evolutes (p. 67).
25. Suzuki, pp. 66–7. This might be termed the acosmic view, in that the Absolute only seems to become (gives the illusion of becoming) the many.
26. Suzuki, chs. 5 and 6. This might be termed the cosmic view, in that the Absolute somehow evolves into the many, while at the same time maintaining its unity and undifferentiatedness. As we have noted, both the acosmic and cosmic views can be found in the Upaniṣads and are echoed in Vedānta (as we shall see in the next chapter).
27. 'The solution of the contradiction lies in the fact that there is no separate efficiency, no efficiency in superaddition to existence, existence itself is nothing but causal efficacy, the cause and the thing are different views taken of one and the same reality. . . . If we identify reality and causal efficiency, we can say that every reality is at the same time a cause.' F. Th. Stcherbatsky, *Buddhist Logic* I (New York: Dover Publications, 1962), pp. 125–6.

28. Edward Conze, *Buddhism: Its Essence and Development* (Oxford: Bruno Cassirer, 1951), p. 156.
29. This, of course, is a philosophical thesis, based on the claim of the sufficiency of the law of karma to resolve the problem of evil and good. In popular practice both Hindus and Buddhists often trace the cause of their pleasure and pain to something other than their past karmic deeds. They appeal to natural causes, other human agents working directly or through sorcery, the anger of spirits and divinities, and astrological conditions. Whether this is to be taken as evidence that they deny the universality of the karmic thesis is debated. The answer depends upon the relation of karma to these other conditions. One view is that, for some at least, it is one explanation among others or a final resort which might be invoked on rare occasions when no other explanation suffices. [Charles F. Keyes, 'Merit-Transference in the Kammic Theory of Popular Theravāda Buddhism', in Charles F. Keyes and E. Valentine Daniel (eds), *Karma: An Anthropological Inquiry* (Berkeley: University of California Press, 1983), pp. 266–7.] With no apparent concern for consistency, the adherent appeals to the causes which at that time best reflect his perspective or the point he wishes to make. Sheryl Daniel refers to this as the 'Tool Box Approach'. 'The Tool Box Approach of the Tamil to the Issues of Moral Responsibility and Human Destiny', in *Karma: An Anthropological Inquiry*, pp. 59–60. One way to attempt to resolve the apparent inconsistency is to claim that the law of karma functions as an ultimate explanation which lies behind other, middle level explanations. [See Paul G. Hieber, 'Karma in a South Indian Village', in *Karma: An Anthropological Inquiry*, pp. 124, 129–30.] For example, it is the person's karma which makes him susceptible to the actions of gods and to sorcery. [Ursula Sharma, 'Theodicy and the Doctrine of Karma', *Man* 8 (1973), p. 358.] Here, where the law works through intermediaries, its universality is preserved.
30. Perhaps the recognition of this is part of the reason some Buddhists deny that all pleasure and pain result from past karmic deeds, or affirm that karma is subjective and hence does not cause material conditions, only the pleasure and pain that we experience. [For a discussion of this in the *Kathāvatthu* and *Milindapañha*, see James McDermott, 'The *Kathāvatthu* Kamma Debates', *Journal of the American Oriental Society* 95 (1975), pp. 426–8, and 'Kamman in the *Milindapañha*', *Journal of the American Oriental Society* 97 (1977), pp. 465–6. To hold to the first contention, the Buddhist must sacrifice the thesis that the law of karma completely suffices to explain good and evil, for if some goods and evils do not result from past karmic deeds, then either they are the product of chance (which the *Milindapañha* seems to accept but which the law of karma was introduced to deny)—or else they occur for some other reason (which is not contradictory but considerably weakens the karmic thesis and the reason for accepting it by destroying its universality). The second contention is problematic in that it is hard to see how

karma could account for our experiences without causally influencing that which produces them (namely, the environment and other agents).

31. Halbfass, p. 290.
32. Śaṅkara, III,2,38 and 41.
33. '[The existence of God can be inferred] from dependence,—from eternity,—from diversity,—from universal practice,—and from the apportionment to each individual self,—mundane enjoyment implies a supernatural cause.' Udayana Ācārya, *Kusumāñjali* I,4; in Sarvepalli Radhakrishnan and Charles Moore (eds), *A Sourcebook in Indian Philosophy* (Princeton, N.J.: Princeton University Press, 1957), pp. 380–1.
34. Uddyotakara, *Nyāyavārttika* IV,1,21.
35. Of course, behind all this lies the critical question of the nature of the God invoked, i.e., whether he is active or immobile, possesses telic will or not, is personal or impersonal, how related to *Brahman*, etc. We sketched this out in the previous chapter.
36. G.R. Malkani, p. 159.
37. Patañjali, *Yoga-sūtra*, I, 29.
38. Kewal Krishna Anand, *Indian Philosophy* (Delhi: Bharatiya Vidya Prakashan, 1982?), pp. 342–3. See also Śaṅkara, II,1,34.

Chapter 7

1. Later interpreters abandoned the imperceptibility thesis, holding that it can be perceived by a person's internal organs. See Karl Potter, *Indian Metaphysics and Epistemology: The Tradition of Nyāya-Vaiśeṣika up to Gaṅgeśa* (Princeton, N.J.: Princeton University Press, 1977), p. 96.
2. Praśastapāda, *Padārthadharmasamgraha*, 44.
3. Sarvepalli Radhakrishnan, *Indian Philosophy* II (London: George Allen and Unwin, Ltd., 1931), p. 603.
4. For Vaiśeṣika-Nyāya, the internal organ is termed the *manas*. It is an atomic substance which is responsible for receiving sensory material and passing it on narrowed down so that the self can attend to it. It transmigrates with the *ātman* but it cannot function in an out-of-the-body state. Expressing the view of Advaita Vedānta, Śaṅkara writes, 'The internal organ which constitutes the limiting adjunct of the soul is called in different places by different names, such as manas (mind), buddhi (intelligence), vijñāna (knowledge), citta (thought). This difference of nomenclature is sometimes made dependent on the difference of the modifications of the internal organ which is called manas when it is in the state of doubt, etc., buddhi when it is in the state of determination and the like.' Śaṅkara, *The Vedānta Sūtras of Bādarāyana, with the commentary Śaṅkara*, tr. George Thibaut (New York: Dover Publications, 1962), II,3,32.
5. Śaṅkara, II,3,18.
6. *Bṛhad-āranyaka Upaniṣad* II,1,16.

7. Kaṇāda, *Vaiśeṣika Sūtra,* III,2,20.
8. Śaṅkara, II,3,53.
9. Gautama, *Nyāyasūtras,* III,1,18–26.
10. Gautama, IV,1,44–45.
11. Śaṅkara, II,3,33. *Kaṭha Upaniṣad,* I,3,4.
12. Potter, p. 35.
13. Potter, pp. 97–9. Śaṅkara suggests a similar criticism. II,3,53.
14. Nyāya, later Vaiśeṣika, and Advaita Vedānta, on the other hand, argued that the self can be known directly by intuition.
15. Śaṅkara, I,1,4. Though Śaṅkara's argument is intended to establish the existence of the *ātman,* since the argument takes place within the context of a judgement and involves ignorance about the true nature of the Self, the most it can establish is the existence of the *jīva.*
16. Śaṅkara, IV,1,2. For the Vaiśeṣika statement to the same effect, see Praśastapāda, 44.
17. Vātsyāyana, *Nyāyabhāsya,* I, 10.
18. Kaṇāda, III,2,6 and 9–18. See also Praśastapāda, 44; Uddyotakara, *Nyāyavārttika,* III,1,Introduction.
19. Kaṇāda, III,1,3–4.
20. Kaṇāda, II,1,13; III,2,5. *The Kaṭha Upaniṣad* (II,1,13) adds the further characteristic of being essentially unchanging.
21. Śaṅkara, III,3,54.
22. Śaṅkara, III,3,53.
23. Śaṅkara, III,3,53.
24. Śaṅkara, II,3,40; II,3,18.
25. Śaṅkara, III,3,54.
26. Śaṅkara, III,3,54.
27. Śaṅkara, III,3,54. See also Praśastapāda, 44 for this argument in the Vaiśeṣika tradition.
28. This should not be thought to contradict my above thesis that spatio–temporal continuity is not a necessary condition for every instance of personal identity. That it is not such a condition is consistent with the application of such a criterion in most instances.
29. Uddyotakara, III,1,25–6.
30. Śaṅkara, III,3,54. See also Praśastapāda, 44.
31. In passing one might wonder why this particular argument was ignored. The answer, consistent with our discussion in Chapter 4, is that the Hindu was concerned with freedom in the sense of liberation from *saṃsāra,* from the toilsome cycle of rebirths. Indeed, ultimately this liberation constitutes the central focus of all Hindu thought. As such, there was little interest in dealing with freedom in the sense used in this argument.
32. Potter, p. 70.
33. Śaṅkara, III,1,1–27; IV,2,1–21.
34. Nathmal Tatia, *Studies in Jaina Philosophy* (Benares: Jain Cultural Research Society, 1951), pp. 225–6. Interestingly enough, Tatia's objection to the other Indian schools is their failure to admit the direct identity-cum-difference between the soul and the material.

If the *manas* is to relate them, it must be related to both. Hence, in the very *manas* there is this feature.

35. Not all Indian schools hold to an intermediate existence. For the Jainas, Yogins, and Theravādins the reincarnation or rebirth is immediate.
36. J. Bruce Long reports that he has 'found no passage [in the Mahābhārata] that attempts to account for the exact means by which each soul finds its way into the womb and thence into the family whose moral and social standing is commensurate with the "merital" status of the *jīva*. Nor is it stated how moral entities such as good and bad acts become attached to and are transported by physical entities such as wind, fire, water, breath, sperm and blood.' 'The Concepts of Human Action and Rebirth in the *Mahābhārata*', in Wendy D. O'Flaherty, *Karma and Rebirth in Classical Indian Traditions* (Berkeley: University of California Press, 1980), pp. 59–60.
37. *Chāndogya Upaniṣad*, V,10,6.
38. Śaṅkara, III,2,41.
39. Wilhelm Halbfass, 'Karma, *Apūrva*, and "Natural" Causes: Observations on the Growth and Limits of the Theory of *Saṃsāra*,' in *Karma and Rebirth*, p. 290.

Chapter 8

1. D.T. Suzuki, *Outlines of Mahayana Buddhism* (New York: Schocken Books, 1963), pp. 204–5. Cassius Pereira ['An Elucidation of Kamma', *The Buddhist Review* 9 (1917), p. 61] speaks of this continuing vitality in the traditional language of 'current-of-being'.
2. K.N. Jayatillake, 'The Case for the Buddhist Theory of Survival and Karma', *Mahabodhi* (Colombo) 77 (1969), pp. 334–40, 371–6; 78 (1970), pp. 2–6, 350–5.
3. *Majjhima-Nikāya*, sutta 63.
4. *Majjhima-Nikāya*, sutta 72.
5. For example, 'The correct view in light of the highest knowledge is as follows: "This is not mine; this am I not; this is not my self."' *Saṃyutta-Nikāya*, xxii, 85. The exact meaning of the Buddha's silence about or refusal to identify the self is somewhat in doubt. For example, some have attempted to show that the Buddha believed in a soul or self, but remained silent about it because it was non-empirical and discussion concerning it did not lead to edification. See T.W. Rhys Davids, *The Birth of Indian Psychology and its Development in Buddhism* (London: Luzac & Co., 1936), pp. 206–14. More recently David Kalupahana writes that what the Buddha denied was that the five aggregates are the permanent and eternal self; he did not actually deny a 'self' that is over and above, or not identical with, the aggregates. 'His silence on these questions was interpreted as implying that there *is* a reality, a transcendental "self", but that it does not come within the sphere of logical reasoning.' *Buddhist Philosophy: A Historical Analysis* (Honolulu: University Press of Hawaii, 1976), pp. 40–1. See also G.S.P. Misra,

'The Buddhist Theory of Karman and Some Related Problems', *The Vishva-Bharati Journal of Philosophy* 8, no. 2 (1972), p. 41. What the Buddha actually believed about the self remains a historical problem. Whatever the case, our thesis that some metaphysical point of view underlies his assertions and denials is sustained.

6. *Saṃyutta-Nikāya*, xxii, 85. See also the Mahā-Nidāna-Sutta, in *Dīgha-Nikāya*, in Henry Clark Warren, ed., *Buddhism in Translations* (New York: Atheneum, 1973), p. 137: '. . . A priest no longer holds the view that the Ego has no sensation, no longer holds the view that the Ego has sensation, [or] possesses the faculty of sensation; he ceases to attach himself to anything in the world, and being free from attachment, he is never agitated . . . and attains to Nirvana in his own person; and he knows that rebirth is exhausted. . . .'
7. *Majjhima-Nikāya*, sutta 72.
8. According to the Pudgalavādins, the law of karma presupposes rebirth of the person who dies, otherwise justice would not be upheld because someone other than the doer of the action would be rewarded or punished. But rebirth is impossible without a person who transmigrates. This person or *pudgala*, which is the agent for a person's actions, is the connecting link between one life and the next. However, in attempting to maintain the *anātman* doctrine, they argued that the ineffable *pudgala* was neither identical with the *skandhas* nor different from them, but a substance which was neither conditioned nor unconditioned but exists through them. Their view was rejected by the Theravādins on the ground that the substratum introduced was nothing else than a soul or self in disguise. See Edward Conze, *Buddhist Thought in India* (Ann Arbor: The University of Michigan Press, 1967), pp. 121–33.
9. Conze, p. 97. In contrast to F. Th. Stcherbatsky and Conze, that *dharmas* are momentary is held by recent interpreters to be a contribution of Abhidharma thought. See David Kalupahana, *Causality: The Central Philosophy of Buddhism* (Honolulu: The University Press of Hawaii, 1975), pp. 71–2.
10. Conze, p. 112.
11. *Milindapañha*, II,1,1; translation from Warren, pp. 132, 133.
12. 'In the ultimate sense the life-moment of living beings is extremely short, being only as long as the occurrence of a single conscious moment.' Buddhaghosa, *Visuddhi-Magga*, viii, par. 39. For a brief account of this conflict, see Y. Karunadasa, 'The Buddhist Doctrine of Impermanence', *Mahabodhi* 77 (1969), pp. 217–8.
13. Jayatillake, pp. 372–3.
14. Suzuki, p. 213.
15. '. . . So too, when there are the five aggregates [as object] of clinging, there comes to be the mere term of common usage "a being," "a person", yet in the ultimate sense, when each component is examined, there is no being as a basis for the assumption "I am" or "I"; in the ultimate sense there is only name and form.' Buddhaghosa, xviii, par. 28.

16. *Milindapañha*, III,4,2.
17. 'For when, in any existence, one arrives at the gate of death . . . and the body dries up by degrees and the eye-sight and other senses fail, . . . then consciousness residing in that last refuge, the heart, continues to exist by virtue of karma, otherwise called the predispositions. This karma, however, still retains something of what it depends on, and consists of such former deeds as were weighty, much practised, and are now close at hand, or else this this karma creates a reflex of itself or of the new mode of life now being entered upon, and it is with this as its object that consciousness continues to exist.' Buddhaghosa, xvii, par. 163; translation from Warren, p. 238.
18. Buddhaghosa, xvii, par. 163.
19. 'Your majesty, to be born here and die here, to die here and be born elsewhere, to be born there and die there, to die there and be born elsewhere,—this, your majesty, is the round of existence.' *Milindapañha*, III,6,9.
20. *Milindapañha*, III,5,5.
21. Paul J. Griffiths, 'Notes Towards a Critique of Buddhist Karmic Theory', *Religious Studies* 18 (Sept. 1982), pp. 283–4.
22. *Milindapañha*, II,2,6; translation from Warren, p. 236.

Chapter 9

1. G.R. Malkani, 'The Rationale of the Law of Karma', *The Philosophical Quarterly* (India) 37, (Jan. 1965), p. 263.
2. Surendranath Dasgupta speaks of this motive with respect to achieving the highest good. '. . . The ethical goal, the ideal to be realized, is absolute freedom or kaivalya, and we shall now consider the line of action that must be adopted to attain this goal—the *summum bonum*. . . . The motive therefore which prompts a person towards this ethico-metaphysical goal is the avoidance of pain.' *Yoga as Philosophy and Religion* (Delhi: Motilal Banarsidass, 1978), p. 122.
3. This argument, if sound, would establish the truth of the principle of universal justice but not its necessity. That is, from 'p implies q' and 'necessarily not-q', only 'not-p', not 'necessarily not-p', follows.
4. I have argued for this in Bruce R. Reichenbach, *Evil and a Good God* (New York: Fordham University Press, 1982), ch. 5.
5. Luang Suriyabongs, *Buddhism in the Light of Modern Scientific Ideas* (Bangkok: Mahumakuta-Raja-Vidyalaya Press, 1954), p. 72; quoted in 'Is There Group Karma in Theravāda Buddhism?' James P. McDermott, *Numen* 23 (1976), p. 67. On the other side, Karl Potter argues that 'it produces more confusion than clarity to allow notions such as "group karma," "transfer of merit," etc. to constitute variations on a common theme. I prefer now to view such "variations" as in fact departures from *the* theory of karma.' 'Critical Response', in Ronald Neufeldt (ed.), *Karma and Rebirth: Post-Classical Developments*

(Albany: State University of New York Press, 1986), p. 110. Despite Potter's disinclination, the prevalence of these concepts requires that they be considered in a philosophical treatment of karma.

6. McDermott, p. 75.
7. 'I call a collectivity an aggregate if the identity of that collective consists in the sum of the identities of the persons who comprise the membership of the collectivity.' Peter French, 'Collective Responsibility and the Practice of Medicine', *The Journal of Medicine and Philosophy* 7, no. 1 (Feb. 1982), p. 70.
8. French, p. 72.
9. 'Performance' here should be understood in a broad sense to include any contributing act, from planning or ordering the deed to actually carrying it out.
10. This would occur, for example, when my intentional decisions for the group to do wrong are mitigated by the group's action, such that the consequences I derive from the group's action are better than what I would have merited had I experienced the results of my own intentions.

Chapter 10

1. 'It is at the point when rebirth in heaven was no longer a process that the individual could accomplish alone, that the idea of transfer (originally of food, but soon after of a combination of food and merit) must have been introduced. For the descendants gave their ancestors part of their own religious merit (including the merit of having performed the *śrāddha!*) along with the ball of seed-rice; this enabled the *preta* to move "up" out of limbo, to the mutual benefit of the *preta* (who could now get on with the task of rebirth) and the living descendant (who could no longer be haunted by the *preta*). Thus the *śrāddha* represents an exchange of food and merit flowing in both directions.' Wendy D. O'Flaherty, 'Karma and Rebirth in the Vedas and Purāṇas', in Wendy D. O'Flaherty (ed.), *Karma and Rebirth in Classical Indian Traditions* (Berkeley: University of California Press, 1980), pp. 10–11.
2. 'On the one hand, throughout much of the Pāli canon there is a strong emphasis on the personal nature of *kamma*. One's *kamma* is said to be his own. . . . On the other hand, a doctrine of transfer of merit—apparently a popular development traceable to the Brahmanic *śrāddha* rites—finds expression in several places in the canon.' James P. McDermott, 'Karma and Rebirth in Early Buddhism', in O'Flaherty (ed.), *Karma and Rebirth in Classical Indian Traditions*, p. 191. For a defence of the thesis that transfer of merit is consistent with Theravāda Buddhism, see F.L. Woodward, 'The Buddhist Doctrine of Reversible Merit', *The Buddhist Review* 6 (1914), pp. 38–50.
3. Padmanabh S. Jaini, 'Karma and the Problem of Rebirth in Jainism', in O'Flaherty (ed.), *Karma and Rebirth in Classical Indian Traditions*, p. 235.

4. Gautama, *Nyāyasūtras*, III,2,39.
5. Karl H. Potter, 'The Karma Theory and Its Interpretation in Some Indian Philosophical Systems', in O'Flaherty (ed.), *Karma and Rebirth in Classical Indian Traditions*, p. 263. For contemporary illustrations, see also David Miller, 'Karma, Rebirth and the Contemporary Guru', in Ronald W. Neufeldt (ed.), *Karma and Rebirth* (Albany: State University of New York Press, 1986), pp. 61–8.
6. Transfer of merit is likewise present in popular Theravāda Buddhism. For a discussion of its presence in a Thai text see Charles F. Keyes, 'Merit-Transference in the Kammic Theory of Popular Theravāda Buddhism', in Charles F. Keyes and E. Valentine Daniel (eds), *Karma: An Anthropological Inquiry* (Berkeley: University of California Press, 1983), pp. 275–84.
7. *Milindapañha*, IV,8,30.
8. D.T. Suzuki, *Outlines of Mahayana Buddhism* (New York: Schocken Books, 1963), p. 206. Transfer of demerit is also found in popular Hinduism. Sheryl Daniel recounts the 'case in which two college roommates in Tiruchirappalli parted company when the health of one boy declined and transfers of bad karma from his roommate (who was of the same caste) were blamed for the illness. The sharing of karma in this case was said to have occurred through co-residence, since the boys did not share food.' 'The Tool Box Approach of the Tamil to the Issues of Moral Responsibility and Human Destiny', in Keyes and Daniel (eds), *Karma: An Anthropological Inquiry*, pp. 29–30.
9. The problem with this, however, is that Bodhisattvas who transfer merit are purportedly beyond the stage of performing meritorious actions. That is, they are eligible for *Nirvāṇa*-entry. Hence, the possibility of their acquiring merit by deeds of merit-transfer is inconsistent with their akarmic state.
10. *Milindapañha*, IV,8,31.
11. Of course, the fact that they are unsuspecting and innocent is really irrelevant. They might suspect the transfer or be guilty on their own account, and the question still arises.
12. C.S. Lewis, 'The Humanitarian Theory of Punishment', in Walter Hooper (ed.), *God in the Dock* (Grand Rapids: William B. Eerdmans Pub., 1970), pp. 287–94.
13. If the desired goal is to attain zero quantity of merit and demerit, it would be contrary to justice for one person to add merit to another's pool of merit, for this would mean that that person would have more merit to exhaust before liberation is possible. But then is it consistent with justice for one person to add demerit to another in order to deplete a pool of merit, so as to enable the person to achieve the desired goal of a null quantity? Though consistent with the general tenor of the expanded karmic thesis, the suggestion surely is counter-intuitive. We will discuss the problem of zero quantity in the next chapter.
14. Edward Conze, *Buddhist Thought in India* (Ann Arbor: The University of Michigan Press, 1967), p. 55.

15. Conze, pp. 91, 81.
16. Conze, p. 57.
17. The emphasis on yogic meditation leading to pure consciousness is developed even farther in Buddhism in the thought of the *Yogācārins*.
18. Eliot Deutsch, *Advaita Vedānta* (Honolulu: The University Press of Hawaii, 1973), p. 100.
19. Deutsch, p. 102.
20. Buddhism makes a similar claim concerning those who have 'crossed over', who are fully enlightened, able to control their mental powers through concentration. Such persons transcend the moral. Yet though they are beyond moral judgement, they do the good spontaneously.
21. '*Mokṣa*, in the positive sense, means the attaining to a state of "at-one-ment" with the depth and quiescence of Reality and with the power of its creative becoming. Spiritual freedom means the full realization of the potentialities of man as a spiritual being. It means the attaining of insight into oneself; it means self-knowledge and joy of being.' Deutsch, p. 104.
22. It goes without saying that it is the retributive rather than the utilitarian juridical system which is in view in Hindu and Buddhist thought. This proposition would not be true of the utilitarian.
23. It might be replied that this is not quite true, especially in Buddhism. The law of karma does not implement the moral law, it determines it. That is, there is no set of prior moral laws which determine right and wrong. Right and wrong are determined in terms of whether they bring about good and bad, and good and bad are understood in terms of liberation from and extension of suffering. 'Whatever action, bodily, verbal or mental, leads to suffering for oneself, for others or for both, that action is bad. Whatever action, bodily, verbal or mental, does not lead to suffering for oneself, for others or for both, that action is good.' *Ambalaṭṭhikā-Rāhulovāda-sutta*, quoted in David J. Kalupahana, *Buddhist Philosophy: A Historical Analysis* (Honolulu: University of Hawaii Press, 1976), p. 62.

    The problem is that in Buddhism there is both relativism and absolutism. Insofar as the quality of the consequences determine the moral quality of the action, insofar as the consequences which count are those related to creating or ending suffering, and insofar as what counts as suffering depends upon the individual person, what counts as instances of right and wrong is relative to each individual. On the other hand, the very claim that the pleasure or suffering produced by the consequences determines the moral character of the act constitutes an appeal to a moral principle which is non-relativistic. Further, there are listings of the moral virtues, such as the Five Precepts—abstaining from killing, stealing, indulging in sensual pleasure, lying, and intoxication—which are presented as absolute or objective, rightful acts. See H. Saddhatissa, *Buddhist*

Ethics: Essence of Buddhism (London: George Allen & Unwin, 1970), ch. 4.

Chapter 11

1. Patañjali, *Yoga-Sūtra,* II,3 & 5. In Buddhism, ignorance leads to the four perverted views: seeking permanence in what is impermanent, seeking ease in what is characterized by suffering, seeking self where there is no self, and seeking delight in what is repulsive and disgusting. Buddhaghosa, *Visuddhimagga,* XXII, 53.
2. Patañjali, II,25.
3. *Saṃyutta-Nikāya,* XII,4,33.
4. As we shall use it in this chapter, the term 'karmic' refers to the sphere of human existence whose operations are governed by the law of karma. As we argued in the previous chapter, the law of karma by itself does not propose an ethic. Neither does it entail any particular or set of moral principles. Rather, by extending the law of universal causation to moral action, it describes the implementation of universal justice. However, though the law of karma neither is nor prescribes a set of moral principles, it is associated with, indeed presupposes, the existence of moral principles. In describing moral causation it contends that right actions will have good consequences, and wrong bad, and that actions can be determined to be right or wrong. That is, it implements the moral principles which are developed and justified by the various traditions. Thus, in this section when we speak about the karmic, we have in view the conjunction of the law of karma with the specific ethics adopted by the particular philosophical or religious tradition being considered.
5. Whether, technically, these are different ethics, or different religious structures, or the one an ethic and the other a religious structure, is debated. This raises two issues which are tangential to our concerns, but important nonetheless, namely, (1) what is ethics and (2) how is it to be distinguished from religion. (1) The study of ethics in modern philosophy, insofar as it has considered normative questions at all, has been concerned largely with interpersonal actions. Yet there is a more classical notion of ethics, recently revived most notably by Alasdair MacIntyre, which also treats of virtue. Of course, not all virtues are moral; there are intellectual virtues as well, and in many respects it is the latter rather than the former which are central to Buddhist and Hindu discussions of liberation. (2) How one distinguishes the moral from the religious is the subject of ongoing discussion. For example, in a recent discussion of the issue David Little and Sumner Twiss suggest that a moral statement is one 'expressing the acceptance of an action-guide that claims superiority, and that is considered legitimate, in that it is justifiable and other-regarding', whereas a religious statement is one 'expressing acceptance of a set of beliefs, attitudes, and practices based on a notion of sacred authority that functions

to resolve the ontological problems of interpretability'. [*Comparative Religious Ethics* (New York: Harper and Row, 1978), p. 96.] For a critique of this, particularly as applied to Theravāda ethics, see Donald K. Swearer, 'Nirvana, No-self, and Comparative Religious Ethics', *Religious Studies Review* 6, no. 4 (Oct. 1980), pp. 301–7.

6. *Aṅguttara-Nikāya,* V,V,47.
7. Winston L. King, *In the Hope of Nibbana* (Lasalle, Il.: Open Court Publishing Co., 1964), p. 92. Conze writes, 'The Abhidharma tradition had set up an opposition between friendliness and compassion on the one side, and wisdom, the highest virtue, on the other. This opposition was probably alien to the original Buddhism, in which the Abhidharmic *prajñā* did not even form one of the states of the eightfold path, much less the highest one.' Edward Conze, *Buddhism in India* (Ann Arbor: The University of Michigan Press, 1967), p. 217. We shall say more about *prajñā* below.
8. Conze, p. 218.
9. *Aṅguttara-Nikāya,* IV,VII,1; VIII,V,9; VIII,VI,4.
10. Buddhaghosa, I,140.
11. Patañjali, II, 30–45. See also *Chāndogya Upaniṣad,* V,10,9–10.
12. Buddhaghosa, XXII, 4.
13. Buddhaghosa, XXI, 66–72.
14. *Aṅguttara-Nikāya,* VII,2,8.
15. Patañjali, I,2.
16. King, p. 95.
17. Patañjali, II,1.
18. 'The three (concentration, meditation, contemplation) are more intimate than the preceding [first five].' Patañjali, III, 7.
19. Patañjali, IV, 30.
20. H. Saddhattissa, *Buddhist Ethics: Essence of Buddhism* (London: George Allen & Unwin, 1970), pp. 64–74.
21. Conze, p. 53. This, however, is probably a later development, since he cites Vasubandhu's *Abhidharmakośa* on this point and since the full emphasis on the transic aspect of *prajñā* comes with Mahāyāna.
22. King, p. 105.
23. Patañjali, III,20; IV, 30–4.
24. King expresses doubt that the salvific or Nirvāṇic really has an ethic. 'In one sense we can scarcely say that there is a nibbanic *ethic.* There is a nibbanic quality of life, and a nibbanic experience, and the hope of final attainment of full Nibbana. But just because of its transcendent position and quality it can scarcely be put in ethical terms. . . . To seek to give it specific form in the nature of a given code of action, precise definitions of what is right or wrong, or even what attitudes one "should" have, is most difficult' (p. 161). Explicit ethical analysis, he contends, is confined almost exclusively to matters of external behaviour. Elsewhere he notes that, strictly speaking, morality and ethics in Buddhism refer primarily to the lowest level of self-development, to the 'minimal external standards of behavior that represent minimal Buddhist morality for the layman' (p. 29). The highest level, on the other hand, though based

on ethical character, is spoken of in non-ethical or only implicitly ethical terms, that is, in terms of psychic development or religio-mystical overtones. Emphasis is placed on mental concentration (*samādhi*) and wisdom or insight (*prajñā*). The Nirvāṇic is concerned with inner psychological discipline, mental concentration, and purity, whereas the karmic links moral action with receiving pleasant or unpleasant experiences. The achiever of *Nirvāña* is the enlightened one rather than the holy one.

But if the Nirvāṇic has no ethic, then his further claim that there is a dualistic ethic must be mistaken. There is only one ethic, namely, that found on the karmic level, and no antithesis between karmic and Nirvāṇic ethics is possible.

Clearly, to discern whether King is correct in his claim that there is a dualistic ethic we must ascertain what he understands by 'ethics'. Though he nowhere defines the term, he does characterize it in reference to Buddhism as 'the steady pursuit of a rationally conceived goodness' (p. 1). This seems a reasonable place to begin. However, on the following page he notes that 'Buddhism is not "mere morality" since it aims at goals which completely transcend the ethical and always places its ethic in that transcendent context'. Besides equivocating on 'ethical', this statement runs contrary to the first. The goals at which the Nirvāṇic aims are goods. How can they transcend the ethical? The answer he gives is that they are psychological in character, not social. But restricting ethics to consideration of interpersonal actions yields too narrow a conception of ethics. 'Ethics' also properly refers to the development of virtues, and the Nirvāṇic, as we have seen, does not dispense with virtues. The virtues recommended for the person in the karmic sphere are presuppositions for Nirvāṇic realization. The *Arahant*, though he transcends moral virtues, does not depart from them, but simply acts from his virtuous character spontaneously.

King might respond that though the ethical aims at producing virtues, it is moral virtues which are the prerogative of ethics, not intellectual virtues. The karmic aims at producing moral virtues (states of character), whereas the Nirvāṇic aims at producing intellectual virtues (states of consciousness, that is, mindfulness, concentration and wisdom). But since the Buddhist conceives of intellectual virtues as goods, they are an appropriate object of human pursuit. They are fitting ends for self-realization, which, as King points out, is the central feature of Buddhist ethics. But if both moral and intellectual virtues are considered human ends and consequently human goods, there is no reason not to see both as the legitimate subject matter of ethics properly or broadly conceived. Indeed, this is the very case in the Buddhist statement of the Noble Eightfold Path. Right speech, action, living and effort are placed alongside right views or knowledge, resolve, mindfulness and concentration.

25. Patañjali, I,33.
26. Criticizing King's placement of meditation to achieve equanimity on the Nirvāṇic level, Aronson writes, 'It is important to note that

the meditative cultivation of these *four* attitudes [love, compassion, sympathetic joy and equanimity] is karmically efficacious for the attainment of rebirth in the world of Brahma. Thus, King is wrong to identify the first three attitudes as karmic and the last [equanimity] as nirvanic. All four create karma leading to future rebirth. Furthermore, because all four karmic attitudes are cultivated in meditation, there is no basis for King's view that meditation is nirvanic and not karmic. . . . Concentration can be of use in securing even more pleasurable rebirth among the higher heavens.' Harvey B. Aronson, 'The Relationship of the Karmic to the Nirvanic in Theravāda Buddhism', *Journal of Religious Ethics* 7, no. 1 (Spring 1979), pp. 30, 34.

27. Saddhattissa, pp. 90–3.
28. See *Digha Nikāya*, sutta X, where after both the discussion on *sīla* and *samādhi*, Ānanda states that there is certainly more to be done. Only after the discussion of *prajñā* does he assert that there is now nothing further to be done, for the Four Noble Truths and the Eightfold Path have been realized, the *āsavas* rooted out, and liberation gained.
29. Saddhattissa, p. 74.
30. Patañjali, IV, 7. This argument trades on an ambiguity in the notion of karma which we noted in Chapter 2. There we questioned whether acts described as producing karma which was neither black nor white could be properly termed karmic, since they produced no fruit at all.
31. *Saṃyutta-Nikāya*, XLV,I,I,ii.
32. Patañjali, III, 22. In Buddhism 'it is maintained that in the higher reaches of vipassana meditation one is able to penetrate into his past lives and become aware of that evil Kamma not yet come to fruition, but which contains a future threat, since all Kamma must come to fruition at some time in the normal course of affairs. But in meditation one becomes increasingly the master, even of inexorable Kamma itself. As detached meditator he sits beside the stream of his own consciousness as it flows by and spots his past evil deed come floating along on its surface, as it were. This identified source of evil he can induce to produce its effect then and there, though in modified form. . . . The result is that the vipassana meditator is thus enabled to overcome all his kammic past, piece by piece, eliminating it once and for all.' King, pp. 164–5.
33. Conze, p. 81.
34. Conze, p. 84.
35. Even Buddhists recognize this, for the result of *deva*-existence is the inability to control the cravings which gradually develop in such an atmosphere. Thus, those who fall from the *deva*-world, their merit exhausted, return often not as humans but as animals.
36. James McDermott shows that there is at least one exception to the zero karmic pool notion in the *Pāli* canon. In the *Khuddakapāṭha*, *Nirvāṇa* is the reward for achieving the most meritorious karma.

He argues that this is a lay document, which suggests an attempted solution to the puzzle was developed outside the community of the *saṅgha*. 'Nibbāna as a Reward for Kamma', *Journal of the American Oriental Society* 93, no. 3 (1973), pp. 344–7.

37. Lambert Schmithausen, 'Critical Response', in Ronald Neufeldt (ed.), *Karma and Rebirth: Post-Classical Developments* (Albany, NY: State University of New York Press, 1986), p. 207.
38. 'Villagers believe that in the beginning Śiva (Katavul) created the vast array of living beings out of his own bodily substance. He molded each creature and determined its nature, be it good or evil, strong or weak. He then wrote upon the head of each entity its "headwriting," which was an exact and very detailed specification of every act it would perform, of all the thoughts it would have in its life, and of every event, good or bad, that would befall it. After creation the activities of the world began with each order of creation impelled to act in accordance with its own headwriting as specified by Katavul. As each entity began to act it began to generate good and bad karma according to the nature of its actions. At the end of each entity's life, Katavul reviewed that entity's karma, and on this record, caused it to be reincarnated in a new form with a new headwriting. The entity then acted accorded to its new headwriting, generated more karma upon which its headwriting in the next birth was determined, and so on through the cycle of births and deaths.' Sheryl B. Daniel, 'The Tool Box Approach of the Tamil to the Issues of Moral Responsibility and Human Destiny', in Charles F. Keyes and E. Valentine Daniel (eds.), *Karma: An Anthropological Inquiry* (Berkeley: University of California Press, 1983), pp. 27–8.
39. See E. Valentine Daniel, 'Karma Divined in a Ritual Capsule', in Keyes and Daniel (eds.), ch. 3.
40. Judy F. Pugh, 'Astrology and Fate: The Hindu and Muslim Experiences', in Keyes and Daniel (eds.), p. 135.
41. It might be thought that this is merely repeating the heresy attributed to the priest Yamaka in *Saṃyutta-Nikāya*, xxii, 85. But careful attention to this text shows that the heresy of Yamaka was not in thinking that the saint does not exist after death, but rather that the saint goes from being a saint, that is, from having a self or identity of being a person who is a saint, to not-existing. Sariputta's response is that even during his lifetime there was no self or person who was a saint. The *skandhas* neither are, nor are not, the person; the *skandhas* are themselves transitory, even during this existence. So what we call a saint was nothing but an ascription of being a saint to certain transitory *skandhas*, and in liberation even the transitory has ceased and disappeared.
42. *Majjhima-Nikāya*, sutta 72.
43. *Majjhima-Nikāya*, sutta 72. David Kalupahana argues that this simply means that there is no way of knowing what happens to the saint after death. It supports agnosticism rather than transcendentalism. Kalupahana, *Buddhist Philosophy: A Historical Analysis* (Honolulu: University of Hawaii Press, 1976), p. 83.

44. Kalupahana, pp. 78–88.
45. Since it is without any determination, Nāgārjuna argues that it is *Śūnya* or Emptiness. And since everything is a (unreal) transformation of or penetrated with *Śūnya*, he can conclude to the paradoxical thesis that *Nirvāṇa* is *Saṃsāra*. *Mādhyamika-śāstra*, XXV. For a discussion of the debates on whether it exists or not, or has or is a cause, see Conze, pp. 159–63.

Epilogue

1. Stanley I. Benn, 'Justice', *Encyclopedia of Philosophy* 4, ed. Paul Edwards (New York: Macmillan, 1967), p. 301.
2. An interesting, contemporary illustration of this can be found in contemporary Indian government policy. In some states as much as 70 per cent of government jobs and university enrolments are reserved for special groups (scheduled castes and tribes, backward classes, women, and so on) who are deemed to have special needs, leaving little for meritorious achievement.
3. This view should be distinguished from aristocratic justice, which would give rewards on the basis of social standing, not accomplishment.
4. For example, in Alasdair MacIntyre, *After Virtue* (Notre Dame: University of Notre Dame Press, 1981).
5. 'The case of the arts and that of the virtues are not similar; for the products of the arts have their goodness in themselves, so that it is enough that they should have a certain character, but if the acts that are in accordance with the virtues have themselves a certain character it does not follow that they are done justly or temperately. The agent also must be in a certain condition when he does them; in the first place he must have knowledge, secondly he must choose the acts, and choose them for their own sakes, and thirdly his action must proceed from a firm and unchangeable character, Aristotle, *Nicomachean Ethics*, II,4.
6. G.E. Moore, 'A Reply to My Critics', *The Philosophy of G.E. Moore*, ed. Paul A. Schilpp (LaSalle, Il.: Open Court Publishing Co., 1942), pp. 546–54.
7. Bruce R. Reichenbach, *Evil and a Good God* (New York: Fordham University Press, 1982), chs 1–5.
8. C.S. Lewis, *The Last Battle* (Harmondsworth, Middlesex: Penguin Books, 1964), pp. 144, 156–65. See also his *The Great Divorce* (New York: Macmillan, 1946).

Appendix

1. These Upaniṣads are quoted with permission from Sarvepalli Radhakrishnan (ed.), *The Principal Upaniṣads* (London: George Allen & Unwin, 1953).

Bibliography

Abhedananda, Swami, *Doctrine of Karma* (Calcutta: Ramakrishna Vedanta Math, 1944).

Anand, Kewal Krishna, *Indian Philosophy. The Concept of Karma* (Delhi: Bharatiya Vidya Prakashan, 1982).

Aronson, Harvey B., 'The Relationship of the Karmic to the Nirvanic in Theravāda Buddhism', *The Journal of Religious Ethics* 7, no. 1 (1979), pp. 28–36.

Arya, Usharbudh, 'Hindu Contradictions of the Doctrine of Karma', *East and West* (Rome) 22 (1972), pp. 93–100.

Balasubrahmanian, R., 'The Theory of Karma and the Philosophy of Advaita', *Indian Philosophical Quarterly* 6 (April, 1979), pp. 567–9.

Beane, Wendell C., 'Buddhist Causality and Compassion', *Religious Studies* 10 (1972), pp. 441–56.

Bhagavad-Gītā, tr. Eliot Deutsch (New York: Holt, Rinehart and Winston, 1968).

Bhattacharji, Sukumari, 'Fatalism—Its Roots and Effects', *Journal of Indian Philosophy* 10 (1982), pp. 135–54.

Bhattacharyya, Haridas D., 'The Doctrine of Karma', *Philosophical Quarterly* (Amalner) 3 (1927), pp. 226–57.

Bhattacharyya, H.M., 'The Problem of Value in Indian Philosophy', *The Philosophical Quarterly* (India) 16 (April 1940), pp. 29–48.

The Book of the Gradual Sayings (*Aṅguttara-Nikāya*), I–IV, tr. F.L. Woodward and E.M. Hare (London: Luzac & Co., 1952).

The Book of the Kindred Sayings (*Saṃyutta-Nikāya*), I–III, tr. Mrs Rhys Davids and F. L. Woodward (London: Luzac & Co., 1952).

Buddhaghosa, Bhadantacariya, *Of Purification* (*Visuddhimagga*), tr. Bhikkhu Ñanamoli (Colombo, Ceylon: R. Semage, 1956).

Chapple, Christopher, *Karma and Creativity* (Albany: State University of New York Press, 1986).

Chatterjee, Satischandra and Dhirendramohan Datta, *An Introduction to Indian Philosophy* (University of Calcutta, 1950).

Conze, Edward, *Buddhism* (Oxford: Bruno Cassirer, 1951).

Conze, Edward, *Buddhist Thought in India* (Ann Arbor, Mich.: University of Michigan Press, 1967).

Das, R., 'The Theory of Karma and its Difficulties', *Quest* (Bombay), 22 (1959, pp. 15–18).

Dasgupta, Surama, *Development of Moral Philosophy in India* (New York: Frederick Ungar, 1961).

Dasgupta, Surendranath, *Yoga as Philosophy and Religion* (Delhi: Motilal Banarsidass, 1978).

Deutsch, Eliot S., *Advaita Vedānta: A Philosophical Reconstruction* (Honolulu: The University Press of Hawaii, 1969).

Deutsch, Eliot S., 'Karma as a "Convenient Fiction" in the Advaita Vedānta', *Philosophy East and West* 15 (January, 1965), pp. 3–12.

Elayath, K.N. Nilakantan, 'Freedom of Will and Action in Sankara's Philosophy', *Vedanta Kesari* 62 (April 1976), pp. 401–6.

Farquhar, J.N., 'Karma: Its Value as a Doctrine of Life', *Hibbert Journal* 20 (1921–2), pp. 20–34.

Further Dialogues of the Buddha (*Majjhima-Nikāya*) I & II, tr. Lord Chalmers (London: Humphrey Milford, 1926).

Gangadeen, Ashok, 'Comparative Ontology and the Interpretation of "Karma"', *Indian Philosophical Quarterly* 6 (January 1979), pp. 203–56.

Ghose, Aurobindo, *Problem of Rebirth* (Pondicherry: Sri Aurobindo Ashram, 1969).

Gokhale, B.G., *Indian Thought Through the Ages* (Bombay: Asia Publishing House, 1961).

Gómez, Luis O., 'Some Aspects of the Free-will Question in the Nikāyas', *Philosophy East and West* 25, no. 1 (1975), 81–90.

Griffiths, Paul J., 'Notes Towards a Critique of Buddhist Karmic Theory', *Religious Studies* 18, no. 3 (Sept. 1982), pp. 277–91.

Gunaratne, Neville, 'A Philosophical Approach to the Doctrine of Kamma', *Mahabodhi* 79 (1971), pp. 8–13.

Herman, Arthur L., *An Introduction to Indian Thought* (Englewood Cliffs: Prentice-Hall, 1976).

Herman, Arthur L., *The Problem of Evil and Indian Thought* (Delhi: Motilal Banarsidass, 1976).

Hick, John, *Death and Eternal Life* (New York: Harper & Row, 1976).

Hillenbrand, Martin J., 'Dharma and Natural Law—a Comparative Study', *Modern Schoolman* 27 (Nov. 1949), pp. 19–28.

Hiriyanna, Mysore, *Outlines of Indian Philosophy* (London: George Allen and Unwin, 1932).

Hogg, Alfred George, *Karma and Redemption* (Madras: The Christian Literature Society, 1970).

Humphreys, Christmas, *Karma and Rebirth* (London: John Murray, 1942).

Indradeva, Shrirama, 'The Doctrine of Karma: Towards a Sociological Perspective', *Diogenes* 140 (Winter 1987), pp. 141–54.

Jayatilleke, K.N., 'The Case for the Buddhist Theory of Survival and Kamma', *Mahabodhi* 77 (1969), pp. 334–40, 371–6; 78 (1970), 2–6, 350–5.

Jhingran, Saral, 'The Problem of Suffering: Some Religio-Metaphysical Perspectives,' *Indian Philosophical Quarterly* 12 (Oct. 1985), pp. 403–13.

Johnston, Charles, 'Karma and Liberation', *Hibbert Journal* 21 (1922–3), pp. 95–106.

Joshi, G.N., *The Evolution of the Concepts of Ātman and Mokṣa in the Different Systems of Indian Philosophy* (Ahmedabad: Gujarat University, 1965).

Kalghatgi, T.G., *Karma and Rebirth* (Ahmedabad: L.D. Institute of Indology, 1972).

Kalupahana, David J., *Buddhist Philosophy: An Historical Analysis* (Honolulu: University Press of Hawaii, 1976).

Kalupahana, David J., *Causality: The Central Philosophy of Buddhism* (Honolulu: University Press of Hawaii, 1975).

Kaṇāda, *The Vaiśeṣikā Sūtras*, tr. Nandalal Sinha (Allahabad: The Panini Office, 1923).

Karunadasa, Y., 'The Buddhist Doctrine of Impermanence', *Mahabodhi* 77 (1969), pp. 213–9.

Kaveeshwar, G.W., *The Law of Karma* (Poona: University of Poona, 1974).

Keith, Arthur B., *Religion and Philosophy of the Vedas and Upaniṣads* I & II (Boston: Harvard University Press, 1925).

Keyes, Charles F. and E. Valentine Daniel (eds), *Karma: An Anthropological Inquiry* (Berkeley: University of California Press, 1983).

King, Winston L., *In the Hope of Nibbana* (LaSalle, Il.: Open Court Publishing Co., 1964).

Knipe, David M., '*Sapiṇḍīkaraṇa*: The Hindu Rite of Entry into Heaven' in Frank E. Reynolds and Earle H. Waugh (eds), *Religious Encounters with Death* (University Park: The Pennsylvania State University Press, 1977, pp. 111–24).

Law, B.C., 'The Buddhist View of Karma', *Aryan Path* 23 (1952), pp. 124–8.

Law, B.C., *A Cultural Heritage of India* I (Calcutta: Institute of Culture, 1958).

Long, J. Bruce, 'Death as a Necessity and a Gift in Hindu Mythology' in Frank E. Reynolds and Earle H. Waugh (eds), *Religious Encounters with Death* (University Park: The Pennsylvania State University Press, 1977, pp. 73–96).

McDermott, James P., 'Is There Group Karma in Theravāda Buddhism?', *Numen* 23 (1976), pp. 67–80.

McDermott, James P., 'Kamma in the *Milindapañha*', *Journal of the American Oriental Society* 94, no. 4 (1977), pp. 460–8.

McDermott, James P., 'The *Kathāvatthu* Kamma Debates', *Journal of the American Oriental Society* 95, no. 3 (1975), pp. 424–33.

McDermott, James P., 'Nibbāna as a Reward for Kamma', *Journal of the American Oriental Society* 93, no. 3 (1973), pp. 344–7.

Macy, Joanna Rogers, 'Dependent Co-Arising: The Distinctiveness of Buddhist Ethics', *The Journal of Religious Ethics* 7, no. 1 (1979), pp. 38–52.

Malkani, G.R., 'Free Will in Indian Philosophy', *Aryan Path* 3 (1932), pp. 387–91.

Malkani, G.R., 'The Rationale of the Law of Karma', *The Philosophical Quarterly* (India) 37 (Jan. 1965), pp. 257–66.

Malkani, G.R., 'Some Criticisms of the Karmic Law by Prof. Warren E. Steinkraus Answered', *The Philosophical Quarterly* (India) 38 (Oct. 1956), pp. 155–62.

Mehta, P.D., *Early Indian Religious Thought* (London: Luzac and Co., 1956).

Neufeldt, Ronald W., *Karma and Rebirth: Post Classical Developments* (Albany: State University of New York Press, 1986).

O'Flaherty, Wendy Doniger (ed.), *Karma and Rebirth in Classical Indian Traditions* (Berkeley, Ca.: University of California Press, 1980).

Pallis, Marco, 'Is There Room for "Grace" in Buddhism?', *Studies in Comparative Religion* 2 (1968), pp. 194–210.

Patañjali, *Yogasūtra of Patañjali with the Commentary of Vyāsa*, tr. Bangali Baba (Delhi: Motilal Banarsidass, 1976).

Parthasarathy, K.E., 'The Law of Karma in Vedanta', *Aryan Path* 40 (1969), pp. 160–4.

Pereira, Cassius, 'An Elucidation of Kamma', *The Buddhist Review* 9 (1917), pp. 54–72.

Perrett, Roy W., 'Karma and the Problem of Suffering', *Sophia* 24, no. 2 (Apr. 1985), pp. 4–10.

Potter, Karl (ed.), *Indian Metaphysics and Epistemology: The Tradition of Nyāya-Vaiśeṣika up to Gaṅgeśa* (Princeton: N.J.: Princeton University Press, 1977).

Potter, Karl, 'The Naturalistic Principle of Karma', *Philosophy East and West* 14 (April 1964), pp. 39–50.

The Principal Upaniṣads, ed. Sarvepalli Radhakrishnan (London: George Allen and Unwin, 1953).

Puligandla, R., 'Professor Deutsch on Karma', *Darshana International* 10 (April 1970), pp. 27–33.

Puthiadam, Ignatius, 'The Hindu Doctrine of Karma', *Theoria to Theory* 13 (1980), pp. 295–311; 14 (1980), pp. 65–74.

The Questions of King Milinda I & II, tr. T.W. Rhys Davids (Delhi Motilal Banarsidass, 1965).

Radhakrishnan, Sarvepalli and C.A. Moore, *A Sourcebook of Indian Philosophy* (Princeton: Princeton University Press, 1957).

Radhakrishnan, Sarvepalli, *The Brahma Sūtra* (New York: Harper and Row, 1960).

Radhakrishnan, Sarvepalli, *The Hindu View of Life* (London: George Allen and Unwin, 1927).

Radhakrishnan, Sarvepalli, *Indian Philosophy* I and II (New York: Macmillan, 1923).

Raju, P.T., *The Philosophical Traditions of India* (Pittsburgh: University of Pittsburgh Press, 1971).

Rāmānuja, *The Vedānta-Sūtras of Bādarāyaṇa, with the Commentary of Rāmānuja*, tr. George Thibaut (Delhi: Motilal Banarsidass, 1962).

Ray, B.G., 'The Law of Karma in Jainism, Buddhism and Sikhism', *Visvabharati Journal of Philosophy* 8 (August 1971), pp. 71–80.

Reichenbach, Bruce R., *Evil and a Good God* (New York: Fordham University Press, 1982).

Reynolds, Frank E., 'Four Modes of Theravada Action', *The Journal of Religious Ethics* 7, no. 1 (1979), pp. 12–26.

Rhys Davids, T.W., 'On Nirvāna, and on the Buddhist Doctrines of the "Groups," the Sanskāras, Karma and the "Paths"', *Contemporary Review* 29 (1877), pp. 249–70.

Rowley, H.H., *Submission in Suffering* (Cardiff: University of Wales Press, 1951).

Saddhatissa, H., *Buddhist Ethics: The Essence of Buddhism* (London: George Allen & Unwin, 1970).

Śaṅkara, *The Vedānta Sūtras of Bādarāyaṇa, with the commentary by Saṅkara* I & II, tr. George Thibaut (New York: Dover Publications, 1962).

Sasaki, Gensun H., 'The Concept of Kamma in Buddhist Philosophy', *Oriens Extremus* 3 (1956), pp. 185–204.

Sharma, Ursala, 'Theodicy and the Doctrine of Karma', *Man* 8 (1973), pp. 347–64.

Singh, Balbir, *The Conceptual Framework of Indian Philosophy* (Delhi: Macmillan Co. of India, 1976).

Steinkraus, Warren, 'Some Problems in Karma', *The Philosophical Quarterly* (India) 38 (Oct. 1965), pp. 145–54.

Stcherbatsky, F. Th., *Buddhist Logic* I (New York: Dover Publications, 1962).

Suzuki, D.T., *Outlines of Mahayana Buddhism* (New York: Schocken Books, 1963).

Swearer, Donald K., 'Nirvana, No-self, and Comparative Religious Ethics', *Religious Studies Review* 6, no. 4 (Oct. 1980), pp. 301–7.

Takakusu, Junjiro, *The Essentials of Buddhist Philosophy* (1949).

Taita, Nathmal, *Studies in Jaina Philosophy* (Benares: Jain Cultural Research Society, 1951).

Tull, Herman W., *The Vedic Origins of Karma* (Albany: State University of New York Press, 1989).

Upadhye, A.N., 'Jainism and Karma Doctrine', *The Jaina Antiquary* 2 (June, 1936), pp. 1–28.

Varma, V.P., 'The Origins and Sociology of the Early Buddhist Philosophy of Moral Determinism', *Philosophy East and West* 13 (Apr. 1963), pp. 25–48.

Vishadananda, Swami, 'Human Soul and Its Sphere of Existence', *Brahmavadin* 14 (April 1979), pp. 54–65.

Wadia, A.R., 'Philosophical Implications of the Doctrine of Karma', *Philosophy East and West* 15 (Apr. 1965), pp. 145–52.

Walhout, Donald, 'A Critical Note on Potter's Interpretation of Karma', *Philosophy East and West* 16 (July 1966), pp. 235–8.

Warren, Henry Clarke (ed.), *Buddhism in Translations* (New York: Atheneum Pub., 1962).

Wayman, Alex, 'The Intermediate-State Dispute in Buddhism', in L. Cousins, A. Kunst, and K.R. Norman (eds), *Buddhist Studies in Honour of I.B. Horner* (Dordrecht: D. Reidel, 1974, pp. 227–39).

Werner, Karel, 'The Vedic Concept of Human Personality and Its Destiny', *Journal of Indian Philosophy* 5 (January 1978), pp. 275–89.

White, J.E., 'Is Buddhist Karmic Theory False?', *Religious Studies* 19, no. 2 (June 1983), pp. 223–8.

Woodward, F.L., 'The Buddhist Doctrine of Reversible Merit', *The Buddhist Review*, 6 (1914), pp. 38–50.

Yevtić, Paul, *Karma and Reincarnation in Hindu Religion and Philosophy* (London: Luzac and Co., 1927).

Zaehner, R.C., *Hinduism* (New York: Oxford University Press, 1966).

Zimmer, Heinrich, *Philosophies of India* (Princeton University Press, 1951).

Index